THE PINOCCHIO
PRINCIPLE

BECOMING THE LEADER
YOU WERE BORN TO BE

The Pinocchio Principle:
Becoming the Leader You Were Born to Be

FIRST EDITION

To order additional copies of this book, please visit www.PinocchioPrinciple.com. To inquire about large quantity discounts or to bring Diane Bolden into your organization to speak, consult or coach, email **Diane@DianeBolden.com** or call (602) 889-2329.

For information on Diane Bolden's workshops, lectures, products and services, please visit **www.DianeBolden.com.**

Inquiries regarding permission for use of the material contained in this book should be addressed to:
Synchronistics Coaching & Consulting, LLC
4148 N. Arcadia Drive
Phoenix, AZ 85018
(602) 889-2329
Diane@dianebolden.com

ISBN # 978-0-9827451-0-6

Library of Congress Cataloging-in-Publication Data has been requested.

Cover and interior design by Jeff Richards, Mesa, Arizona.

THE PINOCCHIO
PRINCIPLE

BECOMING THE LEADER
YOU WERE BORN TO BE

DIANE BOLDEN

Intention

———————◆———————

May all who read this book be uplifted and inspired to reach their pure potential, to see through any illusion that may keep them feeling stuck or trapped, and to emancipate their true selves and give them expression in the world.

May this work allow people to find meaning and purpose in their lives and return them gently to themselves and the Spirit that animates us all.

May it serve as a bridge that allows its readers to bring more of who they are to what they do, and unleash their unique talents and other gifts into the communities, organizations, and circles of family and friends they are a part of – in ways that bring about the greatest good.

May its writing uplift, enlighten and delight its writer as well, and lead her gently back to herself and her Spirit.

Let this book be a conduit of light, love and inspiration. Let it be easy, and let it be fun!

Dedication

---◆---

This book is dedicated
with love and gratitude to
the lights of my life ~

Tim, Zeke, Ryan and Ally

Acknowledgements

It has been said that you teach best what you most need to learn. I have been fortunate to have the opportunity to work with a number of incredibly talented people from whom I have learned so much. Throughout the book I have integrated some of their stories of self-discovery and renewal, as well as a few of my own. To protect their anonymity, their names have been changed. I wish to thank each of them for enriching my life with their own.

I am also grateful for the inspiration, guidance and support I have received from the amazing coaches I have worked with over the years. As my very first coach, Suzanne Allard was a wonderful model who helped me fine-tune my coaching style and approach and integrate it with my organization effectiveness background. Melanie Strick taught me what being a successful entrepreneur is all about and helped me rediscover my true path when it began to become obscured. Vickie Champion has been a constant source of inspiration and wisdom, helping me listen to and act on my intuition, move through my fear, and accomplish things I previously only dreamed of — including writing the book you are now reading. Generous appreciation also goes to my editor, Adryan Russ, whose enormous creativity and diligence were matched by her patience and good humor.

I wish to acknowledge and thank Dr. Michael Foley, Dr. Lisa Dado and the entire community of the Center for Humane Living (CHL), from whom I have learned so much about leadership, life and myself, as well as about the martial arts and what it means to be a peaceful warrior. A portion of the proceeds for this book goes to the CHL, a remarkable organization committed to enhancing the personal and spiritual growth of individuals through an innovative approach to martial arts education, whose vision is to inspire all people to live peaceful and compassionate lives. You can learn more about CHL at www.CenterforHumaneLiving.com.

And of course, I want to express my deepest love and gratitude to my family and dear friends, who have been a constant source of inspiration, support, and humor — especially my incredible husband who, in addition to being the love of my life, is a tremendous leader as well. Our children, Zeke, Ryan and Ally have been some of my greatest teachers. I love you all!

About the Author

---◆---

Diane Bolden is passionate about working with leaders to unleash human potential. An executive coach and organization development professional with more than 19 years of experience in leadership development, coaching and consulting, Diane has worked with managers, directors and officers in Fortune 100 and 500 companies and nonprofit organizations to achieve higher levels of performance and success by helping them bring out the best in themselves and everyone around them.

In December 2004, Diane founded Synchronistics Coaching & Consulting, an organization dedicated to helping leaders unleash the extraordinary in themselves and others. An Arizona native, she received her undergraduate degree from the University of Arizona and her Master's in Business Administration from Arizona State University. She lives in Phoenix, Arizona, with her husband and three children.

Visit Diane's website at **www.DianeBolden.com***, where you can subscribe to receive free articles and learn more about her workshops, lectures, products and services.*

Contents

Acknowledgments		ix
About the Author		xi
Preface		xv

| Chapter 1: | **Unearthing Your True Leadership** | **1** |
| | The Story of Pinocchio | 6 |

Chapter 2:	**Pinocchio's Polar Personality**	**10**
	Animating Genius: The Core of Who We Are	12
	The Puppet: Who We Learn to Be	20

Chapter 3:	**Reconciling Puppet and Genius**	**27**
	Embracing Our Puppet Qualities	29
	Implications for Leadership	33

Chapter 4:	**The Adventure Begins**	**42**
	Finding Your Vision	44
	Life's Perfect Classroom	47
	The Blue Fairy: A Source of Wisdom	52
	Practicing Responsibility	53
	Connecting Actions with Results	54

Chapter 5:	**Navigational Tools**	**59**
	Pinocchio's Nose	63
	Jiminy Cricket: The Voice Inside	70
	The Dove: A Quiet Messenger	71

Chapter 6:	**Strings**	**79**
	The Dangling Nature of Assumptions	80
	Types of Assumptions	86

Chapter 7:   **Stronger Than String**   **108**
                 Doorways to Greater Understanding   110
                 Dismantling the Strings   117
                 Finding the Truth   124
                 Changing Habits and Thought Patterns   127
                 Implications on Leadership and Conflict Resolution   131

Chapter 8:   **Pleasure Island**   **135**
                 Trying to Meet Needs Externally   136
                 Recognizing When You Are on Pleasure Island   149
                 Escaping Pleasure Island   153
                 Helping Others Escape from Pleasure Island   158
                 The Adventure Continues   162

Chapter 9:   **The Belly of the Whale**   **164**
                 Rising Up: The Call to Lead   167
                 Heading into the Fear   173
                 Life's Sudden Storms   183
                 Beyond the Mind   186
                 A Space for Transformation   187
                 Inspiring and Motivating Others   190

Chapter 10:   **The Fairy's Wand**   **193**
                 The Power of Thought   194
                 The Law of Attraction and Living the Dream   210
                 Our Inner Leader   214
                 Navigating the Course   216
                 Pinocchio's Dream Come True   218

Chapter 11:   **Finding Geppetto**   **221**
                 Making Time for What's Important   222
                 Marking Passages to New Doors   230
                 Silencing the Roar of Activity   235
                 Becoming More Focused, Effective and Strategic   236
                 Learning to Let Go   240
                 The Gift of Presence   244

Chapter 12:   **The Adventure Never Really Ends**   **250**

Preface

I have always been amazed by the number of people who seem to think of work as something of a necessary evil — simply what must be done in order to earn a paycheck. For so many who toil through their workday, the primary goal is to make it to the weekend so they can really live. Going through the motions, working side by side with others whose hearts and minds they seldom truly connect with, they withhold the very parts of themselves that make them come alive.

For some it wasn't always this way. Many began their careers ignited with passion and optimism, only to find that their flames began to flicker as they encountered obstacle after obstacle that kept them from achieving what they believed would be success. Succumbing to the unwritten rules of the organizations and other environments they found themselves in, which suggested they needed to act or think in a certain way to get ahead, they may have slowly sold out on their dreams and relegated themselves to quiet complacency.

Many of us were not brought up to expect that work would be fun or gratifying in any way – nor should it be. That's why they call it work, we may have been told. As a result, we may have never really expected much from our careers or professional lives. And as the saying goes, life has a way

> *When we don't enjoy what we do, we only nick the surface of our potential.*
>
> *~ Dennis Wholey, American TV host, producer and author*

of living up to our expectations. In just about every corporation, nonprofit or other organization, you will find people in jobs that do not ignite their talents and passions. Some remain dormant in those jobs because they fear that if they pursue their hearts' desires, they won't be able to put food on their tables. Many don't realize that there might be a better alternative.

Most of us have learned how to turn ourselves on and off at will, in an effort to spare ourselves the pain of disappointment or frustration — or to maintain what we have come to believe is a professional demeanor. It is not uncommon to hear people say that they are very different at work than they are at home. Those golden parts of ourselves that we think we are protecting suffer when we do not let them breathe and interact in the very realms that provide us opportunities to learn more about who we are and what we are here to do in the world. We miss the chance to become a part of something greater than ourselves. And the organizations and communities we are a part of miss out on the unique contribution each of us has the potential to make.

The master in the art of living makes little distinction between his work and his play, his labor and his leisure, his mind and his body, his information and his recreation, his love and his religion. He hardly knows which is which. He simply pursues his vision of excellence at whatever he does, leaving others to decide whether he is working or playing. To him he's always doing both.

~ Lao Tzu,
Chinese Taoist philosopher
(604 BC–531 BC)

We can no longer afford to fragment ourselves in this way, denying the fulfillment of our secret dreams and downplaying the insights we have about what we can do to make life better — for ourselves, and everyone around us. As more and more of us feel the pain that accompanies the denial of our spirits, we start to realize that the time has come for us to bring the totality of who we are to what we do, no matter our vocation, title or role.

We are beginning to awaken to our unique calls to service, creativity and innovation. As we find ways to unleash our distinctive talents and passions at work, we will significantly increase the quality of our own lives, as well as the lives of everyone around us. Corporations that take steps to create environments that allow people to thrive will be met with rich rewards as ingenuity pours forth in ways that lead to increased profit and market share, as well as the creation of self-sustaining cultures that inspire people to succeed by doing what they do best.

**There are people among us who have the ability
to snap us out of our trances —
our states of quiet desperation —
and help us bring more of who we truly are
to everything that we do.**

**They can do this for others because they
have done it for themselves.
They are called *leaders*.**

You may be one of them. *The Pinocchio Principle* is dedicated to allowing you to play a bigger, more significant and meaningful part in the world by unearthing your own leadership in ways that bring about a greater good — and showing others the way to rise through your own example.

*It is never too late to be
what you might have been.*

*~ George Eliot,
English novelist (1819-1880)*

I hope you enjoy reading it as much as I have enjoyed writing it.

Chapter 1

---❖---

Unearthing Your True Leadership

"Come to the edge," he said.

"No," they said.

"Come to the edge," he said.

"No," they replied.

"Come to the edge," he said.

They came. He pushed them and they flew.

~ Guillaume Apollinaire,
French poet, playwright and art critic (1880-1918)

Our foundations are shaking. Corporations are going under. People are losing their jobs and having difficulty finding new ones. Frustration is finding its way into every crevice of our daily lives. The ground that so many stand upon is crumbling.

It can be a scary time. But these changes can also be an exciting time of adventure and reinvention. For years, many of us have been living in ways that are inauthentic — doing jobs that are not a match for our true talents, striving to achieve pinnacles of power, prestige or wealth. And each step has increased the chance of us falling further away from our true selves and from what truly satisfies and nourishes us. As our foundation collapses, we are forced to ponder what is left, what truly has value, and what is actually genuine and meaningful in our lives. This dissolving façade, while painful, enables something more powerful to emerge and bring with it gifts that will benefit all of humanity. We are becoming real again.

With the dramatic changes the world is experiencing, perhaps now more than ever, it is time for each of us to recognize that we no longer need to rely on others to show us the way to genuine "success" — however it is to be defined. We are wired for it. It is in our blood, in our DNA, in our spirits. We have everything we need to get there. And to find ourselves, we must become engaged in the greatest adventure of our lives. In fact, we have already begun this adventure, and through it we are reaching a place of creative tension, where the plot thickens and we are sitting on the edge of our seats to see what will happen next. We are the stars of our own shows, the heroes of our own stories.

The changes for greater peace and true prosperity and the happiness we have been praying for are coming about. Lasting change must come from the inside out. Our world is made up of many nations, many communities, and at its core, many people. The truest change must start from within each of us. We can no longer wait for something or someone to rescue us, to solve all our problems, or to make right what is not working. The greatest thing a leader can do is help us unearth our own authentic leadership so that we, in turn, can do the same for others.

True leadership is about bringing out the best in people. We can all be leaders. And we all must be. There is something greater ready to emerge. And it is within each of us. It is the treasure we have been dancing around in our own backyards.

The old structures are crumbling to make way for the new. And as uncomfortable and challenging as it is, this falling away is an essential part of our own renewal and liberation from whatever no longer serves us, to everything that allows us to bring to fruition our greatest visions and dreams. Seeds cannot sprout from hardened ground. The ground must first become soft and fertile. And that is what is happening now. The old protection mechanisms we relied upon may have kept away the things we feared, but they also kept us from our greatest selves. In the end, we will realize we never really needed that protection anyway. We are much stronger than we thought we were. And now is the time to truly experience that strength, that fortitude, that determination, and that grace.

In many ways our journeys are a lot like that of the legendary story of Pinocchio, a puppet who longs to become real. Like Pinocchio, at our core we too have a burning desire to become real, to bring into creation the greatness that resides somewhere within us. We are born with these impulses — to give form to our distinctive blends of talent, energy, passion and style. We come into the world equipped with far more than we are immediately able to utilize or even comprehend. And though these rich parts of ourselves are always there, they have a way of becoming latent over time. There are people among us who have found ways to tap that well, drawing forth bits of the magic we are all capable of. These are the people we love to watch and be around — who do what they do so well that it is an art. As they tap their inner reserves and unleash their own greatness, they inspire each of us to do the same. In this way, they are true leaders.

In Walt Disney's rendition of *Pinocchio*[1], the puppet encounters a Blue Fairy who tells him, "When you prove yourself

---

[1]*Pinocchio* is a 1940 American animated film produced by Walt Disney, and based on the story *The Adventures of Pinocchio* by Carlo Collodi, a Florentine children's author.

to be brave, truthful, and unselfish, Pinocchio, then you will become a real boy." One could imagine what Pinocchio might have been thinking upon hearing these words. What are these things this fairy speaks of? How do I get them? What must I do? How long will it take? Where do I start? With the promise of a dream fulfilled, he endeavors to do whatever is necessary. And the odyssey begins. The twists and turns it takes are trials we can all relate to, and challenges that I believe are a part of our human experience.

The qualities that the Blue Fairy encourages Pinocchio to demonstrate are not things he must acquire. They are attributes he already possesses. But in order to activate them, he must endure a series of events that allow him to realize these qualities are there and to exercise them accordingly. In order to return to himself — his true self — Pinocchio must endure a journey of trials and tribulations that first lure him away from himself. And the same kind of drama seems to unfold in one way or another for each of us.

So, what does Pinocchio have to do with leadership?

Every one of us has within us an animating genius, which yearns to take different forms depending on who we are. Real leaders could be defined as those whose animating genius longs to create something for the greatest good, which is ultimately accomplished for, with and through others. It has a keen ability to look around, see possibilities and utilize resources in a way that brings something into existence that benefits others, whether that is a family, a community, a non-profit organization, a corporation, or the world at large. To accomplish this, leaders have the distinct charge of working with others in a way that brings out their best — that allows those we can impact to find the animating genius within them and apply it in service of accomplishing a common goal.

Many of us associate the primary meaning of "to lead" as directing something on a given course or being in charge, and this can be one of the functions of leadership. But the essence of leadership is much more than this. The Merriam Webster Dictionary has the following entry as the first definition listed for the word "lead": "a: to guide on a way especially by going in advance." If one of the essential functions of a leader is to bring out the best in others, this definition would suggest that to do this, leaders must first bring out the best in themselves. This, in and of itself, is the very same odyssey our friend Pinocchio finds himself on: to discover and liberate within himself what is real— divinely inspired genius — and to courageously apply it in a way that is truthful and unselfish.

The Pinocchio Principle was written as a roadmap to help each of you bring to fruition your greatest dreams and visions and better navigate through the perils and possibilities along the way. Reading it will help you better differentiate what is true within yourself from the conditioning that would have you acting in ways that are inauthentic and self-defeating. You will learn methods for gaining clarity on your unique call to leadership and leveraging your experiences to prepare for something bigger. Navigational tools explored within the book will help you determine the extent to which you are on or off course and the direction you need to take next on your journey to becoming a real leader.

As you begin to recognize and prevent assumptions and beliefs that keep you from your greatest work, you will learn to utilize ego in service to spirit. With this vital partnership, the elusive promises of Pleasure Island that divert you from your truest fulfillment are easier to recognize and work through. And facing your greatest fears in the belly of the whale becomes a transformational experience that will reunite you with your own determination, courage and heroism. In the end, you will rediscover the power that lies within us all to create and live our dreams. You will also find ways to return to the quiet places within yourself that nurture and inform your greatest visions.

What lies behind us and what lies before us are tiny matters compared to what lies within us.

~ Ralph Waldo Emerson, American philosopher, lecturer, essayist and poet (1803-1882)

The ultimate odyssey is always that of self-discovery. Every challenge, every opportunity gives us a chance to learn more about who we really are and to utilize our inherent gifts in service to something greater than ourselves. When we give ourselves completely to the journey and find meaning in each step along the way, we will truly live. And through our example and the unique contributions we all have to make in the world, we will truly lead.

The Story of Pinocchio

To fully explore the analogy of Pinocchio's odyssey to what real leaders face, we would do well to briefly recount his story. There are at least two versions of the story of Pinocchio out there — one, the original creation by Carlo Collodi, and another, Walt Disney's popularized version. Though each version has differentiating characteristics, at their core they are both about a puppet who is much more than wood and strings, and the adventures he encounters on his journey to become real. To simplify things, and since most people are more familiar with the latter version, this is the one we will explore in greater detail now, though we will make reference to Collodi's original version in upcoming chapters.

The story opens with Geppetto, a lonely clock and toy maker, who creates Pinocchio in an effort to earn some money as a puppeteer. Upon completing his creation, the lonely Geppetto dreams of how wonderful it would be if Pinocchio were a real boy. That evening, the Blue Fairy appears and speaks to the puppet, explaining that though his strings have suddenly disappeared, the true test for Pinocchio in becoming a real boy is to show that he is "brave, truthful, and unselfish, and can choose between right and wrong." She appoints Jiminy Cricket with the charge of teaching him right and wrong, and instructs Pinocchio to listen to Jiminy as the voice of his conscience.

Geppetto, who awakens the next day delighted to see that his wish has been granted, sends Pinocchio to school to "learn things and get smart," so he can be a real boy. On his way to school, Pinocchio meets J. Worthington Foulfellow, a cunning fox, and Gideon, a clever alley cat, both who see in Pinocchio an opportunity to become rich. The two of them convince dear Pinocchio that the theater is much easier and more fun than school. Despite Jiminy's protests, Pinocchio trusts them and happily follows along singing, "Hey, diddley dee, an actor's life for me."

Pinocchio enjoys brief success as a stage performer, and then soon finds himself trapped in a small cage, where he regrets his actions and longs to see Jiminy and Geppetto. After concerted effort, Jiminy finds Pinocchio, and the Blue Fairy appears once again. In response to her inquiries, Pinocchio invents a long story about having been kidnapped by two monsters and suddenly experiences his nose beginning to grow. As he elaborates on his story, his nose becomes a long branch that sprouts leaves. The Blue Fairy explains to Pinocchio that he is telling a lie "as plain as the nose on his face is growing." Upon waving her magic wand, Pinocchio's nose returns to its original size and form, and the Fairy explains that this is the last time she can help him.

On his way home, Pinocchio again meets the fox and cat who convince Pinocchio that he needs a vacation for the sake of his health. They hand him over to a wicked coachman who "collects stupid little boys who play hooky from school," and takes them to Pleasure Island, from which they never return — at least as boys. While there, Pinocchio makes friends with a tough boy named Lampwick, who explains they can fight and wreck things, and eat all the cake, pie, and ice cream they want. They destroy things, set things on fire, smoke cigars, play cards and chew tobacco. "Being bad is lots of fun!" Pinocchio proclaims. Jiminy finds him there, and scolds, "How do you ever expect to become a real boy?" Even so, Pinocchio refuses to leave.

Jiminy then wanders to a place where he sees a coachman loading a boat with boys who have turned into donkeys, whipping them as they slowly file on board. Horrified, Jiminy returns to Pinocchio to find that his friend has grown ears and a tail, beginning the transformation into a jackass. Jiminy gets him to shore, and they swim for the mainland. They return to

Geppetto's house to find it empty. A dove drops a note at their feet that explains that Geppetto has been swallowed by Monstro the Whale, and is in the whale's stomach at the bottom of the sea.

Pinocchio decides to save Geppetto, despite Jiminy's proclamation that Monstro is "a whale of a whale," and other warnings of eminent danger. They swim until they see Monstro, and maneuver themselves into his mouth. Once they find Geppetto inside the whale's body, they get busy figuring out how to escape. The two of them set a fire inside the whale causing him to sneeze, enabling them to make their getaway. Upon seeing Geppetto and Pinocchio as they swim to shore, the whale is outraged and smashes their raft into splinters with his tail, knocking Geppetto unconscious. Pinocchio rescues his father and tries to divert the whale while Geppetto is carried safely to shore by a big wave. Pinocchio gets trapped under some rocks, but is finally washed ashore, half drowned.

Geppetto carries Pinocchio home and puts him to bed. He sees Pinocchio's donkey ears and thinks of how brave he was. Suddenly, the room turns blue, and the Fairy appears to address Pinocchio. "Pinocchio, you have been brave, truthful, and unselfish," she tells him. He sits up and opens his eyes saying, "Father, I'm alive!" Upon examining his hands, he says "And I'm real! A real boy!" Geppetto and Pinocchio hug. On Jiminy's breast appears a badge that says "official conscience," and when the cricket goes to thank the fairy, all he sees is a brilliant star winking at him. The scene closes with Jiminy singing, "When you wish upon a star, your dream comes true."

Each character and event in Pinocchio's story holds symbolic meaning for real leaders who are determined to unearth their genius and apply it in ways that benefit others. Some of you may be only beginning your journey, recognizing the call to lead, or the persistent, playful urge to create something or embark upon an adventure to new, unfamiliar territory. Others are already well onto your journeys, pursuing a dream, heading up an organization or a team, leading a charge, or creating something that will change your family, your community, or your world for the better. It is not always an easy path. Obstacles abound. And some of them are not visible to the naked eye. Yet it is a blessed one, filled with excitement, gratification, and promise.

Are you ready to take a look at the leader's odyssey, using Pinocchio as our mascot and visionary hero? If so, let's begin where all great things begin — in the realm of desire.

❖

Chapter 2

Pinocchio's Polar Personality

Geppetto was a lonely woodcarver trying to earn a living by working his trade. Pinocchio began in the same manner that each of his many creations did. But this particular one was a bit different. In it, he saw possibility — something out of the ordinary. Rather than selling this puppet as he originally intended, he kept it for himself, and saw in his creation a reflection of his desire for companionship. "If only Pinocchio were a real boy," he sighed. And his desire took on a life of its own.

There is some Geppetto in all of us. As the creative aspect of our true selves, it longs for a connection to something bigger — something to nurture, to love, and to shape, which has the ability to take on a life of its own. We may be fleetingly aware of this desire throughout our lifetimes. It may remain latent in us for years, until finally it emerges, more often than not, out of a need for its own expression. Once expressed, or intended, it can become a holding place for a whole new life experience.

Pinocchio is the manifestation of this desire — a divine spark that takes an earthly form. Pinocchio is the part of us that holds our most precious dreams, visions, and possibilities. It has enormous potential for greatness. And it realizes it has access to everything that is necessary to achieve that greatness. The irony is that Pinocchio doesn't consciously know this at first. In order to realize it, Pinocchio must endure trials, tests, disappointments and successes — a whole variety of challenges that bring out the essence of who he really is. And so, too, do we.

Like Geppetto, Pinocchio must also make his way through the world. The vehicle that he uses to get around is wooden and perhaps hollow in places. It is painted, and can be manipulated by strings. The part of our Pinocchio that longs to become real is the innate talent, vision, and dream of greatness we were all born with; the same dream that was the object of Geppetto's desire. It is the animating spark of Pinocchio — the essence that comes from a place that goes deeper than the wood. It is the part of Pinocchio that is capable of demonstrating bravery, honesty and unselfishness — the three qualities that were required of Pinocchio to become real, that is, to transcend the stiff, wooden frame that differentiated Pinocchio from being a mere puppet.

This duality has been the subject of texts from ancient to modern civilization. The part of Pinocchio that longs to be real can be compared to what has been described as "higher self," "true self," "authentic self," or simply "Self" with a capital S. It has also been referred to as "spirit," or "divinity," and "inner child." You might have additional ways of thinking about it and understanding it. This inner self, whatever you choose to call it, is accompanied by another aspect of self that is the wooden, painted puppet side of Pinocchio. This version of self has been described using such words as "ego," "personality," "identity," "social self," and "shadow self," to name a few. Let's look more closely at each of these two aspects of Pinocchio's persona.

Animating Genius: The Core of Who We Are

For the purpose of simplicity, let's refer to Pinocchio's inner essence — that which is real within him, as his animating genius. In Carlo Collodi's version of *Pinocchio*, the wood that Pinocchio was created from was given to Geppetto by another carpenter who heard it speak as he endeavored to make a table with it. Animating genius is the ghost in the machine — the essence of what we were created from. It is the very life within us, and the core of who we really are — our unique blend of talent, energy, and style. Just as a great oak begins as a tiny seed, animating genius contains the blueprint of everything that we are capable of achieving along with all the intelligence we will need to bring it into existence. Each of us has animating genius within. It is the masterpiece in the marble — what stands after everything that is not the masterpiece is carved away. Let's take a closer look at the various elements of animating genius to achieve a better understanding of what it truly is.

Connected to a Higher Intelligence

If you think of everything that has been created as having an origin in something else, you can begin to conceive of the idea that we came from something bigger than ourselves. Our bodies are the offspring of our parents and our minds are a part of our bodies. Yet we are more than body and mind. There is something greater in the mix that occupies the body and the mind and orchestrates their movements and thoughts. Regardless of your religious or spiritual beliefs, one can surely describe this higher intelligence as being divine. It carries all the seeds of our potential and, as a product of divine origin, it is pure, boundless and connected to everything that emanates from that divinity. In this

If you are willing to accept the notion that we are all deeply interconnected, then compassion naturally arises.

~ John Kabat-Vin, author, founding director of the Stress Reduction Clinic and Center for Mindfulness, Medicine, Health Care and Society at the University of Massachusetts Medical School

way our animating genius as our truest self is connected on some level to a higher intelligence, as well as to the animating genius or spirit of each and every person we will ever come in contact with. Because of these connections, animating genius always urges us to do things that are for the greatest good.

Heart-Based and Intuitive

Animating genius is the purest and highest level of our being. Many great musicians, poets, writers, artists and inventors have experienced this connection to something greater. This calling beckons them to explore, innovate and create. They have mastered the art of letting this energy funnel through them to take its own unique form. It is not uncommon to hear composers talk about hearing in their heads the music they eventually wrote. Many of the world's greatest inventions and creations started as a vision or a dream. Albert Einstein's theory of relativity came to him in a flash of insight — he even had to go back to school to learn language through which he could capture and communicate it. Every one of us at some point or another has felt a gut-level instinct to do something, often something that doesn't make a lot of sense at the time. An accountant may find herself daydreaming about writing a screenplay. A mechanic may tinker with spare parts and end up building something he never planned on creating. These nonlinear promptings come from our animating genius. And though they often cannot be explained, they tend to be very compelling. We feel them more than we think about them.

None of us will ever accomplish anything excellent or commanding except when he listens to this whisper which is heard by him alone.

~ Ralph Waldo Emerson, American philosopher, lecturer, essayist and poet (1803-1882)

Our animating genius instinctively knows what we need to do to realize our own unique potential. Just as a seed has within it the unique blueprint of all it is destined to become, so do we. It beckons to us in ways that we can feel in our hearts and our bodies more so than our minds. The vehicle animating genius uses to communicate with is intuition. *Merriam Webster's Dictionary* defines intuition as: "1: quick and ready insight; 2: immediate apprehension or cognition; 3: the power or faculty of attaining direct knowledge or cognition without evident rational thought and inference." In short, we know something, but we do not know *how* we know — it defies explanation. Its source is of divine origin. And as beings of divine origin, we are connected to it.

Present, Playful, Focused on Being

Animating genius lives in the moment and wishes to truly experience everything first hand. Not wanting to miss a thing, it becomes completely immersed in what is happening right now — sounds, sights, feelings, sensations — that add up to raw, unadulterated experience. Rather than wanting to label, categorize or even explain the experience, it simply becomes one with it. When this occurs, time can feel as though it is standing still. Animating genius relinquishes any need to control what is happening and relaxes into the faith that all is exactly as it should be.

Animating genius plays at things in such a way that even the most arduous task can become interesting and enjoyable. It takes itself and everything around it lightly, and easily finds humor in situations that could otherwise become overwhelming. Being so intensely present, it doesn't concern itself with what may happen tomorrow or what took place yesterday. In this way, it can truly enjoy what is unfolding in each moment. It is far more focused on the way things are done than on what it has to show for it. Being unattached to results in this way, it has the ability to

There is one thing we can do, and the happiest people are those who can do it to the limit of their ability. We can be completely present. We can be all here. We can give all our attention to the opportunity before us.

~ Mark Van Doren, American Pulitzer Prize-winning poet, author, critic and professor (1894-1972)

accomplish anything. Whenever we operate from this true self, we will feel a sense of peace, joy, and unbridled enthusiasm that allows anything we do to become somewhat effortless.

Animating genius in one person is inherently connected to animating genius in others. Engaging in our experiences with such a high level of consciousness elevates the consciousness of other people. Perhaps no better example of this connection exists in the twentieth century than Mahatma Gandhi, India's political and spiritual leader, who pioneered resistance to tyranny via mass, nonviolent civil disobedience. Through his animating genius he held the ability to merge and bond deeply with others. His animating genius and all animating geniuses recognize a union among all souls that can become mysteriously delightful.

Animating genius is the part of us that is able to listen deeply to what people are saying, as well as to what is not being said. It listens with the heart, and as a result can comprehend what goes beyond rational understanding. In the presence of this kind of deep listening, one cannot help but feel nurtured and validated.

Focused on Possibilities

The easiest way to see animating genius in action is whenever something one is doing moves from action to art. There is a state of flow to it, as it seems as though whatever we are witnessing has become the work of something greater that has taken on a life of its own. And that is exactly what has happened. Animating genius is an expression of love in its highest and purest form. It has a transformational quality that leaves you feeling different somehow — more connected, inspired and in touch with your own greatness and all the possibilities that are before you. Because animating genius has as its origin something divine, being in its presence evokes the divinity within each of us.

Similarly, animating genius recognizes divinity in others and everything that surrounds it. It has the ability to cut through illusion to perceive what is real, which is of course, animating genius in itself and others. Animating genius knows there is always more than meets the eye — things aren't always

*Trust men and they will
be true to you; treat them
greatly, and they will show
themselves great.*

*~ Ralph Waldo Emerson,
American philosopher,
lecturer, essayist and
poet (1803-1882).*

what they seem. Where others see limitations, animating genius sees possibilities and is inspired by them. It has the ability to reframe challenges into opportunities, and to bring out the latent talent in others that is required to rise up to those challenges in innovative and empowering ways. Acknowledging the greatness in others, it treats them in ways that allow that greatness to emerge. The flow must by its very nature continue; as others find their own animating genius, they act in ways that continue to inspire and uplift. It is in this way that one person can make an exponential impact in the world.

Takes Courageous Actions

Accompanying the animating genius's ability to creatively conceive of infinite possibilities is the courage to take action to bring these lofty visions and dreams into reality. Animating genius has no fear, which is one reason it tends to take itself and others so lightly. It is free of any doubt that would suggest something is not possible. This courage is fueled by love and a desire to contribute

*You see things; and you say
'Why?' But I dream things
that never were; and I say
'Why not?'*

*~ George Bernard Shaw,
Irish playwright, co-founder
of the London School of
Economics (1856-1950)*

to a greater good, which is so strong that it can overcome any obstacle. Having no need to prove itself, it is quietly unassuming. It does not have to make others wrong to build itself up; instead it strives to help others rise up and summon the determination and resilience to face their own challenges with grace and to find solutions that bring about the greatest good.

There is an interesting paradox to the courage possessed by animating genius. Though it has the ability to make us strong and even invincible at times, it also allows us to be vulnerable and to share that vulnerability with others, which breeds trust.

- Animating genius is not afraid of being wrong. It innately knows that wisdom comes from many sources and that learning happens when we are willing to acknowledge that we cannot even begin to have all the answers.

- Animating genius welcomes the knowledge and insight of others. And in so doing, it drives others to find within themselves resources they may not have realized they had.

- Animating genius is more comfortable with listening than talking. When it does speak, it shares its truths without any attachment to the way others will respond.

- It treats mistakes as discoveries and is able to quickly leverage and learn from them.

- It innately knows that no one and no thing can take from it what is at its core. No matter what happens, it will always have the bare essentials to survive — even when we are battered and believe all has been lost.

- Its infinite creativity and divine guidance will always allow it to create or recreate whatever it needs. Knowing it can never truly fail, it is not afraid to take risks. Having an inherent desire to expand rather than contract, animating genius knows that the only real failure is the failure to try.

Unending Source of Power

Animating genius has at its core an inexhaustible supply of power. Because it always seeks to elevate others and serve the greatest good, this power becomes connected to and renewed — as clichéd as it may sound — by the power of goodness that it elicits from and ignites in others. As animating genius reveals itself, it encourages the animating genius of others to come forward. Because its purpose and inclination is to unite rather than divide, it does not become fragmented. It has no need to defeat anything. As a product of divine origin that is connected to everyone and everything, it knows that any attempts to alienate are unproductive and self-defeating. When faced with what may seem to be opposition, it seeks to look beyond appearances to understand what is really happening. Its chief task is not to banish undesirable qualities in others, but rather to emancipate and connect to what is true and divine in them. This power is similar to that of light. Light does not take anything from the darkness; it only illuminates what is hidden inside it. In the light of understanding and compassion, the darkness of illusions of fear and insecurity — cast by the ego — vanish.

Life is a pure flame, and we live by an invisible sun within us.

~ Thomas Brown, English author (1605-1682)

Unlike other forms of power, we are born with this one. We need not rise to positions of prestige, fame or fortune to acquire it; we need only look within. There is nothing to prove, nothing to earn. No matter your job, your status, your role or vocation in life, you have the ability to exercise this power in yourself and to connect to and evoke it in others. And the animating genius in each one of us contains unique talents and gifts that allow each person's contribution to be distinctly different, yet beautifully complementary. We are all pieces of an elaborate and exquisite puzzle; there are no spare parts.

The beauty of this journey we are all on is that when we come into this world, we are in our purest states. Having yet to learn the ways of the world we are wholly and completely aligned with the source from which we came. We have a beginner's mind and heart. This is the reason that babies and small children captivate us so — they awaken in us our natural states of curiosity, playfulness, and love.

Wisdom begins in wonder.

~ Socrates, classic Greek Athenian philosopher (469 BC–399 BC)

It is easy to recognize animating genius in children. They are in touch with their intuition and have no need for explanations or proof to validate what they see and believe with their hearts. Small children can become

Animating Genius	The Puppet
Our inner essence — what is real inside us — who we really are	Product of conditioning and external environment — who we are taught to be
Connected to a higher intelligence, infinite	Our creation, limited by our conceptions
Urges us to do things for a greater good	Interested in self preservation
Complete, knows it has everything it needs	Feels incomplete — seeks power, money, status, approval and fears losing them
Heart-based and intuitive, trusts	Head-based and rational — needs evidence and cannot trust
Present and playful, lives in the moment and is focused on being	Rushes to the future based on the past — focused on doing
Connects with others, likes to listen	Separates itself from others, prefers talking
Inspired and inspiring — sees possibilities, reframes challenges into opportunities	Skeptical and inhibiting — sees limitations and deficiencies
Courageous, not afraid to be vulnerable or wrong; inspires courage in others	Fearful, tears others down to build itself up; must prove itself, win and be right
True sense of power, inexhaustible; elevates and encourages others; its light illuminates our darkness	False sense of power, temporary and fleeting; fear and insecurity create darkness

perfectly fascinated watching ants march in a straight line down the sidewalk. They do not fret over what happened yesterday or what might happen tomorrow — until they are taught by others to do so. They are perfectly content to absorb themselves in the now, and tend to bring out the best in everyone around them wherever they go. Children often say whatever they are thinking in whatever way it wants to come out, which tends to endear them to us, even when their reason for not eating the meal Grandma spent three hours preparing is, "It's yucky." Unconstrained by limiting beliefs, they feel they are capable of doing anything and often have trouble understanding why we do not feel the same way (about ourselves and them).

The Puppet: Who We Learn to Be

Our parents, teachers and other adults around us shared the essential task of helping us survive and learn how to function in the world. After all, though we may have thought we could fly, jumping off a tall building with our arms spread wide would have had very negative consequences. In addition to learning to avoid things that could physically hurt us, they endeavored to teach us what would spare us (and them) mental or emotional pain as well. Somewhere in our development, around the age of three or four, we began to recognize behaviors that would get us certain things — a cookie, approval, love; or a time out, a slap on the hand, a disapproving look, or worse. Over time, we developed a version of ourselves that allowed us to get the kind of response that felt best — and that was reinforced positively and negatively by all kinds of people through the course of our lives — parents, teachers, friends, romantic interests, bosses, coworkers, and others. This is analogous to the wooden part of Pinocchio, which is our puppet.

Created by Human Conditioning

Just as animating genius is the most divine part of our being, the puppet is the most burdened by material wants and desires. Rather than deriving from a divine origin as animating genius does, our puppet is the creation of human conditioning. It develops within us as a survival mechanism, which helps us make sense of the world around us and keep us from harm. It becomes the personification of messages we first received from others, and then internalized and expanded upon. In contrast to our animating genius, which has within all that it needs to realize greatness, our puppet is focused on deficiency. It believes that in order to be complete, it must prove something, acquire something, or change something.

Being predominantly focused on lack, the puppet is centered in fear — mostly fear of losing some external source of gratification: control, influence, power, money, status, approval, or recognition. This fear of loss is augmented by a scarcity mentality, which tells us that if someone else wins (or gains something), we will lose (or get less of what we want). Where the animating genius is interested in the greatest good, the puppet is interested in itself. It doesn't see, as the animating genius does, its inherent connection to others. In fact, it prides itself on being different — rising above the crowd and, at times, taking care of itself at the expense of others.

Head-Based and Rational

Our puppet is a product of rational thinking. It responds to what it sees, hears, touches. It needs "hard evidence." This logical, linear thought emphasizes cause and effect and requires data. As the puppet grows more rigid, anything that lacks concrete proof is quickly dismissed. In the absence of an explanation, our puppet will create one, and then find evidence that supports that story, even if it is not true. Often the evidence it puts the most stock in consists of the limiting beliefs it has carried with it over its life that suggest it is not smart enough, worthy enough, lucky enough or important enough to do whatever it wants to do. Though these beliefs are not true, they become valid pieces of data, which create the very result the puppet fears. Armed with the experience that proves the belief to be legitimate, the puppet exalts in being right.

The puppet dismisses gut instincts and intuitive feelings. Flashes of inspiration become subjected to a logical analysis of the chances something has of success or failure. Our puppet is single-handedly responsible for slowly crushing our most brilliant ideas and dreams. While our animating genius is inclined to trust inspirations and gut feelings and allow itself to be guided by them, our puppet would much rather figure everything out and try like hell to make things happen the way it thinks they should. The puppet does not trifle itself with anything that would suggest a higher intelligence. It considers itself king, and as a result tends to create a lot of work for itself and others.

Rushes Restlessly to the Future, Based on the Past

Because our puppet strives to control, it has a hard time allowing itself to simply be, as our animating genius does. Our puppet keeps itself occupied with orchestrating everything it believes should happen, which is often different from what *is* actually happening. As a result, our puppet gets caught up in judgment and labeling. Things are either good or bad and require a certain predetermined response.

The trouble is that the stories our puppet creates about what is happening rarely take into account the whole picture. They are based only on what the puppet is able to see from where it is standing, and that vision is almost always enhanced or altered by stories related to a previous experience. As the puppet endeavors to prepare for something that has not yet happened, the only data it has comes from the past. Consequently, the plans it so cleverly constructs and endeavors to carry out often entirely miss what is happening in the moment.

The puppet has difficulty simply being, because it believes it is inadequate the way it is. Consequently, it occupies itself with proving itself, whether through acquiring things, winning or being right. Our puppet would have us believe that rest is for the wicked, and gives credence to messages it has heard that validate this belief. As a result of this tumult, it keeps itself continually busy, often creating work that didn't really need to get done and hopping from one activity to the next without really investing itself in anything. When we find ourselves enslaved to our "to do" lists, doing things that allow us to check off boxes without truly evaluating whether the task was appropriate or even necessary, we have succumbed to our puppet.

Where animating genius inherently feels a connection to and desire to bond with others, our puppet often has us too busy, proud or fearful to stop long enough to listen. During conversations, our puppet impels us to think of responses to what people are saying before they are even finished talking. The puppet also has a way of filtering what it hears through its own judgments, stories and perceptions so that the message can become obscured. The nuances of conversation that go beyond words are often lost on the puppet, who is more consumed with wanting to talk than truly listening. This separation leaves people feeling alienated and misunderstood.

Focused on Limitation

Where animating genius has a tendency to be expansive and inspiring, our puppet has the opposite effect. Rather than seeing possibilities that exist in people and situations, it focuses on limitations, and potential failure. In so doing, it draws out insecurities and weaknesses in others as well. In the presence of the puppet, others may feel inclined to either shut down or become a bit deflated as they begin to question their own abilities. In some cases as the puppet gains strength, it consciously or subconsciously elicits responses of fear and anger in the face of what others may feel is an attack.

Being naturally skeptical, the puppet will immediately find reasons that the best laid plans could go astray and supply several worst-case scenarios. While it can sometimes keep us out of trouble or save us from uncomfortable situations, our puppet tends to cast dark shadows that keep us from recognizing and bringing out the gifts of the animating genius — both those of ourselves and others. It is the wet blanket that suffocates sparks of brilliance and inspiration. "Who are you to think you could pull that one off?" it slyly suggests. "You'll look like a fool when your plan fails." And with thoughts and comments such as these, many of the most beautiful ideas and dreams die on the vine.

We've become enamored with deadlines. We want to feel an adrenaline rush. We believe that if we're always chasing the next deadline, we must be important. A lot of our 'busyness' is a way for us to avoid thinking about what is most important. There's a difference between being busy and being productive.

~ Kristen Lippencott, astronomer, Director of the Royal Observatory, Greenwich, London

Laden with Fearful Thoughts

When Franklin Delano Roosevelt said, "The only thing there is to fear is fear itself," he could very well have been speaking to the tendency our puppet has of propagating hysteria and engaging in other self-defeating behavior. As mentioned, the puppet is a creation of our own thinking and the conditioning we have received over the years. Because it believes it is all there is, the puppet is detached from the greater intelligence of divinity. Where our animating genius inherently trusts that appearances are not always what they seem, and has faith that there is a greater purpose behind the most dire of circumstances, our puppet only believes what it sees. And if that isn't bad enough, it tends to create and buy into stories that suggest that things are far worse than they appear. Wayne Dyer wrote in his book, *You'll See It When You Believe It*, that the word "fear" can be used as an acronym for "false evidence appearing real."[1] The more fear there is, the more evidence there seems to be to suggest there is something to fear, which of course elicits more fear. Perhaps that is why doom and gloom seem to sell more papers and magazines than hope and optimism. And in turn, when a thought pattern of fear is activated, it tends to attract similar thoughts, which can result in large numbers of people who believe with strong conviction something that others from a distance can see is merely an illusion. With today's means of viral communication, one fearful thought can easily snowball into baseless mass hysteria. We have all seen the blogs and Internet stories that beat the drum of fear whose sound, before long, becomes deafening.

One of the ways the puppet deals with conflict is by tearing others down to build itself up. Priding itself on being right, it delights in making others wrong. Another way the puppet responds to conflict is by cowering and withdrawing. Both responses emanate from fear. The puppet will not risk appearing the fool. As a result, it tends to engage in everyday experiences in ways that allow it to maintain control, minimize

---

[1] Wayne Dyer, *You'll See It When You Believe It: The Way to Your Personal Transformation* (New York, NY, Harper Paperbacks, August 21, 2001).

discomfort, and increase its chances of winning and being right. The behavior the puppet employs tends to alienate others and cut itself off from the wisdom of the animating genius, which is often activated when one realizes he does not actually know it all and has no need to prove anything to others. The puppet has a way of calling attention to itself to cover up a deep sense of inadequacy and fear. The irate driver who honks and screams at someone who unintentionally cut him off in traffic has succumbed to the puppet. In contrast, operating through animating genius, this same driver would have graciously allowed the other person to move into his lane.

Operates Under a False Sense of Power

The puppet is mostly concerned with self-preservation. It is wired to mitigate the risk of losing. It defines itself in terms of separation — better than, or worse than. This can take the form of superiority or inferiority complexes (which are often two sides of the same coin). The puppet who feels inferior often tries to compensate for deep-seated feelings of lack and shame by making itself feel superior in some way. It may quickly judge and dismiss others, zeroing in on their faults and weaknesses (which are often a reflection of the puppet's own inadequacies) and call attention to itself. What the puppet fails to realize is that because the animating spirit of each person is connected to something divine, by extension each person is also connected to every other person. Therefore, any attempts at elevating itself at the expense of others are ultimately self-defeating. They are based in illusion.

The puppet often judges its own success by the number or quality of possessions it has, its accomplishments, title, prestige, or ability to control others. While each of these things will bring temporary satisfaction, the problem is that in and of themselves they are never enough. Today's star becomes yesterday's news. Managers, directors and vice presidents are replaced and in danger of losing their titles and even their jobs at any moment. Possessions lose their appeal over time and must be replaced with something that holds more luster. Misapplied authority over others creates even more peril. It breeds compliance, but not commitment. Authority exercised without any of the trust, optimism and faith that animating genius brings eventually sours people and leads them to do only what is absolutely required. People go through the motions with their bodies but not their hearts, and everybody loses.

In recent years, we have witnessed the self-implosion of many houses of cards built by the illustrious puppet, whose true power always seems to elude him. We see executives who have created empires — by stealing from, defrauding or otherwise taking advantage of others — come tumbling down along with their corporations. Their organizations, which may have at one time been sound and strong, lack the strong foundation that animating genius contributes. Consequently, when the ground shifts beneath them, they topple over into piles of debris. This is not to say that all organizations or people experiencing hardship are operating from the puppet, only that doing so seems to be a major causational factor in their demise.

At this point, it would be easy and even logical to draw the conclusion that our puppet represents something within us that is bad, while the animating genius is everything in us that is good or redeeming in some way. A logical extension of this would be that to reach our true potential we must learn to overcome and even dismiss our puppet selves like old smelly clothing. But this is not the case. In the next chapter, Reconciling Puppet and Genius, we will explore methods for harmoniously integrating the two, so that puppet and animating genius can work constructively together.

Chapter 3

Reconciling Puppet and Genius

Geppetto, who awakens the next day delighted to see that his wish has been granted, sends Pinocchio to school to "learn things and get smart," so he can be a real boy. On his way to school, Pinocchio meets J. Worthington Foulfellow, a cunning fox, and Gideon, a clever alley cat, both who see in Pinocchio an opportunity to become rich. The two of them convince dear Pinocchio that the theater is much easier and more fun than school. Despite Jiminy's protests, Pinocchio trusts them and happily follows along singing, "Hey, diddley dee, an actor's life for me."

Our puppet gives us a safe vehicle in which to move around in the world. And because the rational mind exists largely within the sphere of the puppet, our puppet selves are not only important, but also essential to our own survival, as well as to our individual and collective development. What we need to do is not overthrow the rational mind, or the puppet, but rather find a way to allow the rational mind and the animating genius to complement each other. Perhaps this is what Albert Einstein was referring to when he said, "The intuitive mind is a sacred gift and the rational mind is a faithful servant. We have created a society that honors the servant and has forgotten the gift."

So the question becomes, how do we allow our animating genius, or what Einstein calls "the intuitive mind," to take its rightful place in the driver's seat? Simply pondering the implications of this thing called "the intuitive mind" may suggest the beginning of a response to that question. As mentioned, Webster's Dictionary defines intuition as "non-logical insight." Intuition is the way our animating genius communicates with us. The insights that come from animating genius, though not necessarily always logical, are the source of our greatest accomplishments, discoveries, creations, and innovations. They inspire us and allow us to rise to new understanding of ourselves, others, and the world around us. Yet, to a large degree, they cannot be explained. In subsequent chapters, we will talk more about the language the intuitive mind uses when communicating to us. For now, let us simply ponder the fact that it does in fact communicate.

The rational mind, or our puppet, is likely in many instances to quickly dismiss these insights, since they seem irrational. Insights show up as hunches, or gut feelings. They often come out of nowhere, and are gently persistent — like a recurring thought or desire. The face of a friend we haven't seen in years shows up in our minds, along with a curiosity or a desire to reconnect. "Where is this coming from?" we may ask ourselves. "It doesn't make any sense. Why would I call this person when he is not even a part of my life anymore?" Some of us are likely to pick up the phone

I don't want to see the day when we are rounded upon by our grandchildren and asked accusingly why we didn't listen more carefully to the wisdom of our hearts as well as to the rational analysis of our heads.

~ Charles Windsor,
Prince of Wales

and call, while others dismiss this intrusion into our thoughts and move on to something more rational. And often, we later find that such people did in fact have relevance in our lives — perhaps they were getting ready to call us, they were involved with something that had direct application to a project we were working on or a vision of something we longed to create, or they were connected in some way to others who are important to us.

Just as our puppet is inclined to reject these insights on an individual level, our collective puppets do so on a larger level. How many of today's greatest inventions or discoveries were initially met with resistance from those who refused to accept that they were possible? Nicolas Copernicus asserted that the Earth rotates on its axis once daily and travels around the sun once yearly, which in 1530 was a fantastic, unbelievable concept. Where would we be as a society and a planet if we had held fast to disbelieving this astonishing notion? Animating genius on the other hand, lives in this world of possibility, creativity, and inspiration. And it is a place where many of our greatest leaders have drawn strength and guidance. They listened to the hunches — hunches that suggested things could be better, that people were capable of more, and that our creations might answer a call to rise up to the challenges that are a part of our everyday existence. However, our animating genius is incapable of bringing these possibilities into reality without its faithful servant, the puppet — home of the rational mind. Being highly attuned to the way of the world that created it, the puppet complements the other worldly component of animating genius's creations with a practical, methodical approach that allows these creations to take form, survive and prosper.

> *It always seems impossible*
> *— until it's done.*
>
> *~ Nelson Mandela,*
> *South African President*

Embracing Our Puppet Qualities

In addition to acting as vehicles for animating genius, our puppet serves another very vital function. In many ways, the puppet actually allows us to find animating genius — much like darkness allows us to see light. Often, we do not awaken to who we fully are, and what we are capable of, until we have spent years trying to appease and win approval from others. Many find they do not have the courage to venture out beyond their comfort zones until they are tired of living in fear. And the desire to reach out and become part of something bigger often does not have much momentum until isolation and loneliness bring the pain that provides the impetus to do so.

Our puppet often contains within it the negative qualities that we pass judgment on in others. Our impatience, intolerance, aggression, cowardice, greed, arrogance and any other weaknesses that keep us from allowing our animating genius to shine forth reside in our puppet selves. These qualities drive us to do things we are not proud of that keep us from being true leaders. And they are the very things that frustrate us in the people we lead and interact with. But before we can have any kind of influence on others, we must learn to be present with these qualities in ourselves. We cannot run from them; we must embrace them and learn what they have to teach us.

Observing and Attending to What Is

We do this by observing our own behavior, and paying attention to what feels aligned with who we really are as well as to what does not. We will talk in subsequent chapters about some of the signals our minds and bodies provide for us that help us recognize the subtle differences. For now, suffice it to say that when you are feeling tension, stress, and discomfort, you are most likely allowing your puppet to take the reins and steer you away from the wisdom of your animating genius.

In states like this, we must learn not to judge ourselves. Often we cannot be present with these qualities until the moment in which they have surfaced has passed. Then we can review in our mind's eye how things unfolded and the ways we behaved. We need to learn to accept and forgive ourselves for succumbing to our weaknesses. We must have compassion for ourselves before we will ever sustain a change. Once aware of our behavior and our thoughts, we can decide what we would like to do instead.

And then we can gently shift our focus and our actions to align with our desired state. This process is gradual and often messy. But we must do it and be patient with ourselves in the process.

> *It is our choices that show what we truly are far more than our abilities.*
>
> ~ *J.K. Rowling,*
> *British author*

You may be asking why this is necessary. Specifically, if there are qualities in ourselves we do not like, why should we embrace them? Why should we give them any portion of our energy and focus? Should we not turn our backs on them and immediately go in another direction? The answer is no. Doing so will actually give them more power, as what we resist often persists. We end up spending more energy focusing on what we do not want than on what we desire. This causes the thing we turn our backs on to grow larger and more powerful.

I'm not advocating that we act on our negative impulses, but rather that we simply be present with them. We must accept ourselves completely before we can change. As Debbie Ford wrote in her book *The Dark Side of the Light Chasers: Reclaiming Your Power, Creativity, Brilliance, and Dreams,*[1] "It is by embracing all of who we are that we earn the freedom to choose what we do in this world. Our shadows exist to teach us, guide us, and give us the blessing of our entire selves." It is as important for us to do this for others as it is for ourselves.

Recognizing Causal Relationships

As much as we wish we could, we cannot banish hatred, intolerance and greed from others by judging and casting them away. We must learn to accept that we all have the capacity to exercise these avarices and pay attention to our choices. We need to recognize how our choices manifest in results and to what degree these results are desirable. Once we begin to truly experience the painful impact of these decisions and recognize their causal relationship, we reach a critical point at which we

---

[1]Debbie Ford, *The Dark Side of the Light Chasers: Reclaiming Your Power, Creativity, Brilliance and Dreams* (Riverhead Books, a division of Penguin Group, USA, June 1, 1999).

*Everything you do has a cost
and a payoff. Make sure your
payoff is worth the cost.*

*~ Alan Cohen,
American inspirational
lecturer and author*

have the motivation and power to choose differently. It is up to us to determine how much pain we must endure before we alter our own behavior. Life-altering decisions that free us of our self-imposed burdens do not happen until we become aware of the undesirable effects of any given course of action.

**At the juncture between
awareness of destructive behavior patterns
and willingness to change,
an opening occurs through which the balance of power
can shift from the puppet to the animating genius.**

This process can take minutes or lifetimes. The catalyst for this transformation is acceptance and forgiveness. We must have patience for ourselves as well as for others, as these are sacred journeys.

When we accept ourselves and all our weaknesses and misgivings, we can do the same for others. When we learn to be present with our own puppet selves and all the uncomfortable things they sometimes drive us to do or feel, we can do the same for others — without judging them, turning our backs on them, or alienating them. When we can be fully present with others, we can help them be fully present with themselves and support them as they make their way through their own processes of transformation.

Our puppet is essential in that it helps us find the way back to our true self. And in doing so we become able to guide others back to their true selves as well. Perhaps this is what T. S. Eliot was referring to when he said, "We shall not cease from exploration, and the end of all our exploring will be to arrive where we started and know the place for the first time." As young children, we identify solely with animating genius, but we do not come to the place where we fully understand and appreciate it until we have explored and allowed our puppet self to divert us from the place of our truest peace and power.

So, we must learn to balance the two, to allow them to commingle, partner up, and dance. Animating genius breathes life into the puppet, and the puppet allows animating genius to find and express itself. Either one without the other is incomplete.

No man remains quite what he was when he recognizes himself.

~ Thomas Mann, German novelist, social critic and philanthropist (1875-1955)

Implications for Leadership

What has all of this to do with leadership? The animating genius and puppet both play a major role. Both are essential, and they need to be balanced. The primary pitfall of leaders is to allow their puppet to take the reins, while their animating genius takes the back seat (or rides in the trunk). Each of us has very likely experienced what it is like to be led by puppets, and many of us also know what it feels like to allow the puppet in ourselves to single-handedly do the leading. The trouble is we are not likely to realize when this is happening.

Remember, puppets take cues from the external environment to determine what behavior will allow them to get some kind of external gratification. As children this gratification may take the form of a cookie, a new toy, or even a pat on the back. As adults, and as leaders, this gratification might take the form of a promotion, a prestigious assignment, or a larger span of control. Sometimes the simple pat on the back that we sought as children is a driver of behavior for us as adults as well. It is not uncommon to get ideas about what it means to be a leader by watching others who have gone before us. It is also not unusual for people to emulate leaders they have worked with in the past, or those who hold positions they aspire to hold themselves.

Consider what most people do upon starting a new job. Eager to succeed, one of the primary objectives tends to be to look around and learn what it takes to move ahead, or to be perceived favorably. "What kind of behavior is rewarded around here? How do people typically operate in order to get things done? What have others done that have allowed them to succeed in this place?" All are fair questions. They feed our puppet, who helps us survive in whatever environment we find ourselves. Our puppet takes these cues, and acts accordingly.

The trouble is that when the puppet is enabled to function without the benefit of its animating genius functioning as co-pilot, the behavior people tend to emulate may not truly serve them, or the organization or community of which they are a part. In some cases, this behavior can prove to be rather destructive.

The Art of Communication and Earning Respect

One of the areas greatly impacted by the self-promoting and self-protecting mechanisms of the puppet is communication. Though many are quick to say they value and practice honest, direct communication, the puppet has clever ways of keeping us from walking our talk. Since our puppets are greatly risk-averse, they tend to play it safe. As a result, they may not say what they really think for fear of rocking the boat, upsetting others, or losing control and looking foolish. Or, believing that they are expressing themselves, they water down their messages to the degree of making them so vague that others do not hear them.

It is very easy in the world to live by the opinion of the world. It is very easy in solitude to be self-centered. But the finished man is he who in the midst of the crowd keeps with perfect sweetness the independence of solitude.

~ Ralph Waldo Emerson, American philosopher, lecturer, essayist and poet (1803-1882)

Another area where the puppet dilutes our effectiveness is one in which we attempt to gain and exert influence. The puppet, seeking validation from others, might be inclined to go to great lengths to win the respect, approval or acceptance of others.

Rather than gaining respect from people as a result of who they are, as our animating genius would have them do, they jump to the conclusion that who they are is not enough, and immediately set out to scheme what they can do to win people over. Of course, people eventually see through this. It dilutes the power of a leader, because it is not truly power at all — and not the good, sustaining stuff that comes from animating genius.

Getting Through It: Tom's Short-Lived Gain

Wanting to get on the good side of his new boss, Tom expressed agreement with a policy even though he had strong doubts about it. Later, eager to ingratiate himself to his team, he communicated the new procedure by prefacing it with the following: "I don't really agree with this decision either. But we have to suck it up. Part of working is doing things you don't want to do, and I don't like this any more than you do. Let's just keep our heads down and get through it."

Though Tom may have succeeded in getting people to temporarily feel that he is on their side, his gain will be short-lived. His people will soon see through his duplicity and conclude that he lacks the courage to be anything but a "yes man." And even worse, by neglecting a discussion of his concerns and potential alternatives with his boss, he has lost out on the opportunity to respectfully demonstrate true partnership and leadership. Even if Tom's boss did not agree with his perspective, engaging in open communication would have helped Tom better understand the rationale behind the decision so that he could better communicate that to the team. And both Tom's boss and his team would know that they can rely on Tom to be honest and supportive.

The desire to seek validation from others is just one side of the coin. On the other side is the drive to demand it. Leaders who fall prey to this drive often identify more with the definition of leadership that speaks to position or authority. "I am in charge," they reason, "so others must respect me. If they don't, I have the power to make them suffer consequences." This kind of leadership emanates from fear — a fear that others might see beyond the façade of an all-knowing, all-powerful icon to the person who doesn't have all the answers but desperately wants others to believe he does. It is a hollow kind of leadership, one that once again may get short-term results in the form of compliance, but will not engage the hearts and minds of people necessary in order to affect a change that will stand the test of time.

Jumping Through Hoops with Claudia

Claudia prided herself on her ability to make people jump through hoops. She secretly liked the way people straightened up when she walked into a room and would drop everything they were doing to act on her requests when she called. As a result, no one around her had the guts to tell her that the direction she was taking the organization was effectively running it into the ground. Her people did not question her, but rather complied with her demands despite their insights into better ways of getting the results she wanted. And when she wasn't around they scoffed at her arrogance and updated their résumés.

Though Tom and Claudia had drastically different styles, their commonality is that they allowed their puppets to do the leading. In seeking validation outside themselves, they cut themselves off from their own animating genius, which prevented them from ever seeing and bringing out the animating genius in others. They both employed a hollow, flat leadership style, devoid of the true power that they so desperately wanted to demonstrate. The paradox is that the more they searched for this power by trying to get it from or exert it over others, the less powerful they really were.

Tom and Claudia are opposite extremes, caricatures that are easy to judge. In most cases, people are much more complex.

They are able to effectively employ small bits of animating genius from time to time, but fall prey to the same temptations and pitfalls we all do. In most cases, they are applying the same behaviors that have gotten them what they wanted all their lives.

For any one of us to truly lead, we must ultimately become aware of the degree to which we are allowing our puppet to point the way, consciously — or more often unconsciously — silencing our animating genius. Our puppets jump into the foreground when fear is present. They take action designed to allow us to win, to be right, or simply to protect ourselves. This action tends to be somewhat one-sided, in that it really operates in the interest of oneself versus being inclusive of others.

Integrating Management and Leadership

The distinction between animating genius and puppet calls to mind the difference between management and leadership. Like the puppet, management is a product of analytical, rational thought. It is concerned with keeping things largely the same, maintaining effectiveness and efficiency through such tasks as planning, controlling, organizing and directing. It also tends to mitigate risk, just as our puppet does, and concerns itself with making sure things happen in a certain way and that they are done right.

Leadership, like animating genius, resides in the heart and is focused on possibilities — in people, situations, organizations, communities, and the world at large. Rather than trying to keep things the same, it challenges the status quo, inspiring vision and empowering others to focus on doing the right things rather than making sure things go as originally planned. Instead of being focused on tasks, leadership is focused on people and on creating strong relationships with people that

The qualities that people look for most in leaders are not infallibility or infinite knowledge, but confidence in themselves and in their group's collective ability to find a solution.

~ Jerry Colonna, American venture capitalist and life coach

inspire trust, and help people realize what they are truly capable of accomplishing. Rather than pointing the way or telling others what to do, leaders model best efforts and allow others to play pivotal parts. Just as you cannot have animating genius without some kind of puppet or vehicle through which it can function, you cannot have leadership without some aspect of management to allow things to happen effectively and efficiently. But the manager must report to the leader, and not the other way around.

The best, most influential and admired leaders are those who have tapped into their animating genius and allowed it to take the driver's seat. Leaders we admire — those we consider extraordinary — are the ones who have learned to be aware of the puppet's self-protection mechanisms and consciously redirect their power by choosing different responses when appropriate. They are strong, yet vulnerable, and willing to be wrong. Most great leaders have failed a time or two and have learned from it. Others want to follow them because they are onto something really big and want to be a part of it. They are inspired, and as a result they are inspiring. They have no need to lead by force because people follow them out of personal choice.

Wayne Sets the Stage for Success

After successfully leading his division to surpass corporate revenue, growth and productivity targets, Wayne was transferred to a new area that had been struggling for some time. He was excited about the possibilities before him and eager to create a strong, high-functioning organization like the one he had just left. He was well aware of the widely held expectation that he would come in and turn everything around. However, rather than using his first few weeks to establish himself as the expert and begin issuing commands, Wayne decided to spend time getting to know the people in his new organization, listening to their thoughts, ideas and concerns and answering their many questions. Wayne knew his vision of what they could create together would be incomplete without their input and commitment.

Intent on building a culture of mutual respect and trust, he dedicated himself to modeling it through his actions. He recapped the insights people shared with him and complemented them with his own observations, thoughts and ideas about what they could create together. Wayne let them know what they could expect from him as well as what he would expect of them and emphasized that because he knew he didn't have all the answers, it was essential that they become part of the solution. He also let them know that when circumstances would require him to act decisively without the luxury of a consensus decision, he was committed to doing so in such a manner that served the highest interests of the organization and everyone within it. Treating them as people who had the ability to do far more than they realized, he set the stage for them to prove him right.

Like Wayne, great leaders know they cannot single-handedly accomplish everything. Rather than trying to do it all themselves, they become devoted to seeing and bringing out the innate talent, strengths, styles and passions of others and ensuring that the work they are charged with carrying out is a good match with what comes naturally to each person. Rather than fostering an unshakeable belief in the leader, they commit themselves to helping each person foster this kind of unwavering belief in themselves. These leaders allow their rational minds to take charge of giving form to greatest dreams and visions of their animating genius and, in so doing, serve as models to others who can learn through their example to do the same.

So, let us return to the leader's odyssey at the place where all adventures begin — that of desire.

THE LEADER'S ODYSSEY

Animating Genius	The Puppet
Our inner essence — what is real inside us — who we really are	Product of conditioning and external environment — who we are taught to be
Connected to a higher intelligence, infinite	Our creation, limited to our conceptions
Urges us to do things for a greater good	Interested in self-preservation, keeping us safe
Complete, knows it has everything it needs	Feels incomplete — seeks power, money, status, approval and fears losing them
Heart-based and intuitive, trusts	Head-based and rational — cannot trust without hard evidence
Present and playful, lives in the moment and is focused on being	Rushes to the future based on the past — focused on doing
Connects with others, likes to listen	Separates itself from others, prefers talking to listening
Inspired and inspiring — sees possibilities, reframes challenges into opportunities	Skeptical and inhibiting — sees limitations and worries about deficiencies
Courageous, not afraid to be vulnerable or wrong; inspires courage in others	Fearful, tears others down to build itself up; must prove itself, win and be right
True sense of power, inexhaustible; elevates and encourages others; its light illuminates our darkness	False sense of power, temporary and fleeting; fear and insecurity create darkness

Reconciling Genius & Puppet

- To maintain a sense of balance, we need both; our animating genius and our puppet must work together and complement each other.

- The intuitive mind provides insight, inspiration and vision; the rational mind provides a practical, methodical approach to give form to creations and allow them to prosper.

- The puppet allows us to find animating genius in ourselves and others.

- The best leaders tap into their animating genius and allow it to take the driver's seat; they are respected for who they are rather than what they do.

- Leadership is to animating genius as management is to the puppet; both are necessary, and the manager must report to the leader.

- Great leaders lead through example; they foster people's unwavering belief in themselves and inspire them to act on it in ways that serve a greater good.

❖

Chapter 4

The Adventure Begins

Pinocchio begins his odyssey with the desire and dream of becoming real — to allow his animating genius to emerge and take the helm from the puppet whose strings have kept him bound and dependent upon the will and action of others. He longs to become the captain of his own ship.

Allowing our animating genius to emerge enables us not only to give form and life to our greatest dreams and visions, but also to liberate and experience our own unique talents, strength, styles and passions. As we do so, we learn who we really are. We unearth treasures in our own backyards. Leaders are people who in one way or another do this not only for themselves, but also for others. Are you ready for this adventure to begin?

The greatest good you can do for another is not just to share your riches but reveal to him his own.

~ Benjamin Disraeli, British Prime Minister (1804-1881)

The call to leadership takes different forms for different people. For some it will mean being at the helm of a large organization, community or nation; for others it might be leading a small team. We often think of formal roles in management or supervision when we hear the word "leadership." But there are countless others out there who are leaders in their own right, who do not bear a title such as supervisor, manager, director, or vice president. They are teachers. They are parents. They are coaches. They are artists, writers, entrepreneurs, healers, musicians, visionaries, community leaders, and people within large and small organizations, communities and neighborhoods that are centers of influence.

As James M. Kouzes and Barry Z. Posner state in *The Leadership Challenge*,[1] "What we have discovered, and rediscovered, is that leadership is not the private reserve of a few charismatic men and women. People make extraordinary things happen by liberating the leader within everyone."

The one thing each of these people has in common is the desire to bring something into the world for, with, and through others. Many of us spend a good part of our lives trying to define what this "something" is. The roads we take to find it contain a number of twists and turns and the signs are not always clear. But something within us spurs us on through all the trials and tribulations, through the fog and the clouds, to keep at it. There are clues everywhere and though the search often takes us outside ourselves, the answers reside deep within. They are a part of the divine inspiration contained within our animating genius.

> *Your vision will become clear only when you look into your heart. Who looks outside dreams, who looks inside awakens!*
>
> *~ Carl Jung, Swiss psychiatrist and founder of Analytical Psychology (1875-1961)*

[1] James K Kouzes and Barry Z. Posner, *The Leadership Challenge* (San Francisco, CA: Jossey-Bass, A Wiley Imprint, 2007).

Finding Your Vision

I have found over the years that the best leaders are not those who have all the answers, but rather those who ask the best questions.

- What are the possibilities?

- What are the opportunities?

- How are we uniquely positioned to make the most of them?

- In what ways can we leverage our strengths to rise up to our challenges?

By asking such questions, leaders bring to the surface answers, insights and knowledge people hold inside that allow great things to happen. Rather than imposing a vision on others, they allow one to develop collectively, with the knowledge that they can't possibly see and accomplish everything single-handedly.

Before these great leaders can do this for others, they must do it for themselves. Here are some questions that can be helpful in recognizing and remembering your life's purpose and allowing your greatest visions to unfold:

- What did you do as a kid that came easily and effortlessly to you?

- What activities have you engaged in over the years that gave you the greatest satisfaction?

- When you look back over all the jobs and/or roles you have had throughout the course of your life, what do you believe you have gained from each?

- What might your experiences be preparing you for?

- What do you stand for in your work? What does your work stand for?

- What interests and intrigues you?

- What books call out to you in the book store?
- What movies do you tend to enjoy?
- What is it that you are stirred to do right now?
- Who are the people you feel drawn to?
- When you envision yourself as successful, what does that mean to you?
- Who are you surrounded by?
- How are you feeling?
- What are the contributions you have made to others?

After spending time contemplating and even writing about the answers to these questions, the larger picture question is whether you notice any recurring themes.

Your work is to discover your work and then with all your heart to give yourself to it.

~ Buddha, spiritual teacher and founder of Buddhism

In Native American cultures, young adults are sent on vision quests. These rituals involve sending the youth on a journey, packed with provisions that allow basic needs to be met. Instructions are simply to wander around and find a place that calls to them. Upon doing so, further direction is simply to sit and reflect. The belief behind this is that we do not necessarily need to actively *find* our vision. When we quiet ourselves and pay attention, our visions find us.

In our complex societies, few of us have the time to go wander around the desert and sit for indefinite periods of time. So we need to make the time in our busy schedules to connect the dots, even if it's just for a few minutes here and there. Our puppet will keep us on the run. It is uncomfortable with stillness because it fears that inactivity will expose emptiness and nothingness. Eager to prove its worth, it keeps us busy hopping from one thing to the next much more occupied with doing than being. It would have us believe that being still is unproductive and lazy. We are a culture obsessed with the next great accomplishment, feat, or acquisition. But we often forget that the greatest accomplishments of our time all started with a single thought. And this thought had to compete with all the other craziness that existed in the mind of its conceiver.

Walt Disney described the conception of his lovable character Mickey Mouse — who has become an indelible part of our popular culture and the cornerstone of a dream that has brightened the faces of millions of people around the world — as follows:

"He popped out of my mind onto a drawing pad 20 years ago on a train ride from Manhattan to Hollywood at a time when business fortunes of my brother Roy and myself were at lowest ebb and disaster seemed right around the corner. Born of necessity, the little fellow literally freed us of immediate worry. He provided the means for expanding our organization to its present dimensions and for extending the medium cartoon animation towards new entertainment levels. He spelled production liberation for us."[2]

The ancestor of every action is a thought.

~ Ralph Waldo Emerson, American philosopher, lecturer, essayist and poet (1803-1882)

You may find yourself repeatedly daydreaming about something, or playfully entertaining an idea or possibility that will not allow itself to be dismissed. These are critical pieces of information that, like pieces of a puzzle, will eventually come together to reveal a bigger picture. Pay attention to them, and do whatever is necessary to nurture and protect them. Capture these thoughts on paper or in your computer, and add to them as new

Cherish your visions and your dreams, as they are the children of your soul, the blueprints of your ultimate achievements.

~ Napoleon Hill, American author (1883-1970)

ideas continue to emerge. Some of these nuggets will become more valuable to you than others — and like gold in the miner's pan, they will begin to shine among the grains of sand.

Life's Perfect Classroom

It has been said that there is nothing more powerful than an idea whose time has come. But these ideas often enter into us long before they are ready to be brought into the world. They prepare us, transform us, and lead us through a myriad of experiences that allow us to develop what we need in order to manifest them.

Consider the path of Rosa Parks. On December 1, 1955, Ms. Parks, a 42-year-old African American woman, initiated a new era in the American quest for freedom and equality when she quietly refused to give up her seat on a Montgomery City bus to a white man, as the Jim Crow laws of segregation mandated at the time. Parks, an active member of the local NAACP, was put off a city bus twelve years earlier for refusing to enter the back door — the same year she was denied the right to register to vote, which she wouldn't be granted until her third attempt in 1945. Her simple, spontaneous action on that December day in 1955 led to a boycott of the Montgomery bus system by a group of local activists and ministers, who chose Martin Luther King, Jr. as their leader. The boycott, which lasted 381 days, ended when the U.S. Supreme Court ruled that the segregation law was unconstitutional. It marks the beginning of a revolutionary era of non-violent mass protests in support of civil rights in the United States.

"When I made that decision," she said later, "I knew that I had the strength of my ancestors with me." In 1995, President Bill Clinton awarded Ms. Parks the Presidential Medal of Freedom, the highest civilian honor bestowed by the U.S. government. In 1999, she received the Congressional Gold Medal.[3]

---

[3] The Henry Ford Museum. http://www.hfmgv.org/exhibits/rosaparks/story.asp

The experiences that pave the way to our greatest successes, like those of Rosa Parks, are not always pleasant. We suffer disappointments, setbacks, and frustrations. During times like these it is easy to feel that life will be just fine as soon as these turbulences subside. But what if these disturbances are the very things we need in order to breathe life into these visions that lie within us? How many of the world's greatest healers once experienced some kind of malady that they needed to overcome before they had what it took to help others through the same challenge? How many people transcended their suffering by finding meaning in it and then went on to help others do the same? How many leaders rose to great heights charged with a mission of improving an organization or a community after having experienced something that needed to be changed?

Pinocchio was charged with the mission of proving himself brave, truthful and unselfish in order to become real. To allow these qualities in himself to come to the surface, he had to experience a litany of challenges and setbacks that may have seemed, along the way, to have little to do with his ultimate goal. However, in order to become brave, he needed to experience and take action despite his fear. Becoming truthful required him to experience the consequences of lying. And before he could truly be unselfish, he needed to experience love for another that would compel him to place the needs of someone else before his own. As Eckharte Tolle wrote in *The Power of Now*, "Sometimes what's in the way is the way."[4]

If your journey as a leader will require you to exercise courage, you may find yourself in several situations that scare the hell out of you. If it requires you to show compassion, you may find yourself in situations where you must learn to transform your anger into something more constructive. You will continue to draw to yourself the experiences you need in order to develop what is required to bring your vision into the world. The blessing and the curse in all of this is that those experiences will continue

---

[4]Eckharte Tolle, *The Power of Now: A Guide to Spiritual Enlightenment* (Novato, CA: New World Library, 1999).

to present themselves until you finally learn the things you need to learn.

Showing Up

Early in my career as an instructor and developer of courses and workshops, I realized that an effective learning experience required a balance of lecture and discussion with some kind of experiential activity that would allow participants to translate into action what they had just learned in theory. Life has a beautiful way of doing this for us. In the classroom no one ever much seems to enjoy breaking into pairs and triads and having to practice something they are not very good at yet. The same thing seems to be true when those experiences present themselves in our daily lives. But life doesn't give up on us. If it doesn't go so well with one person or situation, we get another to practice on. And it doesn't matter how well we do with these challenges. As long as we show up and do what's in front of us, we will continue to be given opportunities to choose different responses, learn from them and adapt our behavior once again.

Think about anything you ever had to learn. You began at the beginning. You started with the easy stuff. Then when you became stronger and more capable, you moved on to a more advanced level, where the challenges were tougher and you had to apply greater skill, muscle and intellect. You emerged from each of these lessons with something you didn't have before. And you couldn't have acquired it through any route other than your own experience.

How can we possibly lead others through challenging times if we are not able to do it for ourselves?

Helping People Discover Their Abilities

As I began coaching executives several years ago,

the emphasis in my work shifted from trying to impart a lesson to helping people learn from their own experiences and see the perfect order in which things are unfolding in their personal and professional lives to help them get where they truly want to go. The pertinent piece was no longer to give people answers, but rather to help them find their own and to recognize that they already possess everything they need to get through whatever challenge is before them. And this is something each of us can do as leaders to help those around us on their own journeys as well.

What is life trying to teach you or prepare you for right now? And how can you seize these opportunities in front of you to bring out your very best so that you can help someone else do the same? Below are some thoughts for contemplation that may help you understand the perfect order of your current experiences.

Notice the people for whom you have feelings of admiration or annoyance. They will tend to demonstrate qualities that you are in the process of developing, addressing or even resisting in some way. When I ask people to identify the qualities in leaders they most admire, what they often see is a reflection of what is already within *them* at some level. Similarly, those who annoy us could represent something that we either need to integrate within ourselves, or resolve at some level. Soft-spoken people who get annoyed with those who are loud and assuming may in turn need to integrate a bit of outspokenness to achieve a better balance. Overly aggressive people who find fault with others who constantly try to steal their stage may very often need to tone down their ways with others.

We see the world not as it is, but as we are.

~ Rainer Maria Wilke, Bohemian-Austrian poet and art critic (1875-1926)

Pay attention to the advice you find yourself impassionedly and repeatedly giving to others. It has been said that teachers teach best what they most need to learn. Often you will attract others to you who may need to learn it as well; however, that doesn't exclude you from the lesson. In fact, it is not uncommon for us to be surrounded by people who mirror our own issues and states of mind. When you are at your most frenzied, you may have a conversation with someone who is having difficulty relaxing and letting go. As this person recognizes what he or she needs to do to overcome obstacles, you may develop great insights into your own as well. You may also have conversations with people who may feel as though someone else needs to start or stop some kind of action. It is not unusual to hear them identify the exact thing they really need to do for themselves, as they project it onto what they think others should do.

Think of the most difficult people in your life as your teachers. This is a tough one. But a funny thing happens when we try to avoid the difficult people in our lives. We can change jobs, organizations and even marriages, but over time we can find ourselves surrounded with variations on the same personalities and situations we fled from. In these situations, we need to look closely and more fully at the challenges these people and situations present. Life only gets more difficult when we resist them. Once we accept these people for who they are and ask ourselves what we can do to make the best of the situation, we find that we inevitably begin to discover qualities and resilience within us that we didn't even know we had (and appreciate the need to attend to some of our potentially negative qualities demonstrated through their example). Lo and behold, we grow and evolve into better people and leaders because of them.

The best way out is always through.

~ Robert Frost, American Pulitzer Prize-winning poet (1874-1963)

As we recognize and embrace the ways life teaches us, we stay in a flow that allows us to get where we need to be with less resistance and more ease and satisfaction. As leaders, we can help others do this for themselves as well. We need to resist any temptation to "save people" from challenging situations and instead help them find and unleash the qualities within them that will most assuredly allow them to rise above their difficulties and discover themselves to be greater than they realized.

The Blue Fairy: A Source of Wisdom

Pinocchio's odyssey began with his desire to become real. His journey took him through several twists and turns that tested his strength and character. And he did not handle them in a manner one would define as "swimmingly." His first challenge landed him in a cage. His second nearly turned him literally into a jackass. Both encounters, however, ultimately led him to take a look at his actions — to contemplate his decisions and to become clearer on the outcome he really wanted, what he would need to do and who he needed to be to get there. During Pinocchio's time of trouble, the Blue Fairy visited him and helped him gain this clarity.

The Blue Fairy represents the connection we all have to the divine, regardless of our religion or creed. She is the embodiment of something otherworldly — an unfaltering source of universal wisdom. She is unencumbered by the weight of humanity and operates solely in the world of thought and inspiration. She cannot really "do" anything for Pinocchio — only guide him gently back to himself — to that part of him that is his animating genius, which must ultimately become stronger than the wooden part of him in order to realize his wish of becoming real. It is the animating genius who knows the way.

We experience this connection to the divine in times of silence, reflection and reverence. We need to slow down and quiet our minds to truly experience its magic. We must be willing to acknowledge that there is something greater than ourselves to which we are connected, that breathes life into us and illuminates our path. Our animating genius is an embodiment of this divinity — spirit in physical form, chartered with a unique and special mission that slowly reveals itself to us over time. And the Blue Fairy accompanies us on our journey, largely unseen.

Sometimes we reach a point where our analytical minds can no longer derive answers. When we have exhausted ourselves with trying like mad to make everything happen the way we think it should, we are near our breaking points. It is often during these critical times of suffering and frustration that our puppet is finally able to surrender and make way for the Blue Fairy to appear. Despite our greatest efforts, we may run into brick walls and find that things seem to be falling apart at the seams. Paradoxically, sometimes this is exactly what is required to allow us to make the necessary shift of allowing our puppet to step back so that our animating genius can take the wheel.

It is not uncommon to hear stories of people who, having experienced some kind of calamity, threw up their hands or cried their eyes out in surrender and felt a strange calmness overtake them. In the eye of their storm, they found peace and hope. These are the messages of the Blue Fairy, reminding us that we have everything we need to endure our trials and emerge victorious, and helping us see solutions to our problems that previously evaded us.

> *Seeds of faith are always within us; sometimes it takes a crisis to nourish and encourage their growth.*
>
> *~ Susan Taylor, American editor, author and journalist*

Practicing Responsibility

Though Pinocchio's Blue Fairy has the power to grant wishes, she does not magically transform Pinocchio into a real boy with a single wave of her wand. "To become real," the Blue Fairy tells Pinocchio, "you must *prove yourself* to be brave, truthful and unselfish." He needs to take action, despite his fear, be honest about his role in each and every situation, and find a way to serve someone other than, or in addition to, himself. The series of events that make up his adventure test Pinocchio's ability to do each of those things, allowing him find and unearth within himself the determination, spirit and talent to effect his own transformation.

We need to approach our own odysseys with the same spirit. We must learn to look beyond those things that trouble us to realize that we have drawn them to us to teach us what we most need to learn. We will experience fear, terror even. We may procrastinate, rationalize and blame. And we will be tempted to take what appears to be the easiest path — one that often benefits us at the expense of others. But each choice we make will bring a corresponding outcome. These choices will either bring us into alignment with our animating genius, or separate us from it. When we are separated, we will be weak. When we are as one, we will be strong. Either way, we will learn and grow.

The word responsibility connotes our ability to respond. Regardless of the situations we may find ourselves in, this is something we *always* have control over. Throughout our daily lives, there will be developments that are disappointing and people who will do things we don't like. Our first impulse may be to try to change all of this by trying to change these circumstances or people. In some cases we will get caught up in dissatisfaction and engulfed in anger or fear. It is not uncommon to blame circumstances or other people for unsatisfactory results. This doesn't get people very far. It provokes defensiveness, alienates people and often makes the problem worse. In fact, it not only cuts us off from others, but also keeps us from accessing our own wisdom.

Connecting Actions with Results

Fortunately, we have another far more productive and constructive response available to us. When we open ourselves up to recognizing the ways we have contributed to the situations we find ourselves in and earnestly learn from them, we can leverage our ability to respond by focusing on those things that are truly in our control — our actions, and perhaps more importantly, our own thoughts. Instead of becoming hardened and resistant, we can relax into the flow of something greater and shift our focus from negativity and skepticism to appreciation and optimism.

When Pinocchio finds himself caged by Stromboli, the "evil puppeteer," one available response is to blame the man for his circumstances and make himself the victim, rendering himself powerless. As Pinocchio begins to tell stories about the situation that absolve him of any responsibility (that he was kidnapped by monsters), his nose

> *It is essential to distinguish between problems that are beyond your control and those you caused yourself.*
>
> *~ Barbara Sher, speaker, career lifestyle coach and author*

begins to grow and his situation becomes worse. The Blue Fairy helps him connect his own actions to the results he is experiencing. We must do the same.

The *Merriam Webster Dictionary* defines a leader as someone who "guides or directs others on a given course of action by going before them."

- If you want people to identify what they need to do to fix or improve things, you need to show them how it is done.

- If you want to create a culture of responsibility, whether in a family, an organization, a community or something larger, you must start by practicing it yourself.

- This requires humility and vulnerability.

**Rather than being signs of weakness,
humility and vulnerability are incredible strengths of leaders.**

**They require far more courage
than projecting a "bullet proof" image.**

Setting an Example by Taking Responsibility

Early in my career as an organization effectiveness practitioner, I would get requests from leaders to come and help them "fix" their organizations. "My people need to learn to work better together," they would tell me. And I would go about interviewing these people to find out what was going on. I asked them questions about what was working and what was not, what they thought needed to be changed, and any other insights they had. Often these interviews generated a great deal of feedback for the leader that suggested that he or she was part of the problem. Perhaps roles were not clear and people were stepping on each other's toes, poor performance was being tolerated, the vision was fuzzy, they didn't have the resources, support, or direction they needed to perform. And the list went on. Granted, there were things others needed to do as well, but I learned early on that to be successful, these leaders needed to take responsibility for their own behavior before they could have any success getting others to do the same.

It is easy for leaders to think that a large part of their work is getting others to behave in certain ways. You can set goals, issue mandates, and give all the pep talks you want, but the best leaders are those who lead others through their own example. "Actions speak louder than words," we have been told since we were children. This could not be truer in the case of leadership. And as we strive to become real — to bring to the surface the greatness that resides within each of us and to help others do the same, we can all practice leadership in one way or another. As Mahatma Gandhi so beautifully said, "We must be the change we wish to see."

This means that when there are problems, we need first to identify our role in them and seek to influence what is truly in our control. This could be with regard to the systems we create, the resources we provide (or withhold), the direction and clarity of expectations we communicate, our vision, our attitudes, and our own openness to feedback. We must also be willing to take a good look at the example we are setting and be honest about whether we are unintentionally modeling the very behavior we do not want to see.

As an executive coach, I learned that I cannot truly help leaders until they are willing to take this kind of responsibility for their actions. Until they make this critical shift, they will complain about the ways others are behaving and try to engage me to help them find ways to make others do things they are not willing to do themselves. Anytime we blame others for things, we conveniently excuse ourselves of the need to change, add to our blind spots and render ourselves powerless. The most powerful way we can keep other people from falling into this trap is to make sure we are not going there ourselves.

Modeling the Ability to Really Listen

It is not uncommon for people to want others to listen more to them. In my coaching sessions, leaders would often tell me that they felt they had tried everything — which usually meant that they had worded things in a number of ways to make their arguments more compelling. And when they felt others were not listening, they talked more or spoke louder.

Upon interviewing people who regularly interfaced with these leaders such as their direct reports, peers, customers and/or bosses, I would often find that what these leaders were failing to do was model the behavior of listening themselves. As a result they were creating the very result they wished to change. Others did not feel heard and were doing the same thing the leaders were doing — talking louder, trying to create compelling arguments of their own, or simply checking out — all of which confirmed the leaders' beliefs that people needed to listen more.

**Leaders who take responsibility
realize that they must be the ones to listen first.
This action has a dramatic effect on the responses
they get from others.**

In the face of what we see as unjust or unkind behavior toward others, we may find ourselves becoming judgmental and righteous. This attitude and the thoughts that accompany it can lead us to feel justified in exhibiting the very behavior we find reproachable in others. We then run the risk of becoming what we despise. Instead of reacting in this way, we can model the behavior we wish to see from others. When we need people to be patient, we must practice patience ourselves. To provoke kindness in others, we must demonstrate how it looks. This does not mean that we should tolerate acts of hatred or violence. It simply means that we must not succumb to engaging in the very mindset that produces those acts, as we seek to rise above them.

Modeling the change we want to see is one way we can endeavor to align our thoughts and actions with animating genius. But the puppet can be sly and cunning. It will lead us to question why we need to be the ones to belly up when the behavior of others seems to clearly be what requires change. Our puppet tends to see things as win/lose propositions and leads us to take action to protect ourselves at all costs. The only way we can rise above the illusion of fear is to defer to animating genius to show us gently back to our true power. But how can we differentiate between actions and thoughts emanating from the puppet and those evoked by animating genius? Like Pinocchio, we have been provided with an array of navigational tools that can greatly help us stay on course. We will explore these in the next chapter.

Chapter 5

Navigational Tools

Geppetto dreams of how wonderful it would be if Pinocchio were a real boy. That evening, the Blue Fairy appears and speaks to the puppet, explaining that though his strings have suddenly disappeared, the true test for Pinocchio in becoming a real boy is to show that he is "brave, truthful, and unselfish, and can choose between right and wrong." She appoints Jiminy Cricket with the charge of teaching him right and wrong, and instructs Pinocchio to listen to Jiminy as the voice of his conscience.

Have you ever had a gnawing sensation in your gut that just wouldn't go away? Maybe it became more pronounced the more you thought about a certain situation or person. Perhaps you were unable to trace it to anything in particular, but noticed that at certain times it seemed to grow stronger, while at other times it may have faded or even gone away altogether. What do you tend to do when you experience heaviness or anxiety such as this? Do you tell yourself to suck it up and increase your intensity to weather through it? Do you become stifled and slow under its weight? Do you try to stuff it down with distractions such as food, alcohol or diversionary activities that allow you to become numb?

Now, think about the times when you have felt light, energetic and strong. Do they have anything in common? Certain people? Activities? Thoughts or associations? During times when you have felt this way, you may have wanted to continue with whatever you were doing for as long as you could — maybe even losing sense of time and space. And the longer you did, the more pleasurable the experience became.

What if these feelings and sensations actually served a purpose?
And what if instead of trying to run from the unpleasant ones, you allowed them to bring you to a place of self-knowledge and discovery?

Getting in Touch with Your Navigational System

One day, I was playing a game with my kids. They had hidden something they wanted me to find. As I walked around the room, they shouted, "Warm!" as I was getting closer, and "Hot!" when I was in striking distance. When I was moving away from the object, they would say "Cool!" or "Cold!" The thought hit me that perhaps this simple navigational system is not all that different from the way our bodies communicate with us every day.

I can recall a time when I was offered a position within the company I worked for that I believed I would be crazy to turn down. Along with increased responsibility and pay came prestige and the opportunity to build relationships with people I believed had the power to substantially elevate my career. However, the nature of the work I would do was quite a change. I tried to convince myself that it would be for the best — allowing me to grow and learn. And as the books and periodicals began to arrive that contained the knowledge I needed to become proficient in this new role, I felt my stomach turn. I wondered if it was my imagination that even a glance at these book covers produced a near gag reflex.

I convinced myself that the reactions were just the jittery feelings everyone experiences at the prospect of taking on something new that requires a journey out of the comfort zone. Each day, I hung in there going through the motions of transitioning into this new position. As I introduced myself to my new customers to let them know of the services I would be providing, I felt a slight sense of incongruence — almost as though I were wearing someone else's clothes and ignoring the fact that they simply didn't fit. As I heard the words coming out of my mouth pledging my commitment, I dismissed a feeling of dissonance that came back to haunt me in my quiet hours.

I was miserable. Over the next few weeks, I had trouble sleeping and felt irritable, impatient, and increasingly superficial as the emotion behind my smile was hardly genuine enough to keep the corners of my mouth turned up. Something had to give.

> *I have learned…that the head does not hear anything until the heart has listened, and that what the heart knows today the head will understand tomorrow.*
>
> *~ James Stephens, Irish novelist and poet (1882-1950)*

"Cold… colder… icy cold." If my kids were there, they would have nailed it. It took me longer than I would have liked to recognize what was right in front of me. I had sold myself a bill of goods whose cost was far too great. And I had numbed myself to that pain with a story that twisted the truth and had me believing that the only losing proposition was not to buy it.

I secretly dreamed of being free of it all, doing the work I loved again, and having the freedom to take that work to the next level. My fear of taking a leap into the unknown was eclipsed by the pain of paralysis and self-deception. Nothing could have been worse than what I was experiencing at the time. And as I allowed myself to believe in a new story — one that told me that if I invested even a portion of the energy I was demanding of myself into following my heart's desire, I would be back on a path that would allow me to restore my sanity and experience congruence with my true purpose once again. The more I entertained these thoughts and ideas, the lighter and more energized I became.

Sure, I dreaded the conversation that came next with someone who would be stunned that I would want to leave a position others coveted. It could have been career suicide — at least that's what the weaker part of me would have had me believe. But career suicide was better than a slow death of a thousand cuts, so I decided the discomfort of this conversation couldn't possibly compare to the misery I had allowed myself to endure. I set my intention on allowing everything to work out for the greatest good — in a way that would let the company and myself win. And as I sat in that chair looking into eyes that stared curiously back at me, I found the words I needed to reclaim my freedom and allow the organization to benefit as well. We were able to identify an alternative that allowed me to apply my true talents within the company and give someone — whose strengths and interests were more aligned for the position I moved out of — the opportunity to come into it and flourish.

Taking that leap was one of many steps I have taken since that moment that has led me to where I am now — in a business that I love, working with clients I am blessed to be associated with, in a continual process of exploration of the wonders of leadership and life. In short, a series of events were set in motion that challenged my fortitude, faith and commitment to putting into practice what I believe. A client of mine once asked, "Do you love every single day? Is it really all wonderful?"

"Of course not!" I replied. I have my ups and downs just

like everyone else. But I have learned to stay in touch with my own personal navigation system; and when I notice I am down for longer than what seems reasonable, I practice inquiry to find out what the emotions and physical cues have to tell me.

Many others have followed their internal guidance to make changes that better aligned their talent and passions to organizational opportunities that they may not have previously known existed, or to those they created themselves. When we stop feeding ourselves lines about what we should be doing and instead do what we know in our hearts to be our true work, we reach a level of freedom, satisfaction and performance we didn't realize we were capable of. The blinders that kept us from recognizing what was right in front of us fall away, and we can step into new, exhilarating worlds of unending possibilities. In the process, we show others how to rise too.

> *As soon as you trust yourself, you will know how to live.*
>
> *~ Johann Wolfgang von Goethe, German author and polymath (1749-1832)*

We are all in some stage of finding ourselves. We discover the path and lose it again, sometimes to learn just as much about ourselves through the diversions as the recoveries. The navigational tools we have at our disposal are often instruments we didn't know we had. There are no instruction manuals, no diagrams, no customer care centers to call and get all the answers from. We learn how to use these tools through simple trial and error.

Pinocchio's Nose

Pinocchio's most obvious navigational tool is his nose. When he lies, it grows. Think back on the scene that showed him imprisoned in a cage. In answer to the Blue Fairy's question of how he got

> *Truth has no special time of its own. Its hour is now — always.*
>
> *~ Albert Schweitzer, Franco-German theologian, organist, philosopher and physician (1875-1965)*

there, he begins to spin a tale of being kidnapped by monsters. As he elaborates on his story, his nose becomes a long branch that sprouts leaves. The Blue Fairy waves her magic wand and sets him free, explaining this is the last time she can help him. This is symbolic of the power that truth can have in our own lives.

Animating genius is truth. It is the truth of our being — our authentic selves and the only thing that is real. It is the one thing we come into and leave the world with. As discussed, our puppet self is a product of illusion, created by assumptions of what it takes to survive in the world. It would have us believe that we are worthless and that in order to become something of value, we must go outside ourselves to prove something, acquire something or exert power over something. As we do these things, we lose sense of our truth, as well as our power. Though we may experience initial success, these deeds are built on illusions that crumble easily to the ground unless we have a more substantial foundation beneath it.

Our navigational systems are not so easily detected, but they are there. The closest and most intimate source of navigation is contained within our own bodies. In the late 1970s, Dr. John Diamond discovered that indicator muscles would strengthen or weaken in the presence of positive or negative emotional and intellectual stimuli, as well as physical stimuli. He wrote a book called *Your Body Doesn't Lie*.[1] Dr. David Hawkins took this work a step further, with research on the kinesiological response to truth and falsehood and wrote a book about his findings called *Power vs. Force*.[2] His findings demonstrated that in the presence of truth, we grow stronger. In the presence of falsehood, we grow weaker.

When we believe and speak truth we are strong — invincible even. When we succumb to the illusion of falsehood, we are weak. This weakness can show up as lethargy, heaviness,

---

[1]Dr. John Diamond, *Your Body Doesn't Lie* (New York, NY, Grand Central Publishing, Hachette Book Group, 1989.).

[2]David R. Hawkins, *Power vs. Force* (New York, NY, Hay House, June 1995)

pain, or even numbness.

The Power of Thoughts and Beliefs

I had the pleasure of attending a retreat facilitated by Martha Beck, author of *Finding Your Own North Star: Claiming the Life You Were Meant to Live*[3] and *Steering by Starlight: Find Your Right Life, No Matter What!*[4] She asked participants to recall a situation that was not pleasurable for them in one way or another, and to think the thoughts they were thinking at the time of the occurrence. While doing this, they were instructed to pay attention to the bodily sensations they begin to feel while they are reliving these experiences. This exercise, which I have facilitated in my own workshops, has varying responses from person to person. People have spoken of feeling anything from slight pressure in their heads to full-blown headaches. Others talk about their chest and shoulders tightening up and often mention that their breathing feels constricted. Some describe a heaviness that weighs them down or a sudden zap in their energy level. Still others talk about their heart racing and describe symptoms of panic.

After that part of the exercise is complete, they are instructed to recall a very positive experience and pay attention to their bodily sensations. What they describe in relation to these positive experiences is often the direct opposite of what they experienced in the first part of the exercise. Someone who talked about feeling heavy and claustrophobic describes feelings of lightness and spaciousness. Those who spoke of feeling lethargic often relayed feeling a burst of energy. People who felt

---

[3]Martha Beck, *Finding Your Own North Star: Claiming the Life You Were Meant to Live* (New York, NY, Three Rivers Press, Random House, January 2002).

[4]Martha Beck, *Steering by Starlight: Find Your Right Life, No Matter What!* (New York, NY:,Three Rivers Press, Random House, March 2008).

tightness in their body many times related feelings of relaxation and calmness.

The important thing to remember in all of this is that the experiences themselves are not what triggered these physical responses, but rather the thoughts and beliefs people had while they were experiencing them. This was beautifully illustrated with the experience one participant shared that he considered one of his best — being stranded at the top of a mountain he was hiking, several thousand feet above sea level. Separated from his hiking companions, he felt bliss and exhilaration at being perched in solitude at the peak of this mountain surveying the earth and sky stretched out before him. This experience could have quite justifiably been anyone else's worst — if feelings of panic and fear set in. What made the difference was what he was thinking and believing at the time. His feelings were generated by his animating genius.

It is neither good nor bad but thinking makes it so.

~ William Shakespeare, English poet and playwright (1564-1616)

With the job opportunity I ended up turning down, my belief that I had no choice but to take the position, and that over time I would come to enjoy the work I was doing, was not based in truth. It was a story generated by my puppet.

You can run from the truth, but you can't hide. Unpleasant sensations may be subtle at first, but over time they become more pronounced, until they propel you into a critical state of awareness that can lead you to realize what you need to do. It is up to us to determine how much misery or discomfort we will endure. If I had continued to fool myself, I likely would have ended up with an ulcer, as my stomach pains would

The body is an astrolabe to calculate the astronomy of the spirit.

~ Rumi al-Jeladdin, 13th century Persian poet, jurist, theologian and Sufi mystic

have increased in intensity and my body reflected back to me the effect my untruths were having. When we feed ourselves lies, our bodies let us know.

Contemplating a Course of Action

In the same way that our bodies can reflect incongruence with our animating genius, they can also help us recognize what will bring us into alignment with our greater selves. While thoughts or behaviors that are not aligned with our own personal truth tend to bring us down in one way or another, those that are a match have a way of bringing us up. When we are contemplating something that is a true match, we find our energy levels elevated with feelings of excitement and enthusiasm. We may also experience a sense of peace and calm.

The next time you contemplate a course of action, try each alternative on in your mind. Put yourself in the place of having made the decision one way or another, and see how you feel.

- Does your energy increase or decrease?

- Do you experience feelings of pressure, discomfort or pain, or are there sensations of expansion, relaxation or increased energy?

- Do you find yourself physically swayed in one direction or another? It is not uncommon for people to speak of feeling drawn toward some people or situations, leaning closer, with a desire to shorten the gap.

- Alternatively, do you feel a desire to get some distance or a general lack of energy around the alternative altogether?

In my coaching practice, more and more I find myself working with people who have lost that little glimmer in their careers. Some experience restlessness or anxiety. Others feel lethargic and empty. At a very deep level, they find their situations lacking the spark that once held their attention. Many cannot put their fingers on it. They are becoming increasingly aware that something is missing and that there is more to life than what they are currently experiencing. They seek a sense of meaning and purpose and know that the time has come for a change. The changes they need may not necessarily require that they change their careers, the organizations they are working within, or even their jobs. They may simply need a subtle shift in the degree to which they allow their animating genius to come out and actively participate. Their intuition often first communicates to them through their bodies.

These people are finding that:

- They are ready to push the envelope a bit more.

- They are prepared to go out on a limb to say things or propose creative ideas they previously feared were inappropriate or risky or to cross the bounds that kept them from connecting more deeply to the people that surround them — their coworkers, boss, customers and subordinates.

- They intuitively recognize the change they need to make when they land upon a course of action that simultaneously frightens and excites them.

- Upon examining these alternatives, they sit up straighter in their chairs, their voices become stronger, and their eyes sometimes seem to sparkle.

- When they contemplate going about things in the way they always have, playing it safe, going through the motions of their ingrained routines, they find themselves anxious and constricted.

Utilizing Your Internal Compass

It is important to pay attention to these sensations. Our rational minds — the home of the puppet — would have us dismiss them, as they are not logical or driven by what most consider valid data. We all get them. The question is: To what degree have you allowed yourself to experience them? Children tend to be very connected to them. They seem to have an innate sense of knowing. Animals have these abilities as well, and can easily sense a situation that will bring them pain or pleasure. Human beings are, in fact, the only species that has the ability to interfere with and disassociate from these gentle promptings by allowing the analytical mind to override.

Intuition will tell the thinking mind where to look next.

~ Jonas Salk, American medical researcher and virologist (1914-1995)

The greatest use of our minds is to utilize these non-linear promptings to complement our ability to figure things out with data and logic. Again, the key is to balance one with the other.

The first time you saw a compass, you may not have understood what the symbols mean or exactly how the tool could be used to help you find your way. Similarly, your level of skill in identifying and decoding the subtle messages your body provides you with will improve with practice and increased levels of concentration and focus. Our internal compass is somewhat buried within us. The more we have disassociated from our bodies and intuition, the harder it is to identify and utilize.

We disassociate from our bodies in many ways. The most common is by numbing pain and discomfort with food, alcohol or other diversionary activities. An uncomfortable feeling in the gut can be misinterpreted as hunger, and easily stuffed down with large amounts of sugary or carbohydrate-laden food that fogs our mind and keeps us from intuiting our body's true signals. Any other method of shutting out our bodies' signals can become a pattern that allows us to routinely disassociate.

Breaking unproductive patterns of any kind requires three elements: willingness, awareness, and action. To break the pattern of disassociating from your body, you must first have a desire to get back in touch with it. Secondly, you must practice awareness by recognizing when you are falling into the routine, what prompted it, and the effect of doing so. As an example, when you see yourself heading for the pantry in search of chocolate or potato chips, rather than judge, simply observe. Similarly, observe yourself sitting in a bloated stupor when you have finished. When you discern that the pain of what you are experiencing is greater than the payoff of becoming numb, you are ready to make a change. As you do so, your mindset will shift and help you to take action that is aligned with your desired result. The benefits you'll experience will supersede any payoffs that engaging in the old routine may have generated. We will discuss this process in more depth in future chapters.

In addition to recognizing and shifting the ways that we muffle our bodies' signals, we can also take action to increase our bodily awareness. This can be done by getting in the practice of deliberately placing your attention on what your body is feeling at any given moment. You can direct your attention to one part of your body at a time, perhaps in this very moment recognizing how your left foot feels inside your shoe or the place at which your backside is resting on the chair you are sitting in. You can practice breathing deeply and notice how differently your body feels with a deep breath versus a shallow one. You can also scan your body to notice where you tend to store tension. Yoga and martial arts can be a wonderful way of helping you become more integrated with your body and increase your level of energy and perception, as can any type of exercise that allows the freeing of the body and mind.

The breath itself can open doors to awareness and help you access your inner wisdom. Bringing more oxygen to your brain and relaxing your body, the breath allows you to literally inspire yourself — breathing in spirit or animating genius, and exhaling the stress and other irritants that keep you from hearing and acting on your own inner voice.

Jiminy Cricket: The Voice Inside

Our physical bodies are only one form of navigational tool available to us. As mentioned, animating genius communicates to each of us via our intuition ——our non-linear insights or "direct knowledge or cognition without evident rational thought and inference" as *Merriam-Webster* defines it. In addition to having his nose as a guide, Pinocchio benefited from Jiminy Cricket, whom the Blue Fairy appointed as the voice of Pinocchio's conscience. Jiminy Cricket can be likened to the voice of intuition itself. While our bodies communicate with us through physical sensations, this little voice quietly expresses itself through our thoughts and emotions.

Intuition can come across visibly, audibly or in a sentient or feeling way. It can also be a simple knowing or cognizance. People whose intuition communicates more visually may actually see images, symbols or words in their minds. They may also find themselves noticing visual stimuli that seem to jump out and grab their attention, like phrases or pictures on a billboard, in newspapers, magazines or on the Internet. Rather than simply being interesting or eye-catching, these images are of importance because they have personal connotations.

Those whose intuition communicates audibly may actually hear words or sounds that communicate in a meaningful way, perhaps through music they hear or things people say, even if the person talking doesn't intend it that way.

When intuition communicates sentiently, it can be felt within the body. It might create a strong attraction or repulsion, or a physical sensation. Still others have a sense of knowing something without understanding where the knowledge comes from. It could be information about a person or situation or a hunch that something has happened or is about to happen, or an understanding of complex principles or theory.

The Dove: A Quiet Messenger

Toward the end of Pinocchio's journey, he returns home to find that Geppetto is gone. A dove flies by and drops a note that tells Pinocchio of Geppetto's whereabouts. At times, each of us encounters signs that contain information for us. Many times, we see these signs and don't think anything of them or write them off as coincidence. Other times, we stop long enough to ponder the possibility that these little occurrences may actually have significance. These little indicators take on increased meaning when they seem to hold information that contains the answers to questions we have been asking ourselves.

A Turn of the Screw

For years I worked as an internal consultant and executive coach for a large corporation in a job I loved. Gradually, I began to recognize my longing to break out to start my own business and have more flexibility and time to spend with my family. Initially, I dismissed these yearnings as something everyone encounters. Then I began looking into what it would take to actually start a corporation. Though I daydreamed of the possibilities, the thought of leaving my job altogether seemed impractical since I was enjoying my work and had wonderful working conditions. I reasoned that I would stay there unless things changed to the point that I didn't enjoy it anymore.

I kept waiting for things to take a turn for the worse — for someone to tell me I couldn't do the work I was passionate about anymore, or for the organization to be restructured in such a way that was no longer optimal for me. None of that happened. In fact, things just seemed to get better and better there. Still, these visions and dreams continued to beckon. They became more and more pronounced, until finally I began to seriously entertain the notion of taking action on them.

I began to find screws everywhere I went. I walked across the kitchen floor and stepped on one. An elevator opened up and I saw another one on the floor in front of me. They were turning up when I cleaned my kids' rooms, and in other odd places. In a meeting, a co-worker and I were pouring over some documents when a tiny screw popped out of her reading glasses and landed on the papers in front of us. Initially, I didn't think anything of finding these screws. But after several occurrences, I became curious as to whether there could be significance.

One day while on the phone with a very good friend, I related my experiences. "Maybe you're screwed," she joked. "Or I have a few screws loose?" I retorted. She suggested we look up the definition of a screw in the dictionary. As she went to get her dictionary, I wandered around the house, phone in hand, straightening things up. When she came back to the phone, among the many definitions she read was one that said "something that must be turned or acted upon in some manner." As she said the words, I reached into the small drawer of a sewing table in our living room and felt my hand wrap around a zip-lock bag. I lifted the bag out of the drawer to find — you guessed it — a bag of screws in assorted sizes.

This act held profound meaning for me, as it seemed to be the crowning event of a series of seemingly coincidental incidents that became more and more pronounced until they finally got my attention. Whether it was my subconscious mind, the screws, or both, I felt sure there was a message for me. The following week, I gave my notice at work (and didn't encounter any more screws after that).

When I finally made the decision to leave my stable job, many people thought I was nuts. One evening, I went out with some colleagues who were in their own business. After telling them my plans, I was surprised and discouraged when they reacted with warning and caution. They told me story after story of friends who had taken the route I was embarking upon who ended up regretting their decisions and experiencing significant financial losses.

Confused and deflated, I went running the next

day on a canal bank near my house while I contemplated my life's direction. A running club training for a 10k race had placed mile markers along the path, and beneath one of them was a quote that said, "Those who believe it cannot be done should get out of the way of those who are doing it." Upon reading this sign, the hair on my arms stood up. I knew this message had significance for me. And it gave me the encouragement I needed to get back on my path.

Many of my clients have had similar experiences of receiving answers to questions they were contemplating. Some got their answers in dreams, one while seeing a movie with a particular message that hit home, and still others spoke of multiple experiences, including conversations and interactions with others that seemed to echo the same theme.

Something magical will happen to you today. Pay attention, because it may arrive disguised as something ordinary.

~ Author unknown

The distinguishing characteristic in all of these events is not the events themselves, but the feelings they evoke and the messages they lead us to discover that resonate with our own inner wisdom. In this way our intuition may speak to us using several channels at once — visual, auditory, cognitive and sentient. We see or hear something (once or repeatedly) and know that it has meaning because of the way it makes us feel.

Our intuition heightens our attention and level of receptivity to them when they do have meaning. It's a little like the experience of seeing people driving the same model of car you do, right after you bought it. They were always there, but you never noticed them before because they had no significance. Regardless of the mechanism through which it communicates, when our intuition urges us to take a particular course of action, there is a sense of lightness, energy, joy and/or congruence. Acting upon these promptings leads us to experience a sense of flow and ease, even in the midst of what might be considered a difficult task.

Any feelings of shame, guilt or discouragement are not a product of our intuition (or animating genius), but rather of our puppet. Taking action in this "puppet" mindset feels heavy, tedious and may lead to the experience of several stops and starts or seeming roadblocks that prevent a sense of flow from taking place. You may feel as though you are running on a treadmill, exerting a lot of effort but getting nowhere. Out of fear, our puppet has a way of sabotaging animating genius. When animating genius shows us that we have within us everything we need to be successful, the puppet steps in, in an effort to show us all we have to lose and convince us that the only way we will succeed is to go outside ourselves to win the approval of or exert power over others. In Carlo Collodi's *The Adventures of Pinocchio*, the puppet actually kills Jiminy Cricket by throwing a shoe at him.

Most of us don't have such an extreme reaction to the voice of our intuition. Our puppets engage in methods of sabotage that are more subtle, such as through messages of discouragement, doubt and even ridicule. When we are in tune with the voice of our puppet, we resonate with voices of others who echo the same refrain. The puppet cleverly tricks us into thinking these deflating messages originate from others. They are simply mirror images of the puppet's illusory beliefs, which lead us to validate the suggestion that we do not have what it takes to succeed. This is why, even after receiving praise from multiple sources, we sometimes put undue weight on messages from the one source that is critical of our best efforts. We will discuss this phenomenon in greater detail in Chapter 6.

When we believe these messages from the puppet, we experience resistance, which leads us to engage in avoidance mechanisms such as procrastination, diversionary activities, or self-sabotage. The noise in our heads grows to the point that the subtle, quiet voice of our intuition (or animating genius) gets drowned out. In an effort to silence the critical voices, we may turn to activities we have mentioned — the ones that keep us numb and disconnected from everything, such as watching excessive television, Internet surfing, eating or drinking in excess or other such activities. We become fixated on a myriad of activities and preoccupations that keep us from practicing awareness — the ability to notice things our intuition would have us see, hear and feel. One of the puppet's favorite tactics is to convince us to engage our heads to try to figure everything out from an analytical standpoint, and control the outcome by focusing on trying to change circumstances or other people. As long as we are doing that, we will not look within, where the real answers are.

The language that intuition uses is sometimes difficult to decipher. It is particularly tricky when we try to understand it using our logical or analytical minds, as doing so is similar to using an understanding of the English language to try to decipher another language entirely. Properly decoding it requires that we get out of our heads. As discussed previously, our intuition speaks softly and can easily be overrun by the loud voice of our puppet (as well as those around us). The more we have oriented ourselves to the external world of noise, conflict and chatter, (and bought into our own and others' messages of what we *should* be doing) the more difficult it will be for us to tune into this internal navigational mechanism.

Rather than being a product of analytical thought, the intuition sends messages that are non-linear and often seeming to come from out of nowhere. You find yourself suddenly thinking of, or being drawn toward, something, or perhaps saying or writing words that surprise you. Additionally, intuition is gently persistent. It is not uncommon for people to describe several occurrences that seem to reinforce the same message.

To increase your ability to discern and translate these inner promptings, it can be helpful to temporarily quiet the outer voices. This is done in many ways. Spending time alone in silence is one of the best, as is engaging in any activity that feeds your spirit and allows you to calm yourself. Examples of activities that people find helpful range from meditation to gardening, fishing, exercising, listening to music, writing, painting, building, playing sports, and even simply driving. The distinguishing characteristics of an activity that will help you access your intuition is that it allows you to be in the moment, get out of your head, and fully experience whatever you are doing in a way that transcends logic — and sometimes time and space as well.

The final chapter, *Finding Geppetto*, will explore additional ways to quiet the mind and reconnect to animating genius.

The key to making the most of these navigational tools is to lean into them — to see them not only as guideposts, but as the doors of possibility swinging wide open. As we walk through them, we find ourselves in new and exciting situations where we have the ability to reinvent ourselves and bring more of who we really are into the world.

These navigational tools are always available to us. They help us determine the extent to which we are on or off course and the direction we need to take next on the journey to becoming a real leader. They can also allow us to discern what is keeping us from moving forward or to finally see invisible pitfalls we repeatedly fall into (and often create ourselves). Anytime we undertake an effort to change in any way, we will encounter equal and opposite forces that will work to keep us where we are. Our navigational tools help us become aware of these forces.

The next step is to learn to dismantle them or to convert the energy that pulls us away from our true desires into something that will serve and support us. That is the subject of the next two chapters, *Strings* and *Stronger than String*.

YOUR NAVIGATIONAL TOOLS

- Do what you know in your heart to be your true work.

- Step into the world of unending possibilities.

- Invoke your Pinocchio nose, and focus on the truth.

- Our indicator muscles strengthen or weaken in the presence of positive or negative emotional and intellectual stimuli.

- In the presence of truth, we grow stronger; in the presence of falsehood, we grow weaker.

- Thoughts and feelings are generated either by our animating genius or our puppet.

- Pay attention to your physical sensations in any situation. Your level of skill in identifying and decoding subtle messages your body provides will improve with practice and increased levels of concentration and focus.

- Commit to not hiding these feelings or numbing pain with food, alcohol or other diversionary activities.

- Develop a desire to get back in touch with your body and its messages.

- Become aware of recognizing when you fall into an old routine, as well as what prompted it.

- Listen to the Jiminy Cricket intuitive voice of your conscience.

- Ponder the possibility of The Dove's message — perhaps signs that contain information for you — messages that resonate with your inner wisdom.

- Spend time alone engaged in activities that nurture your spirit — gardening, fishing, exercising, listening to music, writing, painting, building, playing sports, among others.

- Quiet your mind and reconnect with your animating genius.

———————◆———————

Chapter 6

Strings

In his early days as a puppet, Pinocchio had strings attached to his head and each of his limbs, all of which could be manipulated in ways that determined how he would move. While these strings gave him mobility, they also limited his range of motion and kept him bound.

We too have strings that determine the direction and extent to which we move. Our strings are our beliefs, fears and assumptions — about ourselves, others and the world around us. They encompass the unspoken rules by which we live our lives.

Our strings are not only a part of the puppet, they are created and sustained by the puppet. While our animating genius speaks to us through our intuition, the puppet speaks largely through assumptions about what we and others are capable of, what is generally possible in any given situation, and what needs to be said or done in order to get what we want.

The Dangling Nature of Assumptions

An assumption is simply a story of the way things are, or should be, that we take to be true. Being an analytical creature, the puppet makes sense of reality by utilizing the data at its disposal, internalizing not only the views and dictates of others, but also forming assumptions based on previous experiences. The stories of our lives are colored by our perceptions, knowledge, values, fears and biases.

An event or person might cause us to feel pain or pleasure, which leads us to associate that event or person with an emotion. Over time, repeated experiences of this sort tend to ingrain these emotions in such a way that they become judgments. We categorize things and invent stories full of assumptions that prepare us for future experiences. In the absence of data, the puppet fills in the gaps based on what has happened before.

"The last time I disagreed with my boss," someone might observe, "I was disciplined for challenging authority and passed over for a promotion." After experiences of this sort, a story takes form, which can become generalized in ways that have implications beyond the initial circumstance we once found ourselves in: "If I challenge my boss, bad things will happen," becomes "if I challenge authority, I will place myself in jeopardy."

This assumption can become so ingrained that the person believing it is completely unaware of the compelling effect it has on his behavior.

Rather than acting from intuition and awareness of the present moment, the puppet's creation of and reliance on assumptions leads us to go to the future based on the past. Though circumstances may have changed and this person may now be in an organization that values open,

Be careful to get out of an experience all the wisdom that is in it — not like the cat that sits down on a hot stove. She will never sit down on a hot stove lid again — and that is well; but also she will never sit down on a cold one anymore.

~ Mark Twain, American author and humorist (1835-1910)

honest communication, he will likely shy away from expressing his true opinions and could end up experiencing what he fears most (career stagnation) not only despite, but because of, his best attempts to avoid it.

We will continue to create these stories throughout our lives. It is a part of being human. The trouble comes when we are unwilling to entertain that perhaps these stories are simply pieces of a larger puzzle. If we act as though they are true, they can more often than not elicit the very behavior we do not want to see (in short, a self-fulfilling prophecy.)

A good example is the common (and deeply flawed) assumption held by many leaders that: "If you want to get something done well, you must do it yourself." This assumption keeps those leaders from delegating effectively (or at all). Those who do delegate while believing this assumption often do so half-heartedly, with the conscious or unconscious thought that in the end they are going to have to redo some of the work anyway (another assumption.) Approaching delegation in this manner subtly communicates doubt to the person being delegated to, which in turn can erode confidence and negatively impact performance. It can also lead the person doing the delegating to skip important details and fail to spend an adequate amount of time ensuring that the desired results are clearly communicated and that adequate resources, direction and support have been provided. When the job is not completed in the desired manner, the puppet's belief in the assumption is validated and reinforced. Consequently, a pattern is established that keeps effective delegation from taking place. In this way, the assumption is a string that keeps the puppet bound to dangle, repeat the experience and blame external circumstances for something it directly contributed to.

> *Man is not the creature of circumstances.*
> *Circumstances are the creatures of men.*
>
> *~ Benjamin Disraeli,*
> *British Prime Minister*
> *(1804-1881)*

When we are unaware of the power of our assumptions, we run the risk of attributing the cause of our greatest disappointments and frustrations to circumstances outside our control. This keeps us in a state of blame and dependency and robs us of our true power. By deferring responsibility for our own actions to others, we conveniently excuse ourselves of any need to change. After all, it wasn't our fault. This places us in a victimization mode that is seductively destructive. We can rationalize all kinds of behavior this way and never feel the need to hold ourselves accountable. And because we never feel the need to change, we remain stagnant.

To move forward with any kind of sustained progress, we must acknowledge that we hold our own strings.

The sooner we catch ourselves telling tales about how other people, things, or circumstances are to blame for our behavior, the more power we will have to move in the direction we ultimately want to go. Once we become aware of our tendency to give our power away, we are in a position to take it back.

One of the reasons that assumptions are so powerful is that they literally determine what we see and do not see. One study suggested that the human brain takes in an average of 400 billion bits of information a second, but has the ability to process only 2000.[1] Assumptions serve as a filter that determines which data we take in and which we screen out. Data most likely to get through confirm whatever we believe. These are the data that keep us locked in a vicious circle, behaving in a way that validates our assumption.

A belief is not merely an idea that the mind possesses; it is an idea that possesses the mind.

~ Robert Bolton, English clergyman and academic (1572-1631)

One example of this filtering process is found in the very common example of someone who, in the midst of an outpouring of compliments, still puts far more weight on the one or two

---

[1] William Arntz, et al., *What the Bleep Do We Know?* (Lord of the Wind Films, LLC and Captured Light Industries, copyright © 2004).

comments that are critical. Often the data we take in aren't even valid data at all, but rather our interpretation of something — such as a facial expression, or a lack of some action, such as a returned phone call. Information such as this seeps in despite the overwhelming presence of data that contradict our assumptions because this "evidence" validates our worst fears about ourselves or others.

Even the most data-driven people can cling tightly to an assumption that has no logical analysis at all, other than what one person says. Many people go through life believing they are not creative. When pressed to provide evidence that this assumption is true, the data presented are frequently unimpressive. More often than not, people's number one substantiation is their lack of evidence to the contrary: "I've never done anything really creative." This is more likely a product of their faulty assumption, which has kept them from trying anything more creative, than anything else. The assumption becomes both the cause and the effect.

> *When you believe something, you have made it true for you.*
>
> *~ A Course in Miracles*

Anything people do repeatedly over a long period of time becomes ingrained. This is good news when you are trying to learn something that serves you. You will start off being unconsciously incompetent[2] — unaware of what you do not know. Many pre-teen children believe they can drive because they do it in their video games. They are in this state of **unconscious incompetence**. Once you endeavor to learn something you do not know, you will enter a state of **conscious incompetence**, where you become painfully aware of what you do not know. This will happen to all unknowing children (as it happened to me so many years ago) the first time they get behind the wheel of a real automobile.

After you begin to learn the basics of the new skill, you will

---

[2]The conscious competence theory is another name for the "Four Stages of Learning," a theory posited by 1940s psychologist Abraham Maslow.

become consciously competent. You'll reach a level of proficiency that requires you to be deliberate about each action you take. You may need to rely on notes or a mentor to help you perform effectively, but you'll be able to act on the necessary knowledge if you keep your full attention on the task at hand. This is the stage of **conscious competence**. The more you practice, the less dependent you become on external resources to help you remember what to do. The knowledge and experience are internalized, and you get

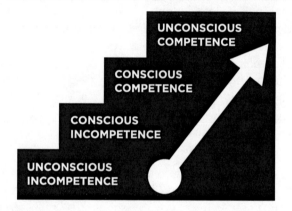

MASLOW'S FOUR STAGES OF LEARNING

UNCONSCIOUS
COMPETENCE

CONSCIOUS
COMPETENCE

CONSCIOUS
INCOMPETENCE

UNCONSCIOUS
INCOMPETENCE

to a point where you can execute the task with little or no effort or attention — **unconscious competence**. Consider, for example, the number of times you get into your car and operate it, practically without thinking.

Assumptions that have become engrained in our thinking operate in a similar manner. We are so accustomed to thinking them, that we have lost awareness (or consciousness) of their existence. When you are unconsciously competent with a particular assumption, it will compel you to act in a habitual way without you having to even think about it. This is a kind of knee-jerk reaction. We take these assumptions as givens and are not likely to stop and question whether they may be true. In fact, the behavior these assumptions drive becomes so automatic that we may not even be aware that it is linked to an assumption at all.

When you combine the habitual and somewhat involuntary nature of our behavior under these assumptions with the tendency to dramatically skew the data we process in favor of what confirms what we already believe, it is easy to live on a kind of "autopilot." You can also appreciate how difficult it is for two people to genuinely connect to and communicate with each other when each is operating on deeply imbedded assumptions that may be conflicting. We really do run the risk of becoming puppets on a string. The irony is that the strings are created and sustained by the puppet, who loves to be in control and will continue to propagate and engrain faulty assumptions in order to maintain it.

The power of these assumptions is so great that unless you can identify and dis-empower the assumption that drives any given action, you will not be able to sustain behavioral change. Going back to the example of delegation, you can read numerous books and attend all kinds of seminars and workshops that teach the steps of effective delegation. You may become so proficient that you can even teach others these steps. However, if your assumption that getting something done right requires that you do it yourself is still operating at the level of unconscious competence, you will not be able to execute on your newfound knowledge. Despite your best intentions and understanding of the proper way to delegate, you are likely to fall back into an old, established pattern that will prevent you from fully letting go so that true delegation can happen.

> *Rule your mind or it will rule you.*
>
> ~ Horace,
> Roman lyric poet
> (65 BC–8 BC)

In addition to preventing us from acting on new knowledge, our ingrained assumptions keep us from accessing and employing our own inner wisdom. In response to the beckoning of animating genius to make positive change in our lives, the puppet pulls those strings and keeps us firmly rooted in habitual behavior and thoughts. The assumptions it propagates remind us of all there is to fear, amplify our limiting beliefs, and keep us entrenched in skepticism and doubt.

The best leaders are those who find a way to utilize the data the puppet offers without becoming dominated by it.

Leaders are by definition change agents — they see possibilities in people, situations and environments they find themselves in and act on them in ways that allow new things to happen.

Assumptions have a way of keeping us unwittingly reinforcing the status quo — even if it is something we do not believe in. We do things because we have always done them — either individually or organizationally. Though we may not have been the ones to create the rules that govern this behavior, we are responsible for internalizing and acting on them. The best leaders know this and realize that the first step in effecting change is to help others see what was previously hidden so that they can recognize and challenge the assumptions they have been taking as a given.

There are many ways of identifying assumptions that operate on a daily basis within yourself and others around you. Let's start with an understanding of all the different forms these assumptions can take.

Types of Assumptions

Limiting assumptions trap us in illusions that keep us from seeing and embracing what is really in front of us — as well as what is within us. The number and types of assumptions people hold are too numerous to count. However, there are two basic categories that seem to drive the majority of our behavior, each related to what we are processing.

The first category comprises assumptions about *what is and what could be*, including, who we are and what we are (or are not) capable of, who others are and what they are (or are not) capable of, and the way life is — and what is possible and impossible in any situation.

The second category is made up of assumptions about *what should be*, including the way we should be, the way others should be, and the way life should be.

Category #1: What Is and What Could Be

Merriam-Webster defines confidence as "a feeling or consciousness of one's powers or of reliance on one's circumstances" and "faith or belief that one will act in a right, proper or effective way." The first three assumptions reflect our level of confidence in ourselves, others and life itself. Let's take a closer look at each of these.

Who We Are And What We Are (or Aren't) Capable Of

When Henry Ford said "Whether you believe you can, or you believe you cannot, you are right," he was alluding to the deeply held assumptions we have about ourselves that greatly determine the results we will achieve in any of our endeavors. Our self-confidence is largely a product of these assumptions. Confidence is both the chicken and the egg. When we are learning something new, we lack the experience that would allow us to know whether we can execute on a given task. However, we can draw upon our belief that we have the ability to learn something new and that given practice, we can become skilled and experienced. This belief is the seed of confidence. The more our experience validates our expectations, the more our confidence grows.

Exercising confidence does not require that anyone else believe we know what we are doing, or even that they witness us doing anything at all. It requires us to do what must be done at any given time, utilizing the resources at our disposal and calling on our own strengths, ingenuity, and discernment to do it. It is easy, however, to fall into the trap of trying to gain confidence from the outside in — undertaking our tasks with an eye on the perceptions of others and allowing their reactions to determine our confidence level.

A positive response increases our confidence, and a negative one decreases it. When we repeatedly engage in behavior like this, we subjugate our ability to perform, and stunt our inherent talent by interrupting its natural flow. We interpret and internalize the reactions of others and allow these to shape our assumptions about ourselves, for better or worse.

As we go about trying to win approval, we allow others to define our sense of self and grow ever more unaware of the treasure (animating genius) that sits in our own backyard. We leave our true fortunes to seek things that glitter and fade. The harder we try to win the confidence and validation of others, the further we get from achieving them and the more deeply buried our inherent riches become. Rather than acknowledging evidence all around us that confirms we are competent, creative, talented, worthy and capable of achieving great things, we waste our energy focusing on what we believe is lacking. Praise and encouragement are often unable to permeate the puppet's strong self-doubt. Criticism, however, is like steel to the magnetic force of our personal misgivings. It validates our feelings of inadequacy, which leads us to act in ways that sub-optimize our potential. This further erodes our confidence and we risk locking ourselves in vicious cycles of deteriorating performance and eroding self-assurance. We not only do not succeed, we actually never really even try.

**Confidence is an inside job.
We cannot expect others to believe in us
if we do not believe in ourselves.**

In the next chapter, we will explore the best methods for disempowering these limiting assumptions about ourselves and replacing them with beliefs based in the truth of our pure potential. For now, it is important to recognize the power these limiting beliefs have over us and the degree to which they serve as strings that both limit our movement and allow others to manipulate us.

Who Others Are and
What They Are (or Aren't) Capable Of

When we harbor doubt about others, we activate their limiting assumptions about themselves, and their confidence erodes. In this way, our limited beliefs about what others are capable of lead us to act in ways that pull their strings. However, our assumptions about other people have power over them only if our assumptions match the assumptions or deepest fears they hold about themselves. This is the dynamic Eleanor Roosevelt was referring to when she said, "No one can intimidate you without your consent." Conversely, when we identify and match other people's positive beliefs about what they are capable of, this dynamic can be used in a very positive way.

Living Up to Expectations — Take 1

Many years ago a famous experiment was conducted with teachers who were asked to work with a group of students who had been identified as high achievers. In reality, these students were randomly selected and there was no indication that their intellectual abilities or development were in any way superior. However, at the end of the school year, their test scores showed significantly greater gains in intellectual growth and development than students in the control group. These students simply lived up to the high expectations of their teachers. [3]

This phenomenon, which is referred to as the Pygmalion effect, operates in corporate settings as well, as J. Sterling Livingston described in a *Harvard Business Review* article entitled "Pygmalion in Management."[4] In the article, he describes numerous studies that indicate

---

[3] *Pygmalion in the Classroom: Teacher Expectations and Pupils' Intellectual Development* (1968; expanded edition, 1992).

[4] Sterling Livingston, *Pygmalion in Management* (Harvard Business Review, September-October 1988).

that people's performance is directly influenced by the expectations managers have of their subordinates. Livingston concludes that superior managers tend to create high performance expectations that their people achieve, while less effective managers fail to develop similar expectations — and their subordinates are less productive as a result.

It is the nature of man to rise to greatness if greatness is expected of him.

~ John Steinbeck, American Pulitzer Prize-winning author (1902-1968)

Not surprisingly, the ability to believe in the potential of others is closely linked to one's ability to believe in one's self. In their book *Leaders*, Warren Bennis and Burt Nanus concluded, after conducting some ninety interviews with CEOs and top public administrators, that "...a key factor [to effective leadership] was...what we're calling... positive self-regard. ...Positive self-regard seems to exert its force by creating in others a sense of confidence and high expectations, not very different from the fabled Pygmalion effect."[5]

Living Up to Expectations — Take 2

As an executive coach, I often gather feedback about my clients from people who are critical to their success — coworkers, customers, subordinates and their boss. Every once in a while I hear widely differing assessments of a given client. By example, in one such case, there were two distinct groups of respondents. One group raved about the leader, praising her ability to make quick decisions and get others to take focused action, while others complained that she was highly ineffective, intimidating people and using fear as a primary motivator. Not surprisingly, those who didn't hold the leader in high

---

[5]Warren Bennis and Burt Nanus, *Leaders* (New York, NY, Harper & Row, 1985).

esteem were people about whom the leader harbored strong doubt or even resentment.

This leader's assumptions that others were not capable of performing without the application of force became an expectation that others lived up to. She may have achieved short-term compliance, but not long-term commitment. She interpreted this response as data that confirmed her limiting beliefs and used it as validation that her approach was merited.

The people who reported to this leader had assumptions about her as well. As long as they believed her intentions were self-serving and that her belief and trust in them was weak, they focused on aspects of her behavior that confirmed those assumptions and felt justified behaving in ways that validated her limiting beliefs about them. As a result, everyone involved was locked into a cycle of largely unproductive behavior.

Our tendency to act on unchecked assumptions about others is one of the primary causes of conflict escalation.

Conflict can be resolved only at the level people are willing to address it. Our judgments and frustrations about people are often impacted more by our stories about them, their actions and their motives than what actually happened.

Steve and Larry

Steve doesn't return Larry's phone call. If Larry assumes Steve is being discourteous, Larry will feel justified treating his colleague in the same manner. This behavior may lead Steve to interpret Larry's subsequent actions as a product of disrespect, which could lead him to respond in a manner that matches Larry's behavior.

As a result, escalation occurs. In fact, even if Larry later learns that Steve lost his cell phone and never even got his initial message, the subsequent behavior each of them engaged in is likely to create conflict that is a direct reflection of each person's unexamined assumptions about the other.

**We create stories about each other,
and act in ways that are likely to make them true.**

The implications of this dynamic are significant for leaders, whose true purpose is to unearth the potential of those they seek to influence. Often leaders are not aware of their limiting assumptions and/or do not realize the impact these beliefs have on others. When we fall into this trap, we risk blaming others for behavior we may have actually contributed to in some way. Our limiting beliefs also keep us from acting upon extraordinary opportunities to see and bring out the very best in others — sometimes before those we lead see it in themselves.

The Way Life Is and What's Possible

Dan Millman, author of *The Way of the Peaceful Warrior*[6] states, "Energy follows thought — we move toward but not beyond what we imagine." This speaks to the power our assumptions about life itself have with regard to the outcomes we will experience.

**Behind every great achievement is someone,
somewhere, who believed it was possible.**

Without that belief, a vision of what could be is never created and the effort required to bring it into reality is never applied and focused. Quantum physics supports this notion with experiments that have demonstrated that we are surrounded by waves of possibility that collapse into particles that correspond with our beliefs about a given situation.

Like our beliefs about ourselves and what we are capable of, our assumptions about what is or is not possible shape our

---

[6]**Dan Millman,** *The Way of the Peaceful Warrior* (Novato, CA, H.J. Kramer, New World Library, September, 2000).

behavior, which in turn influences the results we achieve. If you believe something cannot happen, you will behave in ways that make that true. This might be a reflection of your own actions as well as the actions of others who are influenced by your beliefs. Harvey Mackay said, "Optimists are right. So are pessimists. It's up to you to decide which you will be."[7]

Faced with a problem, two leaders may have widely differing approaches. One, believing that reality prohibits a favorable outcome, will speak and act in ways that keep people locked in a paradigm that reveals only limitation and amplifies the dynamics that created the problem. In doing so, he will construct a box whose walls continue to be crashed into by those he leads. The answer to the problem lies waiting, beyond the limited assumptions that construct the reality of the paradigm this leader and all his followers are locked into. As long as they believe these assumptions, they will never look beyond them.

His colleague, on the other hand, believing that anything is possible, focuses his attention beyond limitations to entertain creative, innovative ideas. He inspires his group to do the same. This leader will encourage his constituents to look at things from many different angles. By setting an example that encourages everyone to challenge what they believe they know, he is able to move the group from their point of view to a higher viewing point — one that sees beyond limitations to possibilities. When Albert Einstein said, "Problems cannot be solved at the same level of consciousness with which they were created," he was referring to the box created by our limiting assumptions that keeps us from seeing a higher plane and broader array of potential solutions.

> *I am looking for a lot of people who have an infinite capacity to not know what can't be done.*
>
> *~ Henry Ford, founder of Ford Motor Company (1863-1947)*

---

[7]Harvey Mackay, *Swim with the Sharks Without Being Eaten Alive* (New York, NY, Ballantine Books, 1988).

What we have before us are some breathtaking opportunities disguised as insoluble problems.

~ John W. Gardner, Secretary of Health, Education and Welfare under President Lyndon Johnson (1912-2002)

Life can have a way of living up to our expectations, just as people do. Have you ever noticed that the quality of people's lives is often commensurate with the beliefs they have about it? Many people who believe life is rough often experience a great deal of struggle. Those who believe it is good tend to have a lot of joy. Their views are a product of their experiences, and their experiences are a product of their beliefs. It is very possible that we can change the quality of our experiences by altering our way of thinking about them. St. Augustine once said, "Faith is believing in that which you cannot yet see. The reward of this faith is seeing what you believe." Rather than basing our expectations of the future on what has occurred in the past, we can open ourselves to the possibility that something entirely different can occur, and allow ourselves the freedom of redefining our assumptions about life itself.

Think for a moment about the beliefs you have about life that may have been with you since you were a kid. Do you believe no good deed goes unpunished? Work is not supposed to be fun? Nice guys finish last? Fear is the best motivator? Success is the product of toil and sacrifice? How might these assumptions be causing you to act in ways that are keeping you stuck in these paradigms? What would you like to experience instead? And what would you need to believe in order to allow it to happen?

Perhaps the only limits to the human mind are those we believe in.

~ Willis Harman, American engineer, social scientist, author and futurist (1918-1997)

Now, think for a moment about all the things you need to do today and in the upcoming week. Which task or project gives you the most angst? If you are procrastinating about something, chances are you have some assumptions that are not serving you. It might be beliefs about what it will take to get the task done, whether or not you can do it, or what will happen once it is complete. The simple act of thinking these thoughts can sap your energy and motivation. When we hang on to our assumptions about how difficult something is, we often act in ways that make it so. Conversely, when we put our focus on the task itself, rather than our beliefs about it, we might find that it wasn't nearly as difficult or onerous as we thought it would be.

Category #2: What Should Be

The puppet is a creature of conditioning whose main goal is self-protection. It plays an essential role in helping us survive and thrive in the environments we find ourselves in. Our puppets are constantly scanning our surroundings to identify the behavior most likely to be deemed appropriate and lead to success. These observations become rules of engagement that take the form of assumptions about the way we should be, the way others should be, and the way life itself should be. Let's look at each of these.

The Way We Should Be

As children, we are taught by well-intentioned people what they consider appropriate and inappropriate behavior, and we do the same with our children. We learn that one behavior leads to a positive response and a different behavior to a negative one. Over time, we become indoctrinated to the rules of our families, our schools, our communities, and our societies. These rules take the form of assumptions about who we need to be and what we need to do to succeed. This dynamic continues throughout life.

Most of our assumptions are a valuable and vital part of our lives. They protect us from engaging in behavior that is hurtful, both to ourselves and to others. However, some of the assumptions we create lead us to act in ways that do not serve ourselves or others well. The school girl who believes she will not be liked or accepted if she does not dress a certain way is not all that different from the new hire who believes that he must choose his words carefully in order to avoid being ostracized. To remain a part of his crowd and stay in good stead, a gang member becomes conditioned to engage in behavior that may contradict the rules of engagement he learned from his mother. And, in turn, an ambitious manager may come to believe that in order to get ahead, he must bring others down.

Some of the assumptions we internalize about the way we should be are aligned with who we really are. Others are not.

When we become overly consumed with who we think we should be, we risk obscuring the truth of who we really are.

We become so identified with our outer world that we forget about the inner one. Assumptions that do not serve us keep us bound — they lead us to focus so much attention on what we have to lose that we are not likely to ponder what we would have to gain. The soft, gentle voice of animating genius is drowned out by the puppet's clamor.

The puppet uses its assumptions as strings that keep us bound, and determine in which direction we will move. The strings are held firmly in place by a fusion of emotions that reinforces their strength and power. These emotions include fear, doubt, regret, guilt and shame. Our assumptions about the way we need to be lead us to negatively judge ourselves when we do not act in accordance with them. In their grip, we fear the worst, question our ability to get by if it were to happen and beat ourselves up if we do not abide by them. Any one of these emotions takes us out of the present; instead we worry about the future and lament the past. We disconnect from our true source of power, our animating genius, who lives and breathes in the here and now. And again, our rules about who we should be keep us acting in ways that are inauthentic, imprisoned

I am an old man and have known a great many troubles, but most of them never happened.

~ Mark Twain,
American author and
humorist (1835-1910)

by preconceived ideas that are based in fear.

Ironically, though the puppet generates assumptions in an effort to keep us safe, these very assumptions themselves create a great deal of suffering. The emotions described above are not empowering and, as mentioned in the previous chapter, our bodies experience pain and discomfort when we believe a thought that is not aligned with the truer parts of ourselves embodied within animating genius. These assumptions lead us to live in ways that are not true to who we really are, which takes its toll on us over time.

The woman who goes to law school because everyone else in her family did may find herself miserable years later, questioning whether the work she does is really matched with her true talent and desires. If you find yourself waking up to the realization that your career is no longer satisfying (and question to what degree it ever was), you are not alone.

The behavior that the puppet tries to regulate through pressure created by its assumptions cannot be sustained indefinitely.

True transformation takes place when a person no longer identifies with his behavior and realizes that the change he seeks to make is motivated internally — a reflection of his true self versus what he and others believe he should be.

The irony is that once we accept and embrace a pattern of behavior within ourselves rather than resisting it (through shame, guilt, etc.), it loses its hold on us and falls away, allowing something greater to emerge.

Our attempts to push ourselves to be the people we think we should be keep us from realizing who we really are, even if we already have what we seek. If a man believes that he needs to be more outgoing and expressive to effectively interact with others, he may become overly critical of himself and not recognize the ways he already connects with people without even having to say a word. In so doing, he'll put pressure on himself to engage in behavior that is inauthentic and unnatural to him — which will ultimately prevent him from achieving his goal. However, if he honors his individual style, he may find that by being himself, he is able to build strong relationships rooted in something much deeper than having something clever and witty to say in every conversation.

Similarly, the assumptions we have about what we should be *doing* in any given moment keep us from being truly present with and focused on what we are doing or who we are with now.

If you believe you should be doing anything other than what you are doing in this moment, you are not really here.

You will not take in the same information. You will not make the same connections. You will not access the same parts of yourself. The lights will be on, but no one will be home.

The tragedy is that many of us live our entire lives this way — constantly planning what we will be doing next, and determining what we should be doing now in order to achieve some future state that is not here yet.

It has been said that, "Life is what happens when we are busy making other plans." Our children outgrow their play sets while we fret about answering all of our email and getting to the bottom of our in-boxes. The romance in our lives and our marriages is put on the backburner. Our greatest aspirations, ideas and dreams wither on the vines of our imaginations while we occupy ourselves with getting to the bottom of "to do" lists or attending "obligatory" events whose importance pales in comparison. If

You must live in the present, launch yourself on every wave, find your eternity in each moment. Fools stand on their island of opportunities and look toward another land. There is no other land; there is no other life but this.

~ Henry David Thoreau, American author and poet (1817-1862)

this strikes a chord with you, chances are that you are believing an assumption about who you should be and what you should be doing that is inconsistent with who you really are and keeping you from enjoying the experiences in your life that are perfectly aligned with who you are becoming.

The Way Others Should Be

Just as our beliefs of who we should be keep us from embracing the beauty of who we really are, our assumptions about the way others should be can keep us from seeing their greatness as well. Often, instead of focusing on their strengths, we put our attention on what we believe to be their weaknesses. Whether these assumptions are made explicit or not, others sense our judgment and dissatisfaction with them and a wall is created that keeps us from truly connecting to one another.

The irony is that even if people already are what we think they should be, as long as we do not believe they are, we will only take in evidence that leads us to believe they need to change. We will fail to see the qualities in others we believe they need to demonstrate. In addition, we tend to display the very behavior we believe others need to change. When we think others should be more kind, we are likely to engage in behavior that could take the form of intolerance or even cruelty. We may justify our behavior as being an appropriate response, but it begs the question of whether our assumptions about the way others should be may actually be more a reflection of ourselves than them. French author Anäis Nin said, "We see things not as they are, but as we are."

The Unseen Cycle

One of my clients expressed frustration over a colleague that he believed was stubborn, rigid, egocentric and insensitive. "This guy doesn't listen to anything I say!" he told me. "And what do you do when that happens?" I asked him. "I have to be more emphatic, talk louder, try to control the situation so I can get a word in," he replied. His unspoken assumption that his colleague should listen more prompted my client to act in ways that could lead his colleague to say the same about him. If his colleague had even a shred of listening ability, my client's behavior surely did not encourage or even acknowledge it. On the contrary, it most likely led him to engage in more of the behavior that originally irritated my client. That his colleague may have "started" the unproductive cycle does not alter the fact that they both became mirrors of each other, and true communication had no chance of taking place.

Without our assumptions about the way others should be, we can shift our focus from what we believe they lack to find something that is already admirable about them. And as hard as that may be, there is always something. Once we begin looking for those redeeming qualities, we may be surprised at what we may learn. Additionally, devoid of our assumptions about what others ought to be doing (which we can never really control), we can put our energy on what truly is in our sphere of influence. Instead of wishing and waiting for others to do something, we can step in and model the behavior we want to see.

Upon reflection, that client realized he was guilty of the same behavior he judged his colleague of and shifted his focus from what irritated him about the guy to what he could appreciate in him. He decided to initiate a conversation with his coworker in which he would deliberately do nothing but listen intently. Much to his surprise, he realized that he and his colleague were not in the deadlock disagreement he thought they were in. Each was using different language to advocate solutions that were actually more alike than they were dissimilar.

When we believe someone should be other than what they are, we are not appreciating or accepting them for who they truly are. Ultimately, they will rebel from our attempts to change them. This might happen during the first conversation, or after years desperately spent trying to live up to our expectations. Those who hold us in high esteem may internalize our assumptions about the way we believe they should be and spend a great deal of their lives trying to be someone they are not, only to resent us later when they realize the futility of these attempts. Our assumptions about how others should be might be more of a reflection of what we want or need for ourselves than what they should do or who they need to be, as when parents expect their children to live the lives they never did.

The biggest drawback of believing that others should be anything other than who they are is that we miss out on the value of their unique gifts.

For years, I facilitated behavioral style workshops in teams and organizations desiring to improve their effectiveness in working together. The classes were designed to help people better understand and appreciate their own styles as well as those of others so that they could leverage their differences to work better together, rather than judge and annoy each other. Those whose natural styles led them to want things to happen right away and in the manner they believed it should often came into the workshops irritated with colleagues who felt they needed more information before taking action. Gradually, each learned that the other offered strengths they themselves lacked. Those inclined to act swiftly helped the others get off the dime and get things done. Those who were inclined to gather more information before making a decision kept the others out of trouble and prevented rework and waste from occurring. But when each believed others should be more like themselves, this understanding and partnership never occurred.

The Way Life Should Be

Have you ever noticed that our expectations of the way things should be often set us up for disappointment? This seems to be especially true, the more detail and specificity we put into our plans and the more attached we are to having things happen exactly the way we want them to. If you find yourself disappointed, resentful or frustrated with your life and what has been occurring lately, chances are you have some pretty clear assumptions about the way life should be that are not serving you.

When we insist on having things happen the way we believe they should, we cut ourselves off from anything that falls outside the sphere of what we want or originally envisioned. Rather than allowing ourselves to appreciate and enjoy unforeseen incidents, we judge and dismiss them and instead occupy ourselves with trying to make our original plans work. We rush to the future based on a plan we created in the past and do not allow ourselves to be in the present.

Dancing with the Flow

Early in my career I designed and taught a lot of classes and workshops. In those days, curriculum was king to me. I spent hours planning what I would say, when, and to whom. Class activities and exercises were carefully placed in a sequence of choreographed events that I believed had to happen in a very distinct way. My biggest fear back then was losing my script or forgetting what it said.

What I realized over time was that the stronger I clung to my curriculum, the less connected I was to the class participants and my own intuition. I'd miss out on the little nuances that were incredible teaching moments and I'd redirect what could have become a fascinating and illuminating discussion so that I could stay on my predetermined schedule.

To have faith is to trust yourself to the water. When you swim you don't grab hold of the water, because if you do you will sink and drown. Instead you relax, and float.

~ Alan Watts, British philosopher, author and speaker (1915-1973)

It is rumored that when Disneyland opened, Walt Disney's assistants were concerned because the guests were walking on the new grass. Disney replied, "They're telling you where they want you to put the paths." Over the years I too have learned to dance with the flow of whatever unfolds. I've traded my assumptions that things should be anything other than what they are for a belief that everything is always perfect just the way it is. When things don't go according to my plan, I rest in the faith that there is a bigger plan, orchestrated by a higher intelligence with much more vision, creativity and insight than I have.

I have learned to detach from my limited ideas of what should be happening and appreciate that life's unforeseen events and curve balls always come with gifts that I will see, only if I am open to them.

**The problem is not having a plan;
it is being too attached to having things go exactly
according to that plan.**

That is when our assumptions about the way things should be keep us from appreciating and embracing the way things are. In this state, we are likely to become resentful and jealous of those whose lives seem to be more like we think ours should be. We may also blame our circumstances for our inability to execute and tell ourselves stories that excuse all kinds of behavior because our lives have not gone the way we wanted them to. George Bernard Shaw once said, "People are always blaming their circumstances for what they are. I don't believe in circumstances. The people who get on in this world are the people who get up and look for the circumstances they want, and if they can't find them, make them." The major thing that prevents us from doing this are our assumptions about the way life should be.

**Life will never be what we think it should be.
It is what it is.
And at its core, like each of us, life itself is perfect.**

I realize that this is a controversial statement. It does not fit with the tragedy in the world, or the suffering and cruelty. But a belief that anything should be other than what it is keeps us from being in a place to summon the parts of ourselves that are truly called for in any given situation.

Think about the tragic events that took place in the United States on September 11, 2001. A plane commandeered by terrorists flew into the Twin Towers of the World Trade Center, killing thousands of people. This event was, by all rational standards, an act of a handful of men driven by evil and unspeakable cruelty. Many of those who were consumed with anger, and beliefs that it shouldn't have happened, engaged in behavior that propagated and even demonstrated the same kind of hatred and judgment with which the horrific act was committed. Those who moved beyond their anger, and their assumptions of what should or shouldn't have happened, were able to focus instead on what could happen. They mobilized people and uplifted them — transforming a crisis and tragedy into an event that awakened us to our true nature, and what is most important in our lives.

Years ago, a friend of mine gave me a refrigerator magnet upon which the words "So what. Now what?" are written. These simple words have such great wisdom. They point the way that allows us to rise above our self-pity and access the wisdom to intuitively make the choices necessary to rise above whatever circumstances we find ourselves in. So what? So what if things didn't go the way we planned? So what if we were beset with unfortunate occurrences? Rather than spending our time and energy trying to find out why, why not focus on what we will do next? Rather than look at what we have lost, we can look at what we still have — and at what, if anything, the current experience has to teach us. Rather than becoming resentful and preoccupied with remorse, regret or anger and frustration at the way things have happened and the way we or others have handled them, we can start anew — right now, shifting our focus from what should be happening to what could be. What will we choose right now, in this moment? If we pause long enough, allowing our minds to become still, we will find that we have all the answers we need. And if even one of us can find the courage to do this, others,

So what? Now what?

seeing the peace that comes from acts of faith this introspection tends to inspire, will follow.

When people we care about experience hardships, we do them very little good by lavishing them with sympathy, conspiring in their rebellion against a course of events that have already taken place. This insurgence does little to help them unless at the core of their rage they find the impetus to rise above their anger rather than react from within it. Our pity reduces them to helpless victims who believe they have cause to lament and despise what they have come to believe is a cruel universe. No good ever comes from actions taken with such a mindset.

Instead, we can help them shift their focus from what has taken place (the past) to what they can do about it (the present). Rather than commiserating in woeful stories, we can help them recognize the opportunities present in every challenge and seize them with vitality and courage. Setbacks can then become platforms from which we, and our loved ones, can dive into our true natures — discovering ourselves to be far greater than we thought we were. This is what the great leaders throughout the history of the world have done that enabled people, countries, even nations to prosper under great adversity. We have the opportunity to do this every day, both for ourselves and others.

Our assumptions have the most power over us when we are unaware of them. We are so good at them that they operate without our conscious awareness, believing they are givens rather than variables. They are the fuel that fires our knee-jerk reactions, closing the gap between stimulus and response and holding us prisoner with the splendid shackles of our own creation. The first step to becoming free of these assumptions is to recognize that they are there and open our eyes to the suffering they create in our lives. Then we can realize that being the people who created them, we have the power to dismantle them as well. In the next chapter, *Stronger than String*, we will explore methods for doing just that.

TYPES OF ASSUMPTIONS

WHAT IS AND WHAT COULD BE	WHAT SHOULD BE
What We Are Capable Of	**The Way We Should Be**
We believe that we have the ability to learn something new.	Since childhood, we learn "appropriate" and "inappropriate" behavior.
We are certain that, given practice, we can become skilled and experienced.	Some assumptions we create lead us to actions that do not serve us or others.
We do what must be done, utilizing the resources at our disposal and call on our own strengths and ingenuity.	We sometimes become consumed with who we think we should be, obscuring the truth of who we truly are.
We cannot expect others to believe in us if we do not believe in ourselves.	We focus on what we may have to lose rather than on what we have to gain.
What Others Are Capable Of	**The Way Others Should Be**
When we harbor doubt about others, we activate their limiting assumptions about themselves.	Instead of focusing on others' strengths, we focus instead on what we believe to be their weaknesses.
When we identify and match others' positive beliefs about what they're capable of, we create a positive dynamic.	When we judge others, we often display the very behavior we believe others need to change in themselves.
Our true purpose must be to unearth the potential of those we seek to influence.	Instead of waiting for others to act, we can step in and model the behavior we want to see.

TYPES OF ASSUMPTIONS, continued

WHAT IS AND WHAT COULD BE	WHAT SHOULD BE
What Others Are Capable Of	**The Way Others Should Be**
Without limiting beliefs, we can act on extraordinary opportunities and bring out the best in others.	The greatest drawback of believing others should change is that we miss out on the value of their unique gifts.
The Way Life Is and What's Possible	**The Way Life Should Be**
Our assumptions about what is or is not possible shape our behavior, which in turn influences the results we achieve.	Insisting on things happening the way we believe they should cuts us off from any-thing outside the sphere of what we want.
A leader will encourage constituents to look at things from many different angles.	We need to make the choices necessary to rise above any circumstance.
When we put our focus on the task itself, rather than our beliefs about it, we are likely to find it's not as difficult as we thought it would be.	We can help our constituents recognize opportunities in every challenge and to seize them with vitality and courage.

Chapter 7

Stronger Than String

Pinocchio finds himself trapped in a small cage, where he regrets his actions. After concerted effort, Jiminy finds Pinocchio, and the Blue Fairy appears again. In response to her inquiries, Pinocchio invents a story about having been kidnapped by two monsters and suddenly experiences his nose beginning to grow.

It has been said that humans use only about ten percent of their brainpower. Perhaps this is because we get locked into seeing and doing things in such a way that we never have cause to tap into the remaining ninety percent. Like a small child that gets so mesmerized by one toy that he never stops to realize he has a whole room full of other equally delightful gizmos and gadgets, we play with only a small subset of what is available to us. We dream of something more, but never relax the grip on our favorite toys enough to embrace anything else.

This chapter is about learning to relax our grip on the tried, true, comfortable ways of being that no longer serve us. As mentioned, our assumptions serve a vital role. They help us make our way through the world. Utilizing the language of our puppet, they serve to keep us safe and are the product of a logical analysis of the world around us. The trouble is that our puppets create assumptions based on what they see – the toys they already know well. When we are ready to delve into that splendid trove of treasures that has until now been out of our reach, we must go beyond the language of the puppet to discern that of our animating genius.

It is important to note that not all assumptions are erroneous or out of alignment with our true selves. Many of our assumptions are empowering beliefs that have strong foundations of truth.

The assumptions that take us away from our true nature and have us acting in ways that go against it are the puppet's strings.

Animating genius can be the source of assumptions too. However, rather than coming from the outside in, the beliefs of animating genius come from the inside out, emanating like rays of light that illuminate the way. These are our truths. Rather than robbing energy, they give and sustain it – both to ourselves and to others. The chart on page 110 shows a comparison between the strings of the puppet and the truths of animating genius.

Journalist Ludwig Borne, who lived in the eighteenth century, once said, "Losing an illusion will make you wiser than gaining a truth." This is because we already have truth. It is inherent in our being, our animating genius. Like a parking brake, limiting assumptions keep us from fully accelerating, from entirely utilizing the power that is already within us. To become free, we must lift the veil of limiting assumptions that keeps us from seeing and acting on our truths. In this way, we become fueled by something stronger than string that energizes us from within and continues out,

The only limit to our realization of tomorrow will be our doubts of today. Let us move forward with strong and active faith.

~ Franklin D. Roosevelt, 32nd United States President (1882-1945)

beyond our individual sphere, to touch the lives of others.

But first, we must recognize those assumptions that are not serving us.

THE PUPPET'S STRINGS	THE ANIMATING GENIUS'S TRUTHS
Keep us trapped in an illusion	Allow us to see beyond illusion
Leave us powerless and victimized	Show us our true power and lead us to act on it
Bring us to the future, based on the past	Open the present moment – making it timeless, infinite
Keep us separate from others	Reinforce our connectedness
Narrow our focus	Expand our vision
Lead us to doubt ourselves and others	Help us trust ourselves and others
Keep us in fear	Allow us to find and exercise courage
Maintain our interest in self-protection and survival	Spark our interest in service to the greatest good
Impose rules	Create possibilities
Are based in scarcity	Are based in abundance
Are head-based – data driven	Are heart-based – faithful
Keep us looking outside ourselves	Lead us to look within
Create suffering	Free us from suffering
Consume energy	Create and release energy
Make us weak	Make us strong

Doorways to Greater Understanding

The body's navigational compass can be very helpful in this regard. In Chapter 5, we discussed Pinocchio's nose as a navigational tool and explored our own physical sensations as indicators of to what degree we are in our truth or not. When our thoughts are aligned with truth, we will experience increased energy, clarity and strength. When we believe something not aligned with truth, our bodies become weak and may experience some kind of unpleasant sensation, such as discomfort, tension, pain, or pressure. These sensations are often accompanied by feelings of low energy. Think of these sensations as the discomfort that comes from straining against the strings of the puppet. When you begin to experience them, the odds are that you've run smack into an assumption (or a few of them) that is not serving you.

These feelings, though uncomfortable, are doorways into greater understanding of yourself that open passages through which you can reclaim your freedom. When you find yourself in them, the most important thing is to stay – to not run away. Our tendency is to find a way to silence or numb ourselves to relieve our suffering. These solutions are always temporary and often exacerbate the cause of our pain. Jack Frost once wrote, "The best way out is always through." Rather than creating distance from the discomfort, we must jump in with both feet and have a good look around.

In the grip of an anxious feeling, ask yourself, "What do I believe?" You will begin the process of making the invisible known. What is operating far beneath the surface is the perfect execution of a thought or assumption that you have most likely engaged in so many times that you now do it without even being aware that it is happening. With lightening speed, our brains make connections between sensory input and memories, previous stories, beliefs and emotions and seamlessly execute predetermined responses that at one point were designed to keep us safe. Before we can dismantle this mechanism, we must slow it down enough to see what is happening. These fabulous machines are a product of our own ingenuity, now performing so flawlessly that we don't even have to be conscious of their activity. They are on auto-pilot. When such programs no longer serve us, we need to perform an upgrade. But first, we have to find the glitch.

Remembering the Phases of Learning

Recall for a moment the four phases of learning:

- Unconscious incompetence (we don't know what we don't know)

- Conscious incompetence (we are painfully aware of what we don't know)

- Conscious competence (we have learned something new that requires effort and concentration)

- Unconscious competence (we are so good at something that effort and concentration necessary to do it are minimized or even eliminated)

When we are learning something new, we will move from unconscious incompetence to unconscious competence. However, when we are "un-learning" something (such as a belief that no longer serves us), the direction is reversed. Our goal is now to move from unconscious competence to unconscious incompetence.

When we find ourselves experiencing anxiety that is the product of an ingrained assumption, we are in the realm of unconscious competence. We are so good at allowing that anxiety to take us over, that we are not even aware we are doing it. We experience only the result and unintended consequences of this thinking – which often shows up in our bodies.

Unconscious Competence: When I took a job that wasn't right for me, the anxiety showed up first in the feeling of a pit in my stomach, and then graduated to full-blown nausea and tension that kept me from sleeping.

Before we can put our finger on what the thought actually is, we must move back to conscious competence. We need to slow down the process by creating a gap in the knee-jerk reaction so that the stimulus no longer leads to an immediate and unconscious response. We do this by becoming the observer of our own thinking. In this way, we come to recognize our thoughts and realize that we are the thinker, rather than the thought.

Conscious Incompetence: **I was believing a number of things that were not serving me.**

When I stopped long enough to trace my thinking, I was able to identify the following assumptions:

- I had no choice but to take the position (and not doing so would have been career-limiting).

- I would have appeared ungrateful if I acted in any other way.

- If I just hung in there long enough I would begin to enjoy it.

Each of these thoughts triggered a negative physical response that was an alert to the fact that I was thinking and acting in a way that was out of alignment with my animating genius. The longer I believed these stories, the more intense the feelings became.

Have you been experiencing anxiety recently? If so, see if you can trace it to a thought.

- Are you dreading a task?

- Feeling guilty because there is something else you believe you should be doing right now?

- Annoyed with something someone did in the last few days?

- Irritated with your own behavior in some situation?

- Worried about something that has yet to happen?

Try to find the thought that elicits the most angst for you. When you begin to feel it, dig even deeper. Assumptions are like weeds. They are often connected, and the deeper you go the more likely you are to discover the mother root.

In workshops I've facilitated over the years, participants are encouraged to come with challenges that are representative of something that tends to recur in their lives.

- Some feel overwhelmed and crave freedom and relaxation.

- Others feel as though they are not appreciated, respected or listened to by their colleagues, boss, customers and even friends and family.

- Some are irritated by conflicts that never seem to get resolved and continue to spiral into greater intensity.

- Others are haunted by projects and tasks that they procrastinate doing, or dreams they fear pursuing.

In every case where these people experience some kind of suffering, they have been able to trace their discomfort to a thought or belief that ended up being illusory – created as a protection mechanism that is sustained out of fear and doubt.

It is easier to spot a limiting belief or assumption in others than it is in our selves. This is because our driving assumptions are so engrained that they become like water to a fish. However, with a bit of distance and objectivity they become visible.

Becoming Your Own Detective

In workshops, I encourage people to become detectives with each other, asking probing questions designed to reveal the logic upon which people's actions and decisions are based. As participants explain themselves, the assumptions often come rolling off their tongues spoken with the same certainty that one could proclaim the sky is blue.

- "Well, if I slowed down I would miss opportunities and be acting selfishly or irresponsibly," or

- "So-and-So obviously doesn't respect me or he wouldn't be doing such-and-such," or

- "If I don't get this thing done perfectly/right away/the same way others have done it/etc., I won't succeed," or

- "I'm too busy to be doing what I really want and if I did do what I really want to, I'd let everyone down."

When people arrive at these assumptions, their shoulders are often up to their ears and their faces are scrunched into wrinkled balls — or they become extremely lethargic, collapsing into themselves and sinking into the furniture as if their bones had suddenly disappeared.

If you don't have the luxury of a partner who can listen to your reasoning about the situation you find yourself in, you can try writing it out or even speaking into a recording device. Often such a writing pad or recording device becomes transformed into a third party who can show us the little glitches in our thinking. The more we write, or speak, the more honest we become until things begin spilling out that we didn't even realize were in play. With a bit of practice, you can learn to distance yourself from your own thinking — playing it out and then standing back a few feet to discern what's really going on. When you hit the assumption that is producing the discomfort, you will intuitively know. Many times the thought, once realized, seems completely irrational — though still very compelling. It's as though one part of us recognizes the fallacy while the other part has been so indoctrinated with it that we never stopped to question its validity.

Some of the most common assumptions:

- If it's not difficult, it's not worth doing.

- If I am not busy all the time, I must be lazy.

- If I don't show others who's the boss, they'll take advantage of me.

- The leader/boss/parent should have all the answers and/or be infallible.

- If I am not winning, I am losing.

- If I don't do it myself, it won't get done right (or at all).

- If I don't please everyone, I will not be successful.

- I don't have what it takes to…

- If I can't do something well, I shouldn't do it at all.

- If I say what I really think/believe/stand for, bad things will happen (I'll damage my relationships, there will be retribution, people will think I'm crazy).

- If I do what I really want to do, bad things will happen (people will think less of me, I'll let others down, I'll be irresponsible, I won't make any money).

Of course, there are countless assumptions in all variations that limit us, like Pinocchio's strings. The deeper you go, the more powerful the assumptions are. A common initial assumption, "I am not capable of performing the task I must now do" can often be linked to another more deeply held assumption: "I am not competent at all and if I don't keep up appearances, everyone will find out." This type of assumption has a way of rearing its head in many situations across the span of our lives, both personally and professionally.

**Assumptions that tend to be most limiting
are those that would have us believe we need to go outside
ourselves – to prove something through achievement,
acquisition or victory over others – to get what we already have
within – respect, approval, worthiness, wholeness,
satisfaction and love.**

**Once we begin to be aware of these strings and recognize that
we are the ones holding them, we can begin to dismantle them
and reclaim our true power.**

See if you can put your finger on a limiting assumption that you believe. It doesn't matter what you pick. Trace any anxiety you are currently feeling to a thought that you can express in the form of an assumption — perhaps an assumption about who you are, what you are capable of, or how you should be; what someone else is or isn't capable of, and how they should be, or how life itself is or should be. If it is truly an assumption, it will match the characteristics of the puppet's strings listed on the left side of the chart on page 110. Write this assumption somewhere so that you can refer to it, as we learn how to dismantle the strings that are holding you in place.

Dismantling the Strings

Once limiting assumptions are identified, we have succeeded in taking a step from unconscious competence to conscious competence. We become aware of what we are doing and have slowed down the process so that we can see it in action. We can now begin to question the validity of the assumptions that have been unconsciously driving our behavior for so long. As stated before, of the 400 billion bits of information we are exposed to every second, our brains process only about 2000. The information that gets past our filters is the information that confirms what we already believe – whatever matches our assumptions. Because that is the only data we have taken in, of course these assumptions have continued to be validated over time. It's as though we have been standing in one corner of a room, believing that what is in front of us is the only thing that is there.

**The first step to challenging these assumptions
and dismantling our strings
is to realize that we have been seeing only a small fraction
of the larger picture available to us —
and take responsibility for that.**

Because our default over time has been to take in only data that validates our assumptions, to become free of them we must deliberately reverse the process. Doing so requires that we shift our focus from what confirms our assumptions to begin to perceive data and information that may not support them, or could actually directly contradict them.

So we move from:

Unconscious Competence: **When I took a job that wasn't quite right for me, the anxiety showed up first in the feeling of a pit in my stomach, and then graduated to full-blown nausea and tension that kept me from sleeping.**

to:

Conscious Competence: **I was believing a number of things that were not serving me.**

to:

Conscious Incompetence: **Is what I've believed really true? Are there other factors I have not considered?**

We begin to ponder how much we *really* know and what else is out there that we haven't been seeing. We now know that we have been standing in a corner and are ready to turn around and take in the rest of the room. Responsibility connotes our ability to choose a response. When we are able to recognize that our previous decisions were made with incomplete data, we see that there is reason to choose a different response – one that will better serve us, and those around us as well.

Poke a Hole

"Don't believe everything you think."

One of the best works I've read on the process of becoming free of assumptions is Byron Katie's *Loving What Is*.[1] In the book, she proposes four simple questions:

1. Is it true?
2. Can you absolutely know that it's true?
3. How do you react when you think that thought?
4. Who would you be without the thought?

The first and second questions – "Is that really true?" and "Can you absolutely know that is *always* true?" allow us to poke holes in what we previously thought were rock-solid cases. We put our assumptions on the stand and become the prosecuting attorney, looking for evidence that disproves or casts doubt upon them. At the very least, we can find a crack in the logic.

Often, when we ask ourselves these two questions, we inherently know the answer is no. Given the opportunity, we can begin to explore why that is the case. Sometimes simply inquiring allows us to focus long enough on something we never allowed ourselves to ponder. The puppet, frightened by animating genius's truth, diverts our attention to our greatest fears, what we would have to lose, and evidence that gives us reason to question and doubt what we know deep inside. When our fears

---

[1]Byron Katie and Stephen Mitchell, *Loving What Is: Four Questions That Can Change Your Life* (New York, NY, Three Rivers Press, 2003).

are activated, it is more difficult to trust in our truth. The illusion is created and the puppet conspires to keep it firmly rooted in our perception. This first step does not require that we turn our entire worlds upside down, only that we begin to question whether our worlds are exactly what we thought they were. We give ourselves permission to pull back the curtain a bit.

We can begin by identifying any exceptions to the rule – any time in our history that the assumption in question may not have been one hundred percent true.

Can you absolutely, positively know that you are incapable of performing the necessary task? Or — going deeper — that you are incompetent? Of course, not. Why not? Because you have done some pretty amazing things over the course of your life; because you have been able to perform in some way adequately enough to get you where you are now.

Is it absolutely, positively true that you will succeed only when you please everyone? No, because there have been times when you had to do what you knew was right to accomplish what was most important, even if it wasn't what everyone wanted.

Assumptions that invoke our rules about the way life is are sometimes easier to poke holes in when we ask ourselves whether we would want our children to believe the same thing. Would you be happy if your kids grew up believing that work should always be hard, that in order to get ahead they must sacrifice what brings them joy? That if they can't do something well they shouldn't do it at all? When we begin to realize that we have been modeling something that directly conflicts with what we want for those we love and lead, the impact can be enough to wake us from the illusions that delude us.

See if you can poke some holes in the assumption you identified above.

- Is it really true?

- Can you absolutely positively know that it is always true?

- Why not?

- What are some exceptions to the rule?

- Is it true for everyone?

- If not, then why would the logic hold for you?

- Can you be absolutely sure about that?

Having raised even a smidgeon of doubt in what was once a rock-solid case, we can move onto the next step in the process of dismantling the strings of our limiting assumptions.

Find the Pain

We are pain-avoiding, pleasure-seeking creatures. The assumptions our puppet creates are designed to keep us from experiencing pain, by generating fear about worst-case scenarios and strategies about what we can do to keep from experiencing them. The irony is that often the assumptions themselves create more pain than the worst-case scenarios would if they actually happened. Somehow, we become desensitized to it until it manifests itself in ways that make us miserable.

The body doesn't lie. Like Pinocchio's nose, our bodies give us signals that something isn't right. These signals may range from slight discomfort to full-blown agony and are often complemented by emotional turmoil as well. Frustration, guilt, shame, worry, resentment — these emotions accompany beliefs that are not aligned in truth. However, we do not often recognize that the source of these emotions and the discomfort they bring are the faulty assumptions we've internalized to the point that we do not even recognize them.

Byron Katie's third question is "How do you feel and act when you are believing that thought?" Asking this simple question allows us to recognize, often for the first time, the true source of our pain. When you believe you are not competent, how do you feel? "Scared, weak, ashamed, worried, inadequate, depressed, lethargic, hopeless." These are some of the answers people who have attended my workshops have shared in answer to that question. "When you feel that way, how do you act?" I ask them.

- "I don't," is a common response.
- Or perhaps, "I try to puff myself up and do what I can to convince everyone that I can perform. But I feel like I'm living a lie."

In these states, no one would be able to do their best work. The fears become self -fulfilling. We play them out – and then what happens?

- "How do you feel after a whole day of doing that?
- What happens when you get home?
- How does it affect the way you interact with your family, your spouse, your children?"

What splendid shackles you have created!

~ William Shakespeare, English poet and playwright (1564-1616)

These questions bring the pain to a head and, in the workshops, even the other participants become uncomfortable, yearning to do something – anything to relieve the tension.

When my workshop participants begin to realize that the pain and suffering is solely linked to the assumption — what they are believing and how it causes them to feel and act — they begin to see beyond the edges of their self-created illusions. They realize that in addition to being the people who created their splendid shackles, they are also the people who hold the key to freedom.

See if you can find the pain associated with your limiting

assumption now. When you believe it, how do you feel and what do you do? How is that playing itself out? Is it working for you? When you believe it, are you the person — the leader — you want to be? Notice that any discomfort or anxiety you feel is linked to the *belief*, and the actions you tend to take when you are in the process of believing it.

Explore the Pleasure

"Who would you be without that thought?" This is Byron Katie's fourth question — one that allows for a shift from pain to pleasure. Once we have established that the pain is linked to a thought, we can explore the pleasure or payoff that comes from moving beyond it. "If you woke up tomorrow, and you could no longer believe that assumption, how would you feel and what would you do?" I ask my workshop participants. It's as though they have suddenly been given a stepladder that allows them to see over the horizon to a whole new field of beautiful possibilities.

"If I no longer believed I was incompetent…" They repeat their assumptions, trying them on for size, moving around like someone who whose corset has just been loosened. And then their animating genius comes out to play.

- "Well, I wouldn't get so worked up about everything," they might say.

- "I'd probably give myself a little bit more benefit of the doubt… "

- "And I'd probably have more fun."

- "I'd try more things, and put less pressure on myself."

"What would you do in the situation you described earlier?" I may ask, referring to the circumstances they spoke of that activated the assumption. Often, to their surprise, out of their mouths come simple answers with astounding power, spoken easily. As these people continue to talk, their inspiration and conviction grow. They are back in touch with their animating genius.

It is not uncommon for these people to come to some of the same conclusions that others had been trying to get them to see and act on for a long period of time. "My wife has been telling me that for years, but I never believed it would work." In some cases, even the advice other participants gave them which previously fell on deaf ears is suddenly a viable option.

What is really exciting and encouraging is that for the first time, these people own the solutions because they have accessed their own inner wisdom, the source of endless creativity and innovation.

They sit up straighter in their chairs and many times look as though they have become a few years younger. There is light in their eyes again as they realize they always had those answers.

Finding the Truth

Once the strings begin to weaken, we are ready to substitute illusion for truth. Doing so does not require that we exert a lot of energy trying to *stop* thinking any particular thought. Often our attempts to resist something end up intensifying whatever it is we are trying to stop. If I go to a party with the intention of eating no sweets, the first thing I'm likely to look for is the dessert table. If I tell you not to think of the color blue for the next thirty seconds — it will likely become foremost on your mind — unless perhaps you decide to think of a different color instead.

Courage is not the absence of fear, but rather the judgment that something else is more important than fear.

~ Ambrose Redmoon, American author (1933-1996)

Rather than resist the thoughts that once brought us down, we can shift our focus to something that holds more power — a thought that brings feelings of lightness and energy rather than heaviness and suffering. We can trade the puppet's strings for the animating genius's truth. How do we get there? It is easier than you might think.

With regard to a thought that does not serve you, in most cases the exact opposite of the original belief or assumption is true. "I am not competent" becomes "I am competent." We can even take it a step further and say, "I am competent and talented too, in my own unique way." The phrase: "If I say what I really think/believe/stand for, bad things will happen (I'll damage my relationships, there will be retribution, people will think I'm crazy)" becomes "If I say what I really think/believe/stand for, great things can happen (I'll strengthen my relationships, free myself of things, people or situations that are not good for me.)"

The key is to shift from your puppet to your animating genius. Believing that you are competent and talented will serve a greater good when it doesn't imply that others around you are not. Saying what you really think becomes constructive when you do it in a manner that is not designed to make others wrong, pass judgment, or win at the expense of others, as the puppet would have us do.

To find the truth that is a better substitute for the puppet's string, we must identify with animating genius and not the puppet.

In *Loving What Is,* Byron Katie calls the truth that is the best substitute for the puppet's strings "the Turnaround." She offers some interesting options for turning around assumptions that involve others, such as: "People should listen more to me." The first of these options is to flip the order of the two nouns in the sentence. "People should listen more to me" becomes "I should listen more to other people." The second option is to flip both nouns toward oneself: "People should listen more to me" becomes "I should listen more to myself."

Both of these methods for arriving at a turnaround allow the thinker of this thought to take responsibility for what is within his control. In the first example, the person stops waiting for others to listen and begins listening to others, interrupting the vicious cycle described in the previous chapter. He refrains from engaging in the very behavior that he wants others to cease (talking incessantly without listening) and begins to model what he would most like to see. This allows people, who previously felt as though they couldn't get a word in, to be heard and increases the odds that they may reciprocate. In the second example, he avoids the trap of trying to get others to believe something in an effort to allay his own doubts and fears. It allows him to stop seeking validation from others and give it to himself.

- How can you turn the assumption you previously identified into a truth?

- Could the opposite of what you believed actually be more true?

- How could you amend the statement to better align it with animating genius?

- If you have believed that someone should be acting in a different way toward you, might it be better to focus on how you could model that behavior yourself?

- If you have been waiting for someone else to give you something (validation, power, attention, respect), might it be more powerful for you to find a way to give that to yourself?

When you land on a truth, your body compass will serve as an indicator that it is indeed aligned with animating genius. You will feel lighter, freer, happier, stronger, and more energized. Once you locate your truth, see if you can find further reason to believe that it is true. Get busy seeking

The real voyage of discovery consists not of seeking new lands but in seeing with new eyes.

~ Marcel Proust, French novelist, critic and essayist (1871-1922)

data that confirms it. Think of what your life would be like with the new belief, and immerse yourself in the powerful possibilities that come with unencumbered thought.

Changing Habits and Thought Patterns

Your turnarounds, or truths, can also become affirmations and reminders that will help you redirect your thought when you find yourself succumbing to old habits and thought patterns. When you put an old, illusory assumption to the test, recognize the undesirable impact it is having in your life, and begin to glimpse the possibilities that exist for you without that assumption, the limiting belief loses its power over you. You may still think that thought from time to time, but it will no longer hold the same charge.

The new belief, which you will discover through your own thoughtful examination and inquiry, will be meaningful to you because of the work you have done to unearth it. Its power goes beyond the affirmations made popular and somewhat laughable by the Stuart Smalley character created by satirist and later Senator Al Franken on old *Saturday Night Live* sketches: "I am good enough, I am smart enough, and doggone it — people like me." Affirmations cannot simply be positive declarations that cover a valley of doubt, like a small bandage applied to a gaping wound. They only work when people believe them with their whole heart and soul, which is exactly what happens when people trade the puppet's illusion for the animating genius's truth using the process just described.

Engaging in the process of dismantling the puppet's strings has a neurological component as well. Research has revealed that whenever we are engaged in thought, neurons in our brains form connections that are reinforced every time that thought is repeated. Over time, these neural networks become hardwired in such a way that they become automatic, allowing us to operate with unconscious competence (and leading us to engage in knee-jerk reactions). However, whenever a given thought pattern is interrupted, these connections begin to lose their connectivity.

At the same time, new connections and even new neurons form with each new thought pattern. The chemicals that cemented the old connections get diverted into the new ones. The less we engage in an old pattern of thought, the weaker the networks become until they begin to dissolve and become replaced by new ones. In this way, whenever you pause long enough to examine your assumptions and trade the illusions for truths, you are literally rewiring your brain. Dr. Joe Dispenza has written at length about this process in his book *Evolve Your Brain – the Science of Changing Your Mind,* and also discusses it in the movie *What the Bleep Do We Know.*[2]

Think of a large flowing field of overgrown grasses. In the center is a path, worn so well that vegetation no longer grows upon it. This represents your old, tired assumption that you have exercised so many times that it now runs on autopilot. When, through inquiry, you substitute the truth for an assumption, you have effectively chosen a new path. The first time you walk it, you will be trudging through knee-high resistance. The grasses will bend and spring back into place behind you. But they will not be the same. The more you walk that new path, the more trodden the grasses become, until they yield and begin to disintegrate. The less you walk the old path, the wilder the grass surrounding it becomes, until the old trail becomes obscured.

It's been said that it takes twenty-one days to change a habit. If you find yourself falling into old patterns or habits, it is important not to become discouraged. Instead, congratulate yourself for becoming aware enough of your patterns to interrupt their automatic nature. You have successfully moved yourself — from unconscious competence in thinking a thought that does not serve you — to conscious competence. You are now aware that you are thinking a new thought and also recognize the impact that thought pattern has on your wellbeing and the effect of the desired result.

---

[2]Dr. Joe Dispenza, *Evolve Your Brain — The Science of Changing Your Mind* (Deerfield Beach, FL., Health Communications, Inc., 2007).

Many of us have a way of beating ourselves up for mistakes. We replay the movie in our heads just as it happened, reliving and even exaggerating the event that causes us to have disappointment in ourselves. And then we watch that scene over and over, feeling ever more discouraged with each repetition. The marvelous thing about the human mind is that we not only have the ability to rewrite the ending, but also to see that movie as though it already happened. We can ask ourselves what we would have liked to do (or think) differently, and play things out from that perspective. Even if all we do is envision the stimulus that triggered our old assumption and knee-jerk reaction and in our minds experience the same event while choosing to replace the illusory assumption with truth, we have made progress.

Research indicates that the mind cannot differentiate between events that happen in actuality and those that occur only in our minds. In 1995, an article was published in the *Journal of Neurophysiology* about a study that involved people learning to play a piece of music on a piano. One of the test groups learned and memorized a specific one-handed, five-finger sequence that they physically practiced every day for two hours over a five-day period. Another test group observed what was taught to the first group until they knew it by memory. Over the same five-day period, they mentally rehearsed the sequence in their minds, envisioning themselves playing it for the same length of time per day. At the end of the study, a technique called transcranial magnetic stimulation was used to measure changes that took place in the brain. Amazingly, the group that only mentally rehearsed showed almost the same expansion and development of neural networks in the same specific area of the brain as participants who physically practiced the sequences on the piano.[3]

What this study suggests is that when you envision your mental movie with a different ending and engage in new thought patterns, your brain will undergo the same process of breaking old neuronets and creating new ones that occurs when you interrupt the thought process and substitute your truth in real time.

---

[3]*Journal of Neurophysiology* (Volume 74, Issue 3, 1037-1045) Copyright © 1995, APS.

Five Days to Awareness

There is a wonderful old story I've heard repeated several times that reminds me of this process. A man walks down a street one day and falls into a large hole in the sidewalk. He is justifiably annoyed. No one told him this hole was there and he has experienced inconvenience and pain as a result. The next day he walks down the same street and falls into the hole again. This time, he is irritated with himself. He knew the hole was there and fell into it anyway. The third day, walking down the same street, he begins to stumble into the hole and catches himself before he falls in. The fourth day, he proudly steps around the hole. The fifth day, he takes a different street.

**Though our progress may not take place as
quickly as we would like,
the more aware we become of our behavior,
the more distance we establish between the trigger and the
response, and the more likely we are to
engage in a new thought pattern.**

The more often we engage in that thought pattern, the more automatic it will become, until it finally replaces the old one. We will have gone from unconscious incompetence with the new thought pattern (falling into the hole we didn't know was there), to conscious incompetence (falling into the hole even though we knew it was there), to conscious competence (stepping around the hole), to unconscious competence (taking a new street).

Using the same logic, the more we get in the practice of habitually identifying and examining our assumptions, the more automatic that process will become. Becoming aware of the way in which we are feeling and getting accustomed to tracing our discomfort to our thoughts is one thing we can practice regularly. Once we have identified what we believe about the situation that is producing the anxious or uncomfortable feelings, we can begin to poke holes in our beliefs by asking whether it is really true and finding evidence to the contrary. We can move into the pain of that belief by objectively observing in our mind's eye the behavior we tend to engage in when we believe that thought, how we feel as we are thinking it, and the way things tend to play out as a result. We can also ask how things could go differently if we no longer believed that thought or substituted it for something that is more aligned with animating genius. All of this can be done in the time it takes most people to commute to or from work, and the more often you practice it, the easier it will come to you.

Implications on Leadership and Conflict Resolution

Your effectiveness as a leader will largely be determined by the degree to which you are able to hold your stories more as hypotheses or possible explanations and are willing to entertain that there may be more to your stories and explanations than you think. Simply said, things are not always what they seem. To rise above this pitfall, get in the habit of asking yourself questions, such as, "What am I believing about this situation (or person)? What do I really know? What am I not seeing?" When you ask questions like these, your brain expands its orientation to allow new information to come in.

Be open to the views of others and go a step further to actively seek out those alternative viewpoints. Encourage people to challenge the way you are seeing things with the knowledge that you could be wrong. When we are able to relax our filters in this way, true learning and innovation can take place. Solutions to problems that were right in front of us suddenly become visible. We are able to go beyond our limited views to see what is really possible — in ourselves and others, our relationships, projects, positions, and organizations. And we are able to connect more deeply with those around us to address our challenges and opportunities in sustainable and mutually satisfying ways.

The best leaders are those who have the ability to raise the level of thinking or consciousness in those they lead or influence.

As previously mentioned, Albert Einstein's assertion that "problems cannot be solved at the same level of thinking within which they were created" alludes to the beliefs we operate within that unwittingly create or contribute to the problems. Until we learn to identify and rise above our faulty suppositions, we will remain locked in paradigms that prevent us from solutions that will result in long-term success. This is particularly relevant in situations that involve conflict.

Most conflict has at its root two people or parties who have widely differing assumptions or beliefs about things. Both will take in data that confirm what they already believe and screen everything else out. Each party believes that the picture it is seeing is the only one there is. In the most extreme cases, each faction will vilify the other, ascribing characteristics and motives that are dark, self-serving, and destructive. In the absence of real data, each group becomes susceptible to exaggerating or inventing stories about the other that further serve to obscure the real picture. The puppet's strings (or stories) allow entire populations of people to be manipulated to take action based on nothing more than conjecture or fear.

In a conflict, when tension runs high, most of us are more likely to immerse ourselves in finding ways to prove that our view is the only right one and that the other's view is somehow wrong. Theoretically, both are right, based on what each is seeing. The problem is that much of it is an illusion.

The key is to recognize that there is always more to the picture.
Our fear keeps us from going there.
The question is not which one of us is right,
but rather what are we both not seeing
that will allow us to find a truth that serves everyone?
How can we raise our sights from fear to love?

The more we become aware of the anxiety that results from believing thoughts not aligned with animating genius, the better we get at sidestepping the traps that our puppets set for ourselves and others. Instead of engaging in behavior that exacerbates the problem, we can consciously interrupt the pattern. One of the best ways to do this when tension runs high is by taking a deep breath. When we become panicked or feel as though we are being attacked, our breathing gets shallow and our brains do not get as much oxygen. We literally go out of our minds, unable to access the reserves of wisdom we always possess. Breathing allows us to inspire — to take in spirit, to regain our connection to something bigger than ourselves and allow it to guide and inform us. In this way we shift our identification from the puppet to the animating genius.

Once we have made this vital shift, we can move from our self-interest (which is what our puppet associates with) to what is in the best interest of all — including, but not limited to ourselves (which is what animating genius is all about.)

No longer having the need to defend or attack, we can practice curious inquiry:

- What is important to each of us?
- What do we have in common that we can both get behind?
- What is it we are each believing in this situation?
- Why does each person (or party) believe that?
- Is it really true?
- What is each of us missing?

We seek to understand each other rather that discredit one another. Being willing to question our initial assumptions does not require that we give in to or totally agree with others. It just means that we don't have to make them wrong in order to make ourselves right. Once we take our blinders off and toy with the idea that we may not be seeing the whole picture, we can begin to discover the truth that is present in both people's viewpoints. We learn to go beyond conflict and even compromise — into collaboration, building on each other's ideas and embracing and leveraging our diversity instead of allowing it to divide us. In this manner, we can habitually recognize and challenge our assumptions in a

Peace is a daily, a weekly, a monthly process, gradually changing opinions, slowly eroding old barriers, quietly building new structures.

~ John F. Kennedy, 35th United States of America President (1917-1963)

way that is aligned with animating genius — one that goes beyond win/lose scenarios to tap into and apply collective wisdom so that everyone can benefit.

The more we individually challenge our own assumptions in a non-judgmental way and shift our perspective from puppet to animating genius, the greater our ability to help others — our families and friends, our organizations, our communities, and beyond — to do the same.

**People around us learn
not from our words and our discourse, but from our example.**

Shifting our balance of power from puppet to animating genius is not easy — it entails a lifetime of exploration, missteps and realignments. The journey requires courage, determination and strength and there are many diversionary paths that have a way of luring us from our true path and keeping us stuck. We are now ready to explore those digressions and what is required to successfully navigate through them.

Chapter 8

❖

Pleasure Island

> *The cat and the fox convince Pinocchio that he needs a vacation for the sake of his health. They hand him over to a wicked coachman who "collects stupid little boys who play hooky from school" and takes them to Pleasure Island, where these boys indulge themselves until they transform into jackasses. While there, Pinocchio makes friends with a tough boy named Lampwick, who explains they can fight and wreck things, and eat all the cake, pie, and ice cream they want. They destroy and set things on fire, smoke cigars, play cards and chew tobacco. "Being bad is lots of fun!" Pinocchio proclaims. Jiminy finds him there and scolds, "How do you ever expect to become a real boy?" Even so, Pinocchio refuses to leave.*

Pleasure Island is a real diversion and temptation for all of us. It represents the puppet's tendency to go outside itself to look for things it doesn't realize or believe it already has. It is also a metaphor for our need for immediate gratification and anything that takes us off our paths to greatness in order to get it. Pleasure Island is like the Siren Song in Homer's *Odyssey*, which seductively lures sailors off course. It calls to our doubt and our desire to be more than we currently are without having to exercise the courage, honesty or service required to be in alignment with animating genius. The pleasure on Pleasure Island is always fleeting and short-lived, leaving one to insatiably desire more in a way that is imprisoning and sometimes abusive.

Like it or not, we have all visited Pleasure Island and may return often. It is where we sometimes go when we lose hope and feel discouraged, doubtful, angry, sad, insecure, restless and small. When we feel daunted by any given task, project or mission, Pleasure Island offers a variety of enticing alternatives that keep us locked in procrastination and avoidance. Pride and envy can also lead us there, as well as any desire to puff ourselves up to compensate for some apparent lack, inadequacy, hurt or fear. When we are there we often do not realize how self-defeating and hurtful our behavior is, because while we are engaging in it we feel temporarily satiated. Our pain is removed, if only momentarily. Unfortunately it always comes back, accompanied by additional pain that has a way of leading us right back to Pleasure Island to quell it. As a result, we engage in addictive and compulsive behaviors that take us from our center and leave us enslaved to our puppets.

As you read this, you may be thinking of various vices that tend to create addictions and undesirable consequences, such as excessive alcohol, drugs or sex, or even aberrant behavior including theft, vandalism and brutality — any practice that robs, abuses or enslaves. While these can certainly take place on Pleasure Island, they are the extreme.

Trying to Meet Needs Externally

On Pleasure Island, there are other, more subtle behaviors that most of us tend to engage in from time to time that lead us in circles and keep us locked in behaviors that do not serve us. These are the product of trying to meet a need externally, rather than finding what we seek within ourselves. We hand over the reigns to our puppet, who bypasses animating genius and goes straight to Pleasure Island. When we do so, the resulting behavior is often unpleasant and sometimes distasteful.

Below is a list of unmet needs the puppet often seeks to fill externally, and corresponding behaviors that can sometimes manifest as a result.

UNMET NEEDS OUR PUPPET SEEKS TO FILL EXTERNALLY	POTENTIAL BEHAVIORAL CONSEQUENCES
Recognition, prestige, fame	Conceit, arrogance, self-absorption, inauthentic behavior, insincerity, vanity
Wealth	Greed, envy, insensitivity, paranoia and fear
To be needed, to be important	Martyrdom, overwhelm, burnout, arrogance
Approval, acceptance, validation	Ingratiation, desperation, dependent relationships, insincerity, inauthentic behavior, manipulation
Respect, to be heard	Disrespectful behavior to others, excessive talking, insufficient listening
Control, power, to be right	Manipulation, domination/force, compliance without commitment, rigidity, closed-mindedness
Pride, perfection, distinction	Arrogance, segregation, loneliness, closed-mindedness
Comfort, security	Whininess, victimization, stagnation, apathy, sloth

There is nothing wrong with money, prestige, power, or any of the needs listed in the left column. The key is the manner in which these needs are met, and whether the desire for them comes from our animating genius or puppet. The puppet feels it is incomplete and seeks to placate its sense of inadequacy by filling itself up with things the animating genius realizes are illusory pursuits. If the aspiration to achieve these things is for a greater purpose – one that is not solely self-serving – the desire is aligned with animating genius and the resulting behavior will be as well. Rather than seek to fill unmet needs, our animating genius, which feels complete, looks to express itself in ways that allow its natural gifts to be of service to others.

If the motive is not in the best interests of others, it is more aligned with the puppet and likely to evoke undesirable consequences such as those listed in the chart on page 137. Those who attain what they seek through animating genius are far more likely to sustain it. Those whose motives and tactics are aligned with the puppet will live in fear of the inevitable loss of their fleeting success. In an effort to keep that from happening, the puppet's default is to continue to engage in ongoing, unfulfilling behaviors.

Often people are drawn to formal positions of leadership for what they have to offer — power, control, prestige, and higher pay. These things feed the puppet, which would have us believe our inherent value is equated with them and that the more we have, do or achieve, the more successful we are. The problem is that no matter how much power, control, prestige, and money we acquire, it never seems to be enough. Life becomes a series of races, battles, and games to be won with little time left to savor the victories, which are often short-lived. Additionally, one can become increasingly consumed with the fear of losing it all. This orientation has many leaders acting in ways that are more about themselves than the organizations and people they lead.

**Simply said, when the focus of leadership
is on what can be gained from a position or title,
any success that accompanies it cannot be sustained for long.**

Let's take a look at some of the most common needs leaders tend to have and the potential consequences of seeking these things via the puppet from their position or organization.

Redefining Power

Some people have a higher need for power than others. People who tend to be driven toward action with a strong task orientation tend to identify more with this need than others. They are prone to want to get things done (right now or sooner) and feel they need a little extra kick to do so. Often, they rely on their authority or position to make mandates or demands. While this tendency does get results, they are often short-lived. In emergency situations where immediate action is called for, these types of mandates are absolutely necessary. There is no time to question what must be done, and someone must be relied on to call the shots in order to ensure consistency and accuracy. The behavior this approach generates is compliance.

But when you need more from people than immediate, short-term action, something with a little more *staying* power is called for. And to get this, leaders must appeal to people's hearts as well as their heads. Think about the last time you fully supported and embraced any course of action. Chances are you believed in it, and/or had immense respect for the person who needed your support. This requires a different interpretation of power than what the ego provides.

True power does not build you up as much as it does others. It looks to influence them to do something they can commit to, not just comply with.

And to get that kind of commitment, you need to relate to people as being capable of doing much, much more than taking orders. The paradox of power is that as you let go of your own need for it, your true power increases because it is fueled by and commingled with the power of others to become a force bigger than yourself.

Re-Thinking Control

The need for control is very similar to the need for power, as it contains an element of wanting people to do what you say. However, control goes much deeper than this. It is about wanting to orchestrate entire chains of events and make things work out the way *you* think they should more often than not. Many people who fall prey to this ego-driven need disdain chaos and take their love of order to an extreme by trying to regulate things around them in a way that can generate a predictable result.

The trouble is, in a given moment, *anything* could happen. The best of plans can go haywire — and sometimes for a very good reason that is outside our immediate ability to understand. People with a need for control block themselves from their intuition, which is always tuned in to the moment. The simple act of having a plan suggests that you are pre-creating a course of action without entirely factoring in what will be taking place at the moment it happens (because nothing can ever be predicted with 100% certainty). Planning serves a vital need in organizations, and leaders need to engage in it. However, becoming too *attached* to any given plan or course of action can become a leader's downfall.

The need for control is sometimes accompanied by a need to be right. Indulging the puppet in getting this need met keeps us from growing.

**When we believe we are right,
we cut ourselves off from the wisdom of others around us
who may have different views, as well as from what we might
learn if we are willing to entertain that we do not actually
know everything already.**

The Need for Approval

The need for approval is closely linked to a need to be liked, or even loved. When we seek this validation from others, we often engage in behavior that takes us away from who we really are in our efforts to become what we believe others want us to be. The need for approval is something that has been with many of us since childhood. From a very young age, many of us are brought up to do things in order to please others, and the rewards we get (inclusion, accolades, affection) reinforce the idea that we can actually act in ways that allow us to be more or less liked based on what we do rather than who we are.

The trouble is that at some point these behaviors become incredibly self-defeating. They breed deep resentment inside us that eventually finds a way of expressing itself, often through passive/aggressive behavior or depression. And they can be disastrous for leaders who hesitate to take action or speak in ways that will not initially be met with approval.

In trying to please everyone,
leaders ultimately please no one.

The need for approval takes many forms. In our efforts to fit in, we often unwittingly engage in behaviors that support a status quo that we don't even believe in. But we cannot progressively change organizations when we become a part of the very problems we are trying to solve. This need also has a way of keeping us from saying what we really think for fear of upsetting others or damaging their good opinion of us. And leadership often requires the courage to speak in ways that are not particularly popular, or to help others recognize and address self-defeating patterns of behavior.

We may never really transcend our need for approval. But we must redirect the source of that approval. When we can supply it from within, what others think of us becomes secondary. And then we are able to speak and act from a place of true power and bring more of who we are to what we do. We also serve as powerful role models that encourage others to do the same.

The Appeal of Prestige

The need for prestige is often another form of approval, only in mass quantities. Like the need for approval, it can be rooted in a feeling of inadequacy that leads people to prove to themselves and others that they really are "someone." It is easy to get lured into and swept away by the star appeal that people in high places generate. Many do not start out seeking this kind of reinforcement. Despite initially being taken aback by it, they can become intoxicated with it over time.

Regardless of how it originates, the need for prestige tends to propel people to do things for the wrong reasons. Rather than becoming engaged in something they truly believe in, they will gravitate toward more popular causes and measure and direct their actions in ways that cause others to take note of them. How many people are you aware of who — despite their accolades, awards, and media exposure — are lonely, imbalanced, or unhappy? These are not the qualities of leaders that inspire others to accomplish extraordinary things.

> **Another problem with the need for prestige is that people who live their lives in order to get it never seem to be able to get enough.**

Even if their prestige is in direct correlation to their good deeds, the end goal often becomes more important than the causes they support and the actions they take to contribute to them. And the people they rely on to help them earn these accolades often become secondary as well.

When we're in our nineties and we're looking back, it's not going to be how much money we made or how many awards we've won. It's really, 'What did we stand for? Did we make a positive difference for people?'

~ Elizabeth Dole, American politician, president of the American Red Cross

There is nothing wrong with prestige. My experience is that it is most satisfying when it comes as a result of work that is its own reward — more of a nice little bonus than the ultimate payoff. The problem emerges when we become too attached to these or any other outcomes and are driven to act in ways that are self-serving rather than of true service to others.

The Driving Force of Wealth

Wealth has been used as a scorecard for success throughout the ages. From its conception, its lure has led many to do things that are not in the best interests of others. We have been conditioned to believe that it is the key to freedom, happiness, and security. People often take jobs that are not truly aligned with their talents because they fear that without them, they will not have the money they need to satisfy their basic needs. Many seek positions of leadership because of the increased pay it has to offer and all the things they could buy as a result.

When money is the sole driving force in what we are doing, we short-circuit ourselves from our true creativity, ingenuity and strength. The energy that fuels us is rooted in fear and lack. We cannot create something of true value when we start from a place of deficiency. As a result, what is created solely from a desire for wealth often lacks substance or value. In the last several years, we have seen the mutation and collapse of institutions whose aim was purely the generation of profit. We have also seen the fall of once affluent individuals whose fortune was generated with the same end-goal. The age of hierarchical structures designed to allow some to prosper at the expense of others seems to be slowly coming to an end. When we look more deeply into the true essence of money, perhaps we can begin to better understand this phenomenon.

> *Moneymaking is about what you can get; perpetual prosperity is about what you can give.*
>
> *~ Ken Blanchard, American author and management expert*

Money is essentially a form of energy. Profit is achieved when the energy of people's creativity, ingenuity, determination and talent is focused on the creation of something perceived to be of equal value to the energy of currency. It is only in mastering the former that the latter can be truly sustained.

The greatest leaders know that there is more to be gained
from generating and harnessing the energy of the human spirit
(their own as well as that of others)
than the tactics and strategies of money-making ventures.

The paradox of money, like happiness, is that when we become fixated upon achieving it at the expense of all else, it has a way of eluding us. It is only when we find the energy of abundance and joy within ourselves that matches what we seek that it comes to us without restraint.

Exploring Elements of Pride

Many of us have been conditioned to believe that leadership means infallibility and perfection. Formal leadership positions are often at the top of a hierarchy and even informal leadership connotes being in a place to somehow be seen as having more wisdom, vision and confidence with which to lead others. All of these aspects play into the puppet's need for pride. Pride can be a wonderful thing. When we take pride in our work and our creations, we are honoring ourselves for the effort, time and energy we have poured into them. However, when pride is sought and guarded for reasons that are more about creating and sustaining an image than what is behind it, the need for pride can be destructive, and the image created as a result runs the risk of being a fragile facade.

Excessive pride keeps people from seeing who we really are and connecting with us on the level that will truly influence and inspire them. Contrary to what the puppet would have us believe, vulnerability is one of the most empowering things a leader can show others. Vulnerability inspires trust. And it is something we can all relate to because we have all felt it before. When we acknowledge our vulnerability and act in the face of our fears, we become an example for others to do the same.

Another pitfall of the bulletproof façade maintained out of pride is that it indirectly communicates that imperfection is not acceptable and that everyone must live up to an unattainable standard. With this unspoken expectation in place, people will hedge their bets and play small. They fear being exposed as less than perfect and consequently do the minimum amount of work required to stay under the radar screen. This behavior often starts with the leader, and becomes reinforced at many levels. Over time, it becomes the culture of an organization. And it inhibits creativity and destroys innovation.

A third pitfall of excessive pride is that it prevents leaders from developing and utilizing the talents of others. Leaders who believe they must have all the answers and do everything themselves put an inordinate amount of pressure on themselves and limit the potential within their organizations. A subconscious message is sent that leaves people feeling undervalued and disposable, ultimately creating a wall that cuts the leader off from the wisdom of the group. People whose talents could otherwise be leveraged and applied to areas that would free the leader up to do something more strategic get bored and frustrated, and they will leave.

Leaders who become known for having all the answers quickly become surrounded by "yes" people who will tell them exactly what they want to hear. And if the leader must always be right, those who have valuable alternative viewpoints to contribute will soon find another place to work. This is a self-propagating dynamic, as it reinforces blind spots leaders often have. The more senior a leader is in an organization, the less people tend to tell him what is really on their minds, for fear of upsetting the leader or damaging the relationship. As a result, the leader risks happily moving forward, thinking he is right, while the effectiveness of his organization slowly erodes.

Great leaders are those who see the greatness in others,
and bring it out.
This quality of leadership is far more important
than any image of infallibility.

When leaders acknowledge their need for partnership with others and admit that others may have pieces of the puzzle they do not possess, these leaders will create strong, self-sustaining cultures, where people work together to produce excellence. The leader does not need to be the hero. In fact, some of the most effective leaders are those who are more concerned about elevating the status of others than improving their own. Lao Tzu, author of the *Tao Te Ching*, said, "When the best leader's work is done the people say, 'We did it ourselves.'"[1]

Finding Comfort and Security

The need for comfort and security is closely related to the need for pride, as it keeps people from trying new things for fear of failing or appearing foolish. It's an interesting phenomenon in that every time we learn something new, we strive to get to that point where we are able to do it naturally — without having to think too much about what we are doing. And when we finally hit that stage, it is nice to settle into a groove. These grooves can be very productive when we are applying new skills and ways of doing things to challenging endeavors. But when these grooves keep us from moving forward and stretching ourselves, they can become counter-productive.

There are risks and costs to a program of action, but they are far less than the long-range risks and costs of comfortable inaction.

~ John F. Kennedy, 35th United States of America President (1917-1963)

If we allow ourselves to stay in our comfort zones too long, over time we will resist anything that could represent a change in equilibrium. The problem with staying in equilibrium is that everything around us is in constant flux. We need to continually reevaluate whether our ways of doing things are aligned with the results we want to produce.

Many organizations find themselves out of business when they continue to do things because they have always done them that way. And the same peril exists for each of us as leaders — the world is at risk of being cheated of the creativity, innovation, and potential we have to offer. We risk cheating ourselves of the satisfaction of discovering more of what we are capable of

---

[1]Lao Tau, *Tao Te Ching* (Dates back to early English transliterations in the late 19th century).

by applying that potential to something worthwhile.

This trap is at the core of the tension that must be balanced between management and leadership. Management is about planning, organizing, directing and controlling. It is largely concerned with keeping things the same.

There is no passion to be found playing small — in settling for a life that is less than the one you are capable of living.

~ Nelson Mandela, former South African president

**Leadership is about raising people's sights
to something bigger and better,
challenging the status quo when it is no longer serving us,
and inspiring people to bring out the best in themselves
to accomplish something extraordinary.**

We cannot do that for others if we do not do it for ourselves.

As leaders, we must resist the temptation to underestimate what we, and others, are able to accomplish, and allow ourselves to be in a constant state of curiosity and wonder. While it is true that any of us could fail if we try to take things up a notch, think where we would be as a society and a country if no one ever looked that fear in the eye and did it anyway. Many of our greatest accomplishments do not succeed without a prerequisite amount of experimental "failure." Consider the following events in each of these people's lives:

- Abraham Lincoln failed in business twice and had a nervous breakdown. He was defeated in eight elections.

- Walt Disney was fired by the editor of a newspaper who felt he lacked creative ideas.

- As a boy, Thomas Edison was told by his teacher that he was too stupid to learn anything. He failed 10,000 times before he had a working light bulb.

- Soichiro Honda, the founder of Honda, was turned down for an engineering job by Toyota.

- Henry Ford went bankrupt five times before succeeding in the auto industry.

- Before becoming a successful actor, John Wayne was rejected from the United States Naval Academy.

- Lucille Ball was dismissed by a drama school with a note that read: "Wasting her time... she's too shy to put her best foot forward."

- Steven Spielberg unsuccessfully applied to film school three separate times.

- Michael Jordan was cut from his high school basketball team.

- Baseball legend Babe Ruth struck out 1,330 times.

- The first novel of best-selling novelist John Grisham was rejected by sixteen agents and twelve publishing houses.

- Robert M. Pirsig's book *Zen and the Art of Motorcycle Maintenance* was rejected by 121 publishers before it was published in 1974 and went on to sell millions of copies in 27 languages.

- The Beatles were turned down by the Decca recording company, who said "We don't like their sound, and guitar music is on its way out."[2]

Many of life's failures are people who did not realize how close they were to success when they gave up.

~ Thomas A. Edison, American inventor, scientist and businessman

While it is true that any of us could fail if we try to take things up a notch, think where we would be as a society and a world if no one ever looked that fear in the eye and did it anyway.

Many of our greatest accomplishments do not succeed without a prerequisite amount of experimental "failure."

---

[2]YouTube, *Famous Failures* (Bluefish TV.com) www.presentoutlook.com/famous-failures.

Recognizing When You Are on Pleasure Island

We will all inevitably visit Pleasure Island from time to time. The key is to catch ourselves and keep our visits brief. The longer we are there, the more difficult it is to identify and reverse its effect on us. Pinocchio was not aware of the fact that he was turning into a jackass until Jiminy Cricket pointed it out. Before he noticed this mutation in himself, he saw it in his buddy Lampwick.

This same tendency is true for us as well. When we judge others for behaviors such as those listed in the chart on page 137, the reaction we have is often an indication that we too are in some way exhibiting the same behavior as those we judge.

Mary's Mirrored Disrespect

Mary was an officer in a large corporation. She was frustrated by the lack of teamwork amongst her direct reports and irritated by the behavior they demonstrated that led her to believe they were jockeying for position. Rather than collaborating to address significant issues that faced the whole organization, she felt they were looking out for their own interests, attacking each other's ideas, and constantly trying to outdo one another. She believed their attitudes were trickling down into the organization, breaking it into fragmented silos, and resulting in plummeting scores on annual culture surveys that indicated people's trust in leadership was at an all-time low.

Convinced that they were incapable of creating a culture of cooperation, she took it upon herself to hold a series of meetings with people in their organizations to discuss issues she did not believe her leaders were handling effectively and give the people an opportunity to express their concerns. Her direct reports were not permitted to attend. In these meetings she conveyed her disappointment in her leaders to their staff and pledged that she would not tolerate their actions. Her language in these and other meetings reflected her belief that her leaders were disrespecting each other, their people and her, and must be stopped.

What Mary did not realize is that she was demonstrating the same lack of respect and disparaging behavior that she saw in her leaders. It was fueled by her need to be right and to single-handedly come in and save the day. The more she passed judgment on her leaders, the more pronounced the behavior she judged in them became prominent in her.

Mary did not recognize this dynamic until she received the results of her 360-degree feedback interviews, which were a part of her coaching process. These interviews were conducted with a sampling of her peers, customers and direct reports. A theme emerged that highlighted Mary's tendency to unintentionally undermine others in an effort to meet her own needs. Some of her peers observed that rather than going to them to address issues that crossed into their organizations, she would go directly to the CEO. Her customers spoke of language she would often use that revealed her lack of faith in her leaders, particularly the use of the word "I" rather than "we" when making promises to them and speaking of why they should have faith in the organization's ability to deliver. Her direct reports, of course, felt completely disrespected. Their reactions to her behavior ranged from outrage to resignation.

When Mary recognized that she wasn't modeling the behavior she wanted to see from others, she began to take responsibility for her actions and turn her behavior around. In subsequent staff meetings, she told her leaders she realized that the changes she was asking them to make needed to start with her. She reiterated these points in one-on-one meetings with each of them, soliciting feedback and making a special effort to listen more than she talked.

They did not trust her right away, but over time she was able to demonstrate her sincerity and commitment to doing whatever it would take to build a strong team. Her focus went from what they needed to do to elevate her status to how she could serve them to improve the effectiveness and culture of the entire organization. In the months that followed, members of her team began to follow her lead, demonstrating more trust of, and willingness to partner with, each other and her. Over time, the organization's culture surveys showed improved ratings of leadership's ability to demonstrate and inspire trust as they truly worked together to creatively address the organization's most significant challenges.

Before we can leave Pleasure Island, we must recognize when we are on it.

Like Mary, we can cultivate self-awareness by paying special attention to the unpleasant behaviors in others that we may be unwittingly engaging in ourselves and take responsibility for our own actions. If, as you have read this chapter, you thought of someone in your life whose actions may be somewhat donkey-like, you may benefit from inquiring what it is about that behavior that irritates you most and how you may be mirroring it in some way yourself.

Another way of recognizing the degree to which we are lured by Pleasure Island is to examine our beliefs about what is required to succeed in life. Take a moment to revisit the list of unmet needs in the chart on page 137, and see if any of them resonate with you. With each need that you identify, see if you can put your finger on any assumptions or success formulas you have that are more aligned with your puppet (who would have you seeking outside yourself to get something it believes you lack) than your animating genius (who knows you have enough of what you seek within you that you could actually *give* it to others in some way.)

Once you have identified these assumptions, you can use the process outlined in Chapter 7 to challenge and dis-empower them. When you begin to identify how you feel and act in the grip of the puppet's faulty assumptions, you will start to see the subtle ways you, like Pinocchio, have begun to deviate from your true form – perhaps even becoming a bit of a jackass. From there, you can transform your thinking in a way that will change your entire course of direction, giving you the nudge you need to begin your escape from Pleasure Island.

Takes One to Know One

One of my personal success formulas for a large part of my life was to keenly identify what people wanted me to be and then go to great lengths to become that person. Like many people pleasers, I engaged in my share of inauthentic behavior. But what is amusing to me now is how irritated I used to become upon observing what I deemed to be phony behavior in others. On the playground when I was a kid, we used to tell each other, "It takes one to know one." And now I know that old adage is true.

When I recognized the assumption my puppet had me believing and acting on for so many years, I challenged it. There was ample evidence to disprove any theory that trying to become someone I am not would allow me to be successful. Topping the list was the fact that doing so usually amplified my self-doubt and zapped my confidence, leading me to act in ways that were not my personal best. Upon looking back, I realized that my greatest successes came when I did things in a manner that came naturally to me — regardless of whether others approved of or even appreciated my methods.

Insist on yourself; never imitate… Every great man is unique.

~ Ralph Waldo Emerson, American philosopher, lecturer, essayist and poet (1803-1882)

The pain I experienced as a result of my inauthentic behavior kept me bound to jobs and roles that were not aligned with my talents and passions. And when I thought of who I could be and what I could do without my old success formula, I began to get excited about the possibilities of truly tapping into my own potential and living life in the way that suited me best. I exchanged my old, worn-out assumption for a new one: To succeed on my own terms, I must be myself in all situations. This new assumption has allowed me to do things I never could have before, including writing the book you are now reading.

Escaping from Pleasure Island

The common theme among all behaviors that lead to the dead end of Pleasure Island is that they ultimately serve the puppet's needs of bypassing animating genius and propagating the illusion that we are not enough in and of ourselves. They keep us locked in behaviors that are self-serving and ultimately self-defeating because they are focused on what we can get rather than what we have to give. The key to escaping Pleasure Island is to reverse this focus and put our energy into something that is greater than ourselves.

The greatest leaders have recognized the larger, more gratifying and empowering side of leadership — that associated with what one has to give. This aspect of leadership transcends position, role and title and speaks to the ability of each of us to exercise leadership wherever we are. In 1970, Robert Greenleaf wrote an essay called "The Servant as Leader,"[3] which explored a concept that many leadership and management writers have since built on. In it, he wrote:

> "The servant-leader is servant first... It begins with the natural feeling that one wants to serve, to serve first. Then conscious choice brings one to aspire to lead. That person is sharply different from one who is leader first, perhaps because of the need to assuage an unusual power drive or to acquire material possessions...The leader-first and the servant-first are two extreme types. Between them there are shadings and blends

---

[3] Robert Greenleaf, *The Servant as Leader* (Greenleaf Center for Servant Leadership, Westfield, IN, 1970, www.greenleaf.org).

that are part of the infinite variety of human nature.

The difference manifests itself in the care taken by the servant — first to make sure that other people's highest priority needs are being served. The best test, and difficult to administer, is: Do those served grow as persons? Do they, while being served, become healthier, wiser, freer, more autonomous, more likely themselves to become servants? And, what is the effect on the least privileged in society? Will they benefit or at least not be further deprived?"

There is a lovely paradox inherent in putting service over self-interest. For years, I've been coaching and consulting with people and organizations that seek to improve themselves — in one way or another. I have noticed that the more they shift their focus from what they can get to what they can give, the more naturally and effortlessly they achieve what they seek, and the more likely they are to sustain their success. Conversely, the more self-absorbed and identified with achieving something that benefits themselves more than (or at the expense of) others, the more likely they are to run into obstacles (many of which they unwittingly create for themselves). The most common hindrances are rooted in the desires of the puppet, whose chief motivation is to defend and differentiate itself, win and be right.

> *The antidote to self-interest is to commit and to find cause. To commit to something outside of ourselves. To be part of creating something we care about so we can endure the sacrifice, risk, and adventure that commitment entails. This is the deeper meaning of service.*
>
> *~ Peter Block,*
> *American author,*
> *speaker and organization*
> *effectiveness consultant*

The puppet unchecked keeps us from truly connecting with those we lead and interact with because it is more concerned with itself than others. As a result, it unwittingly acts in ways that bring about what it most fears. Wanting to be right, it makes others wrong and keeps them from listening and buying in. Needing power and prestige, it steals the show and relies on force to gain compliance that lacks commitment. Fearing that it will not be respected, it demands respect from others who may well feel it has not been earned.

When our focus shifts from self-interest to service, we transcend our fears and doubts because we have something beside ourselves to engage our time, talent and resources in. Our orientation moves from the work — to what is worth working for.

We align with the desire and intention of others and can pool our energy and focus in ways that allow us to do more collectively than we could alone. People of like mind feel compelled to participate and contribute because they share the end goal. In this way, our combined energies become aligned with a force that is much greater than us. Additionally, the energy we tap into when we strive to do things for a greater good can move the mountains of fear that we experience as we venture out of our comfort zones.

It takes generosity to discover the whole through others. If you realize you are only a violin, you can open yourself up to the world by playing your role in the concert.

~ Jacques Yves Cousteau, French explorer, ecologist, scientist, author (1910-1997)

The paradox is that in letting go of our grip on our own needs, we find what we most seek — only better. Philosopher Jean-Paul Sartre once said, "All which I abandon, all which I give, I enjoy in a higher manner through the fact that I give it away. To give is to enjoy possessively the object which one gives."

This is because much of what we really want, we already have. Power, control, prestige, wealth — all of these things are not ends in and of themselves, but rather lead to a state of mind we can achieve on our own. As an example, many people

*Only a life lived for others is
a life worthwhile.*

~ Albert Einstein,
German-Swiss Nobel
Prize-winning physicist,
philosopher and author
(1879-1955)

associate prestige with feelings of importance, or of being respected or revered. When we identify with a feeling of being important and respect ourselves as well as others, we no longer crave that attention and validation in the same way. Instead, we are able to act in ways that allow others to feel important. In the end, what we give to others comes back to us in ways we may not have originally expected.

The puppet believes that to achieve its desired result, it must engage in some kind of action. After all, this is how the puppet was created in the first place — in an effort to ensure that our behavior leads to positive outcomes rather than negative ones. From its inception, the puppet associates the source of what it believes it most needs as being external to itself — something that must be won, earned, achieved, fought for, and defended. In contrast, animating genius would have us identifying with and embodying the feeling and experience we seek. As we embody the state the puppet believes it must knock itself out to acquire from the outside in, we act in ways that attract circumstances that align with that state of being.

Those who have occasion to speak to large groups of people often find that their presentations become much more engaging, inspiring and influential when they stop worrying about what people will think of them and whether they look good (getting their needs met from others) and instead focus their energy on what they can give to people in their audience that will in some way help those people (starting from a place of wholeness that can only be created from within).

In conflict situations, people are often so intent on speaking their piece that they do not pause long enough to engage in the behavior they most want from others — listening. And yet, it can make all the difference in the world. Often what they really want most goes deeper than just winning or being heard —

most of the time there is some kind of interest common to both parties. When they approach these situations with an intention that in some way benefits everyone involved, they find the way to achieve that success becomes much more accessible — and it is far more likely to be sustained. Rather than trying to find the perfect words to say, they can focus on truly connecting with the other person in a way that achieves a common goal. As a result the words they need find *them*.

Planning Your Escape from Pleasure Island

- Take responsibility for your actions; turn your behavior around. Acknowledge that new behavior begins with you.

- Reiterate this and solicit feedback, making an effort to listen more than talk.

- Strengthen your leadership by focusing more on what you can give than what you can get.

- Cultivate self-awareness by paying attention to unpleasant behavior in others that you may be unwittingly demonstrating as well.

- Examine your beliefs about what's required to succeed in life.

- Revisit your unmet needs and explore any assumptions that may be aligned with your puppet.

- Proceed to challenge and dis-empower negative needs and assumptions that are getting you the opposite of what you truly want.

- Revisit your animating genius to help remind you that you already have so much of what you seek within you that you could give it to others and still have plenty left.

- To transcend your fear and doubt, shift your focus from self-interest to service. Your orientation moves from the work — to what is worth working for.

- Focus on connecting with others in a way that achieves a common goal.

- Ask yourself what you most want. Think of a way you can give it to others — not in order to receive it in return, but simply for the experience itself.

- If you wish others would reach out to you more, try reaching out to them.

- If you want more respect, show more of it.

- If you want a little more happiness, see if you can bring some to others.

- In the act of giving, you may find that you had what you were truly seeking all along.

Helping Others Escape from Pleasure Island

In order to compel Pinocchio to leave Pleasure Island, Jiminy Cricket had to see beyond the jackass that Pinocchio was becoming to the true essence of the boy he really was. To save ourselves, and help other escape from Pleasure Island, we must do the same. Once we begin to realize how easy it is to succumb to its lure and engage in the destructive behavior it propagates, we can rise above our judgment of others when they do the same. Doing so is an exercise in respect.

In her wise and enlightening book, *The Four-fold Way: Walking the Paths of the Warrior, Teacher, Healer and Visionary*,[4] Angeles Arrien points out that the Latin roots of the word "respect" are quite telling. "Re" means again or back. "Specere" means to look. So the literal translation of respect is to look again. We respect both ourselves and others when we recognize that, upon a second glance, there are redeeming qualities and enormous potential waiting to be tapped.

---

[4]Angeles Arrien, *The Four-fold Way: Walking the Paths of the Warrior, Teacher, Healer and Visionary* (New York, NY, HarperCollins, 1993).

Great leaders know that there is always more to people and things than what they see at first glance.

Those who are masters of turning poor performance around will tell you that the key is to see beyond people's behavior to their potential and treat them as though they are capable of achieving it.

Rob Learns the True Meaning of Respect

Rob, one of my clients, became so good at turning around poor performance that his span of control tripled within the course of a year through a gradual restructuring done to allow him to take over fledgling departments and turn them around. How did he get there?

For a good part of his career, Rob was a bit of a hothead. He was extremely passionate and had strong feelings about the way things should be done, which he voiced often — using tough language and a loud voice. In division meetings, he would frequently stand up and offer searing comments reflecting his belief that the methods management was using to solve problems were just making them worse. He had little awareness that his impassioned outbursts were actually drawing more attention to himself than the message he was trying to deliver. Because what he said sounded more like an attack than a suggestion, his comments were often met with resistance, which only served to strengthen his disdain for people whose partnership and support he needed to create the change he envisioned.

Over time, Rob realized he wasn't getting the reaction he wanted and decided to try working with a coach. Through the process of raising his own self-awareness, he began to realize that his need to be right and differentiate himself was superseding his desire to be part of a solution that would be embraced and supported by management and his colleagues. For the first time he saw the effects his behavior was having on his ability to influence people. With practice, he learned to ask more questions to better understand the intentions behind decisions he didn't agree with and to appreciate and acknowledge the efforts of others.

Gradually Rob also learned that when he expressed this appreciation rather than launch his customary attack, he was able to help people see that, despite their best intentions, their solutions were falling short. As he shifted his focus from his own interests to include those of others, he found that people were willing to consider his alternative approaches, and he learned to integrate their ideas and insights into his own.

Rob's approach is a great example of practicing respect by looking again to see that there was more to the situation and the people involved than what he originally believed.

Rob took this newfound knowledge and awareness into each area of the organization he headed up and began to dig a little deeper to get a true assessment of what was there. He spent time observing and getting to know people, their motivations, intentions and desires. What he found was that behind much of what others would consider "problem behavior" were passionate people who really wanted to do something of value, but felt they were not appreciated or that their efforts wouldn't make a difference.

In response to what they perceived to be unfair treatment, their passion became funneled into acting out in rather unpleasant ways. Having been in their shoes to some degree, Rob understood that there was more to the story. After getting to know them and learning what was really most important to them, he was able to appeal to desires they had that were aligned with the goals of the organization. In so doing, he was able to partner with these people in such a way that they listened to and acted on his feedback about their performance and what they needed to do to turn it around. These turnarounds involved helping them do the same thing that Rob did for himself — going beyond the puppet's methods of getting ego needs met and finding a way to give to others by tapping their own internal reserves.

With some, he discovered that low performance levels were a product of low self-esteem. He worked with these people to help them recognize and better apply their distinct strengths and talents in ways that would benefit the organization, often changing their roles or job descriptions to allow for a better fit. Rob believed in many of these people before they were able to believe in themselves. His actions engendered respect both for and from others.

Once we have found a way to rise above the temptations and shallow promises of Pleasure Island and rediscover the greatness that has been within us all along, we can help others do the same. Doing so requires that we exercise respect, looking beyond the jackass to reveal raw potential. Just as Jiminy lovingly helped Pinocchio see the effects of Pleasure Island, we too can help others recognize the impact their behavior is having and ignite their desire to put an end to it. Treating people as though they are capable of reversing the process and returning to their true form allows them to find the courage and strength to believe in themselves.

Helping Others Escape from Pleasure Island

- There is always more to people and things than what we see at first look. Get to know people around you — their motivations and desires.

- Ask yourself if your need to be right and to differentiate yourself supersedes your desire to be part of a solution that would be embraced by others.

- Ask more questions to best understand the intentions behind decisions you may not agree with, and also to fully appreciate and recognize the efforts of others.

- Express your appreciation when people, despite their intentions, are falling short.

- Shift your focus from your own interests to include those of others; integrate their ideas and insights with your own.

- Recognize that most people are passionate about doing something of value and need to know that their efforts make a difference.

- Partner with your associates to best turn around challenging situations. Work with others to help them better apply their individual strengths and talents in ways that benefit everyone.

- Believe in people so they find the courage and strength to believe in themselves.

- Help others recognize the impact of their behavior and ignite their desire to change any behavior that isn't respectful, productive or desirable.

The Adventure Continues

Destination Reached

There is a Zen story about a master who was walking up and down the sandy bank of a lazy river, breathing deeply, enjoying the feel of sunshine on his skin, and taking in the beauty all around him. Just across the river one of his students was walking anxiously back and forth, scanning the perimeter of the river and the surrounding land. When the student saw his master, he began waving his arms and shouting, "Master! Master!" The Master looked up and waited silently for his student to continue. "Master," said his student, "How do I get to the other side?" The master simply replied, "You are already there!"

Zen stories have multiple interpretations. One of the insights that can be gained from this one is that of learning to recognize the many ways we already have what we seek. This is the place of wisdom we come to when we recognize Pleasure Island for the diversion that it is. As long as we believe what we seek is outside ourselves, we will be enslaved to it and drawn away from the place of our true riches.

When we, like Pinocchio, are ready to let go of this belief and go within to discover and learn to utilize our inner reserves, the illusions of want fall away and we get closer to reclaiming our true selves. We become ready to embark upon the next leg of our personal adventures — one that requires us to act in the face of our deepest fears.

> *If we go down into ourselves*
> *we find that we possess*
> *exactly what we desire.*
>
> *~ Simone Well,*
> *French philosopher,*
> *Christian mystic and social*
> *activist (1909-1943)*

Chapter 9

The Belly of the Whale

After escaping from Pleasure Island, Pinocchio and Jiminy Cricket return to Geppetto's house to find it empty. A dove drops a note at their feet that explains Geppetto has been swallowed by Monstro the Whale, and is in the whale's stomach at the bottom of the sea. Upon hearing the news, Pinocchio knows what he must do. Despite Jiminy's warnings of eminent danger and his proclamation that Monstro is "a whale of a whale," Pinocchio is determined to save Geppetto.

They swim through the sea until they see Monstro, and maneuver themselves into his mouth. In the belly of the whale, they occupy themselves with identifying ways to escape. Together, they create an opening for their getaway by setting a fire inside the whale that causes him to sneeze. Upon seeing Geppetto and Pinocchio as they swim to shore, the whale is outraged

and smashes their raft into splinters with his tail,
knocking Geppetto unconscious. Pinocchio rescues his
father and tries to divert the whale while Geppetto is
carried safely to shore by a big wave. Pinocchio gets
trapped under some rocks, but is finally washed ashore,
half drowned.

If you have ever endeavored to do anything beyond your current level of ability and experience, you surely have encountered Monstro the Whale. He is the embodiment of all our greatest fears and doubts, and he swims far beneath the surface in the watery world of our thoughts and feelings. The shadowy basin that he rests in magnifies his size, and his reputation precedes him — each tale growing more ominous than the last. He sits, patiently waiting, for someone with the courage to venture into his dark, cold waters. Within his belly is also the key to what we seek. To succeed in our greatest endeavors will require that we face and cleverly outwit him, time and time again.

Our puppet knows the peril of Monstro the Whale. In Monstro, it sees its own demise and would do anything to avoid it. The puppet's greatest weapon is its ability to inspire sufficient fear to prevent animating genius from getting anywhere near the whale. So it does what it does best — creates and propagates stories that would keep us from venturing outside the bounds of our comfort zones. With Pleasure Island the puppet's stories were designed to lure us in — with the promise of getting needs met — needs such as those covered in Chapter 8, page 137. With Monstro the Whale, the puppet's stories are designed to keep us away — with the threat of *losing* what the puppet believes it most needs. The story of Pinocchio and Monstro the Whale is not unlike a Bible story.

Jonah and the Whale

In this story, Jonah was a prophet from Galilee sometime between 780 B.C. and 760 B.C., when Assyria was a powerful nation and Israel's most dreaded enemy. The Lord spoke to Jonah and told him to go to Nineveh, the capital of Assyria, and preach to the Ninevites — people who had committed terrible atrocities against his own — in an effort to get them to repent.

Instead of going to Nineveh, Jonah took off on a boat for Tarshish, Spain, attempting to hide from God. At night, a huge storm arose and tossed the boat wildly, striking fear in the hearts of all the sailors, while Jonah slept soundly below the deck. The captain roused him and brought him to the deck, where the sailors said to one another, "Come, let us cast lots, that we may know for whose cause this trouble has come upon us." When the lot fell on Jonah, they asked him what he had done to bring the storm on them. He confessed running away from God's will and told the sailors to throw him overboard to spare their lives.

As Jonah sank into the sea, he was swallowed by a whale, where he sat for three days and nights praying and thanking God for saving him. God, seeing that his prayer was sincere, ordered the whale to spit Jonah out on shore. He then told Jonah again to go to Nineveh and preach repentance. This time, Jonah did as asked and the people of Nineveh repented. (Jonah 1:4-17 and 2:1-10)

Always do what you are afraid to do.

~ Ralph Waldo Emerson, American philosopher, lecturer, essayist and poet (1830-1882)

Anytime you make a decision to go out of your comfort zone to do something that is new or unusual, you will most likely experience a tinge of fear, hesitation, or anxiety.

This fear may lead you to question your ability, your likelihood of succeeding, and the possibility of your demise — whatever that may mean for you. It is essential to realize that this fear is a part of your journey as a leader.

Our first impulse, motivated by the puppet, is to do whatever it takes to alleviate the fear. Rather than venturing into the unknown, it would have us acting in ways that are comfortable and safe, running away or hedging our bets and maintaining the status quo. But maintaining the status quo is not the job of a leader. Leadership is about taking things to new heights — and the greatest leaders know that before they can do this with others, they must start with themselves.

> *Life is either a daring adventure or nothing. To keep our faces toward change and behave like free spirits in the presence of fate is strength undefeatable.*
>
> *~ Helen Keller, American author, activist and lecturer (1880-1968)*

Rising Up: The Call to Lead

The call to lead is often ushered in by a period of discomfort, where one slowly begins to realize that the outer world does not match the inner one. We may begin to feel a sort of incongruence accompanied by increased discernment of our current course of events and questions about what it is all for. A greater purpose looms on the horizon, but the way things are currently set up doesn't quite allow that vision to live. And so it is time for a change.

**Some call this an awakening. Others call it a crisis.
It is a doorway to greater meaning and contribution,
and the beginning of a transformation
that happens from the inside out.**

Change like this can happen in a variety of ways. Some find themselves becoming slowly discontented with their current state of affairs, perhaps bored with their jobs, or preoccupied by visions or daydreams that quicken their heartbeats a bit. One of my clients, Brad, found himself talking about the same thing in many of our coaching meetings — his growing desire to take on more responsibility and his increasing awareness that though he was very successful in his current role, it no longer held the charge for him that it once did. Another client, Sophia, would repeatedly question the significance of her job and whether anything she did within it was really making a difference. She dreamed of doing something that would have a greater impact on people's lives than the middle management position she was currently in that had her shuffling papers and managing crisis after crisis.

For others, the change comes in more sudden and jarring ways. Bill is another person who was contemplating what he could do to allow the organization he led to rise to new heights. After more than twenty years with the same company, he went into work one day to find that his 11:00 am meeting with someone from the Human Resources department would be his last. Bill was told that the company was restructuring and he was given until noon the following day to gather his belongings and exit the building. The rug upon which he had been walking was suddenly yanked from beneath him, and he was left to ponder not only what was next, but also how he would manage to survive the indefinite gap between the life he had become accustomed to and what was yet to come.

As I write these words, I realize that I myself am in the midst of this kind of transition and transformation. As 2009 turned into 2010, I was faced with the realization that many of my coaching contracts were coming to an end. Though I had been longing for more time to write and explore new creative endeavors, I don't know that I was quite prepared to have my slate wiped as clean as it had recently become. My first inclination was to fill this void with new clients, to recreate the same kind of work I had been doing. But my heart (and my own animating genius) knew that this change was a rare opportunity to break away and begin again — to venture bravely into the world of writing and speaking and begin a new chapter in my life.

**Regardless of who you are and what you do,
there will come a time when the path you have been walking
takes a steep turn in one direction or the other
and you will be required to do something
that stretches you beyond your usual way of doing things.**

Perhaps it will be in your career. The work that fulfilled you at one point in your life may no longer be enough. You might find yourself doing something very well but suddenly devoid of the gusto you once had doing it. It could be the company you keep — people who at one time shared your interests and passions but whom you now suddenly find yourself no longer wanting to spend a lot of time with. Maybe it will be your lifestyle. The objects and material possessions that once gave you joy could one day feel more like clutter or distractions. These things become like shells that the hermit crab has outgrown. The crab must release its previous home and step bravely and vulnerably into the unknown in order to find something more spacious.

The quest for a new shell and even the new shell itself may feel daunting, clumsy and overwhelming. But the act of letting go of the old to make room for the new allows us to evolve and realize our true potential. Anything less will ultimately become imprisoning. Succumbing to the puppet's urges to stay put or withdraw from the challenges before us is ultimately self-defeating. There is truth to the words uttered so eloquently by Lou Holt, "If you are not growing, you are dying."

> And the day came when the risk it took to remain tight inside the bud was more painful than the risk it took to blossom.
>
> ~ Anais Nin,
> French author (1903-1977)

Many of us have lived in states of quiet desperation for quite some time, going through the motions, getting through the days and weeks, shrinking from the possibilities that shimmer just beyond the horizon and yielding instead to complacency. In this state, we are likely to buy into the puppet's skeptical and critical summation of what is at stake if we step outside of what we have become accustomed to. We can easily become convinced that our greatest pursuits are likely to fail and not worth the effort. As we allow our spirits, our animating geniuses to become obscured, the puppet dominates and we become wooden and hollow, heavy, stiff, and at the mercy of everything around us. But deep within, the small, still voice of animating genius still calls, hopeful, faithful and longing to be heard.

What you really want for yourself is always trying to break through, just as a cooling breeze flows through an open window on a hot day. Your part is to open the windows of your mind.

~ Vernon Howard, American spiritual teacher, author and philosopher (1918-1992)

People I coach who desire greater satisfaction and fulfillment at work often believe they may have a better chance of finding it in a different job, with a different boss, or even in a different organization or company altogether. Some believe they must leave their current situation in order to make a bigger impact. While this may be true, once they have decided they cannot find what they seek where they are, they risk cutting themselves off from achieving it at all.

**We cannot put conditions on
our ability to be the people we were meant to be.
Either we are doing it, or we are not.
We can begin anywhere, anytime.**

When we are aligned with our true selves — those parts of ourselves that are creative, unique, strong, inspired, connected, passionate, present and of service to others — we will find joy and satisfaction wherever we are. We can zone in on what we would most like to be doing in the future, and find small ways to embody it now — no matter our circumstances. In the process, we will touch people's lives and improve the quality of our own. Challenges that require what we do best will find us, and as we rise up to meet them we will attract additional opportunities, resources, and people of like mind

He who does nothing renders himself incapable of doing anything; but while we are executing any work, we are preparing and qualifying ourselves to undertake another.

~ William Hazlitt, English author and philosopher (1778-1830)

to assist us in rising to greater heights.

The call to greatness may take many different forms. It could involve anything from founding an organization, leading a special cause, executing a project, creating a work of art, writing a book, raising children or changing careers to simply speaking our minds, championing an idea or a person, taking a stand, making a presentation, getting involved in a special project, learning a new skill, or saying "I'm sorry." In any case, rising up to the call requires that we are willing to bring more of our true selves to whatever it is we are doing. We can start by showing up fully — sharing those parts of ourselves that are real: our humor, our vulnerability, our dreams, honest opinions and wildest ideas.

In one way or another we are all challenged and invited to do something that pushes us out of our comfort zones and encouraged to take the next step toward the lives we are meant to live. We are called repeatedly to rise up in this way — to *lead* in this way, regardless of our position, vocation, title or role. Even those who have become accustomed to looking the other way are continually given opportunities to turn things around and seize the day.

I worked as a consultant for a company where the phrase "retired in place" was often thrown around by frustrated executives. These words were used to describe people who showed up to work in body, but not mind or spirit. The lights were on, but it was questionable whether anyone was home. People who were put into this category were often perceived as doing the least amount of work possible to get by until they could finally retire, and said to have a bit of an entitlement mentality, as though the company owed them in some way. They could be quite pessimistic, sometimes bringing down people around them too. Determined that nothing was worth a whole lot of effort, some of them led others to feel as though their efforts were fruitless as well. I believe this is the ultimate effect of living a life that denies the animating genius its place in the sun.

Many of the leaders I coached in this and other companies came to our meetings wanting to find ways to get performance out of people they saw in this way, or others who demonstrated similar behaviors. They would speak of these people with disdain and irritation and often felt as though their organizations would be better off if those in question simply left the company — ideally by choice, but if necessary through termination.

While these outcomes sometimes *are* in the best interests of both the individuals and the organization, there is much to be gained by first looking beyond them to recognize other, more promising options. These alternatives can only be seen with eyes that are willing to look beyond appearances to realize there is always more to things than what can be seen. The possibility for greatness that we readily recognize in those we call superstars in our corporations, schools, communities and families also exist in those deemed "retired in place." The difference between those who achieve great things and those who do not can be traced to the decisions they have made at some point in their lives to either follow their call to greatness, or to run away from it. And if we are honest with ourselves, I believe we can all admit we have been in both of those categories at various times in our lives.

Before we can lead others to rise up to the challenges before them, we need to be willing to do the same with our own. When we become frustrated with someone else's lack of effort, initiative, or willingness, we can begin by asking how we ourselves can demonstrate the behavior we would like to see. Upon examination, there will always be possibilities beckoning all around us — to live more fully in all aspects of our lives, to be more present, more courageous, more creative, and to bring out and apply more of the true talent of our animating genius — in short, to become real. Saying yes to our own calls to greatness will require each of us, like Pinocchio (and Jonah), to be willing and courageous enough to allow ourselves to explore the belly of the whale — to face our fears and proceed through them.

I learned that courage was not the absence of fear, but the triumph over it. The brave man is not he who does not feel afraid, but he who conquers that fear.

~ Nelson Mandela, former South African president

Heading into the Fear

Going out of our comfort zone doesn't require that we do what we are most afraid of right away. We can begin gradually, easing into the practice of stretching ourselves. In fact, moving beyond what is tried and true is a lot like literally physically stretching.

A Lesson from Yoga

It wasn't that long ago that I had trouble touching my toes. I started doing yoga, and in one of the classes I attended we were asked to bend our bodies in a somewhat unusual way. The instructor effortlessly folded herself in half while I leaned slightly forward and came to an abrupt halt. It wasn't really pain that I experienced as much as plain old discomfort. I wanted that part of the class to be over.

We were told to relax and breathe. Everything inside of me resisted even the idea of this crazy position that was the furthest thing from what I thought I or any other reasonable human being would consider restful. My muscles were tense and my body felt like it was in a knot. But I did my best to follow the directions — relax and breathe into it.

And as I did, a funny thing happened. After a short time, my muscles seemed to soften in spite of themselves, and I found myself gradually dropping more deeply into the stretch. The longer I held it, the (dare I say?) better it felt, until I was actually kind of enjoying this strange new sensation.

And then the thought occurred to me that this whole process is analogous to doing something — anything — that takes us out of our comfort zone.

We see something that beckons, perhaps something we know will be good for us, and yet we resist. Often we move tentatively into it and then hit a wall of discomfort. In this discomfort a myriad of unsettling doubts and related thoughts barrage us: "I'm no good at this..." "This was a bad idea..." "I'm wasting my time..." and on and on. And the resistance itself seems to intensify the discomfort. We tighten up, literally and figuratively, and block ourselves from moving into the experience. But if we can remain patient and open — if we can allow ourselves this initial period of discomfort and stay present with it, relaxing into it and breathing through it, we might be surprised at the results we experience. Think of the last time you tried something really different — something new, exciting and kind of terrifying all at the same time. If you stayed with it, chances are that over time the discomfort gave way to exhilaration and over more time, perhaps deep gratification. And the longer you kept at it, the easier and more satisfying it became.

Every artist was first an amateur.

~ Ralph Waldo Emerson, American philosopher, lecturer, essayist and poet (1803-1882)

Dismissing the Perfectionist

Some of my most valuable experiences in learning to move into my fear and discomfort came when I began taking karate lessons with my children. Initially, I thought it would be something fun to do together that would allow us to learn self-defense techniques and build strength and coordination. To my surprise, it turned out to be an arena that allowed me to explore and move beyond many of my self-imposed limits. The experience has been one that I have learned to transfer beyond the dojo (classroom) into my everyday life.

In one karate class, I was placed in a small group of people who were far more advanced than I was. The Sensei (instructor) was teaching us to do techniques that I had never even heard of, let alone seen or practiced. As the session continued, we were asked to build on these techniques and combine them with others, all of which seemed incredibly difficult to me. I found myself standing between martial artists of great prowess and grace who glided effortlessly while executing spinning, jumping, hooking kicks only to land and do it again and again. They looked like something out of a Jackie Chan movie. I, on the other hand, felt a lot like Chris Farley in the movie *Beverly Hills Ninja* as I clumsily made my way across the floor, getting no air under my feet when I tried to jump, losing my balance, and doing all I could to keep from crashing into the people next to me.

I flashed back to a time in college during the first session of a dance class that I didn't realize was about two levels too advanced for me. I remember feeling great during the warm-up (which I, of course, thought was the class itself) and then pirouetting (or more accurately, spinning out of control) across the floor and right out the door when I realized I was *way* out of my league. Back then, I felt the sting of shame and embarrassment and dropped the class within minutes of returning to my dormitory. This time, that old familiar feeling crept up, but I didn't give in to it.

In that instant, an entire lifetime of perfectionist patterns caught up to me. I couldn't help but laugh, and though I didn't actually see anyone laughing at me, I wouldn't have blamed anyone who did. I'm fairly certain that I looked ridiculous. And then I realized that this is what perfectionists (and recovering perfectionists like me) worry about most — looking like a complete idiot and not being able to master everything in a minimum of time. I wondered:

> *The only victory that counts is the one over yourself.*
>
> ~ Jesse Owens, American Olympic Gold-winning track and field athlete (1913-1980)

- How many times did I procrastinate something only to leave myself such a small time frame to complete it that no reasonable human being could get it perfect?

- How many things did I never even try for fear that I wouldn't be able to do something well?

- And when I did try something new, how often did I berate myself for not being able to perform flawlessly?

Not this time. I began to feel exhaustion creep in, and found myself looking at the clock. I hung in there, overcoming my temptation to track the remaining minutes by immersing myself in the experience. I dug in my heels and kept at it, trudging through, giggling to myself. If I looked like a clumsy fool, so be it. I would be the beginner, and give myself license to do those moves in whatever way they came out, as long as I actually made an attempt to do them.

And then a funny thing happened. That little voice in my head that has a way of sabotaging me lost its fervor, and I learned a thing or two. I heard the Sensei say, "That's it – you have the basic motion. Now just do it about two hundred more times and you'll have it down." About two hundred more times?

Isn't that like life, though? Just when we think we're good at something, events change and we find ourselves in uncharted territory, doing things we have little or no concept of. When we take ourselves too seriously, we end up getting in our own way.

> *If you would give your inner genius as much credence as your inner critic, you would be light years ahead of where you now stand.*
>
> *~Alan Cohen,*
> *American inspirational*
> *author and lecturer*

Our worlds become smaller and we become the center of them. We lose touch with reality — and instead of hearing and seeing what is really going on, we give our attention to the voices in our heads that sap our confidence and lead us to question our abilities — and in some cases our very worth itself. In that state, any kind of criticism, real or imagined, seems to have infinitely more weight than positive, supportive feedback. We screen the good stuff out and take in the junk.

**It's not that we need to silence the voices.
I think they will always be there.
We just need to focus on something more empowering.**

**We've got to give ourselves credit for showing
up and not running away.
And we need to embrace the experiences that
put us back in beginner's shoes,
with beginner's eyes, for they are the mark of
another cycle of growth.**

When I reflect on my karate experience, I realize how in so many ways it mirrors the place most of us have been in repeatedly over the course of our lives — where we feel drawn to do something so different from what we have previously done that we question whether we really have what it takes to succeed. The little puppet commentator in our heads would have us believe that what we strive toward are domains reserved for a special breed of people, to which we do not belong. We always begin in the stage of conscious incompetence with it — painfully aware of just how much we do not know.

Thinking back to what my Sensei taught me in that karate lesson, I realize that it doesn't matter if I don't know something right now. What is most important in this moment is to show up and do what is in front of me — despite my fear — and to do the same in the next moment, and the next one.... As I build on what I am learning and keep at it, the unknown will become the known. And if I do it long enough, the known will become engrained enough that I can draw on it in creative ways.

Unless you try to do something beyond what you have already mastered, you will never grow.

*~ Ralph Waldo Emerson,
American philosopher,
lecturer, essayist and
poet (1803-1882)*

The puppet would have us believe that we must resist or battle fear, in an effort to overcome it. The true test is not to eradicate it, but rather to move through it with patience, determination and grace. Like Pinocchio, we must learn to swim toward it. In the belly of the whale that contains our deepest, darkest fears, we can sit courageously, looking that fear in the eye.

When we resist our fear, we give it credence and power, creating something in our minds that we need to run from. However, when we remain present with it — moving into it, we realize that it is more of an illusion than a reality. As mentioned in Chapter 2, the word "fear" can be seen as an acronym for False Events Appearing Real. Creating false events that appear real is what the puppet does best — in an effort to maintain control and avoid moving into a realm that would allow us to see through its power and, rather than react to fear, act instead on the initiative of our animating genius.

At bedtime, when my kids were young, they would get scared, seeing shapes in their room that they couldn't make out. In the absence of information, they created their own stories about what they were seeing, which usually involved some kind of monster or other unwelcome guest. But once the lights were flipped on and they realized the shadows were simply the product of a jacket thrown over the back of a chair or a teddy bear with a large hat, they settled back into their beds and slept peacefully.

This is what our puppet does with the projects and tasks we face on a regular basis — and sadly, also with our grandest dreams and visions. In the light of day, we see them glimmer with promise and possibility. But in the dark, our doubts and fears creep in and have a way of distorting things. This is the point where the skeptics welcome the optimists to reality. But it isn't reality at all. It is an illusion that has been created by a frightened mind.

Never doubt in the dark what you saw in the light.

~ Author unknown

The stories we tell ourselves in the dark are those of peril and potential failure. In the absence of knowing exactly what it will take to accomplish the task, project or dream and whether we will be able to execute on it, we begin to identify with our doubt which amplifies the enormity of what lies before us. The shadow of a task magnified becomes a feat that feels insurmountable. But flip on the lights and challenge the assumptions that make a creation feel heavy, and it becomes a collection of smaller pieces that can be gradually assembled over time. As Lao Tzu once said, "The journey of a thousand miles begins with a single step."

Whenever I feel the heaviness that comes with trying something new, I know that I have entered my dark room. In the absence of light, I am prone to question my ability and my nerve, compare myself to others, and amplify the work it will take to pull it off. The darkness has a way of casting shadows on everything else that needs to get done as well. But in the light, I realize all I need to do is take one simple step toward my goal — and then another — and then another. And each seemingly insurmountable task can be broken down into a simpler component that I can get through with even just a little effort. I can breathe through my fear and move into each experience, letting go of the outcome and enjoying the process itself.

Out on a Limb

Anne, one of my clients, longed to widen her sphere of influence and felt that her discomfort with people in positions of high authority and prestige was holding her back. Her fear of not being able to hold a conversation with them that would provoke and maintain their interest led her to shy away from the numerous opportunities she was regularly presented with to practice. Even in meetings I observed Anne having with her peers, she often held back on voicing her true opinions and would later tell me what she was thinking but didn't have the nerve to say. In many cases it was exactly what the rest of the group needed to hear to move forward.

Anne is a delightful, charming, thoughtful and intelligent woman who was contributing only a small percentage of the wisdom, insight and knowledge she had to share. What held her back was her doubt in her own ability and lack of faith in herself. This was coupled with fear that if she were to go out on a limb, she would not be well received. She was her own worst critic, editing and judging everything she said — many times before she ever uttered a word. She continually second-guessed herself and downplayed the impact she thought she could make.

Over time, Anne's desire to advance and make an impact became greater than her fear. She began to recognize that the stories she was telling herself — the ones that created doubt and hesitation — were a product of her frightful imagination and doubts that were largely unfounded. At the same time, she started giving more credence to her ability to convey her understanding of what the group was trying to accomplish and build on their ideas in ways that helped them get closer to their goals. Each step she took in becoming a bit bolder gave her the courage to continue.

Anne began accepting roles she previously turned down that put her in a sphere where she was expected to converse with people in other companies to identify and establish connections with people of influence. With each engagement she attended, she made a game of seeking people she most wanted to connect with and ended up creating networks that would later greatly benefit her career path. By moving into her fear, she was able to dis-empower it and find something worth focusing her time and energy on that was far more productive. Anne is the first to admit that her fear is still always there, but she has learned to be present with and use it in a way that works for her. When we

We can't become who we need to be by remaining what we are.

~ Oprah Winfrey, American television host, actor, producer, and philanthropist

last spoke, she was one of a handful of internal candidates being considered for an officer level position in her company.

When we are able to move into our fear, we can use it in ways that serve us, rather than hold us back. Think of the last time you were on a high dive. You may have felt flip-flops in your stomach or a strange surge of energy through your core. Perhaps you turned around and climbed back down. Or maybe you stepped forward, entered the unknown, and bravely leaped off the board.

After having done it once, depending on your experience, it may have been a bit easier for you to do it again. As leaders, we are repeatedly called to dive into the unknown, despite our fears about it.

We must use the fear the puppet generates to inform us of the dangers, and to provide us with data that will help us make good decisions. But we must not allow this fear to make our decisions for us.

Having faced our fear and moved forward in spite of it, the experience may be positive or negative. Regardless of the outcome, we must acknowledge the progress we have made. If our experience is less than desirable, we can evaluate it and learn from it. Having had the experience, we are wiser for it — far more than we would be if we simply continued to contemplate taking that leap or safely learn from the experience of others instead. And if we are successful, we can build on this experience and use it as a platform for further growth.

A life spent making mistakes is not only more honorable but more useful than a life spent doing nothing.

~ George Bernard Shaw, Irish playwright, co-founder of the London School of Economics (1856-1950)

There will always be an abundance of people who will tell you why things cannot be done, what there is to fear, and why it is just not worth the risk. Let them speak, but do not be swayed by their doubt. It is based on their own experience of the world,

The spirit, the will to win, and the will to excel are the things that endure. These qualities are so much more important than the events that occur.

~ Vince Lombardi, American football coach (1913-1970)

not yours. If you are to lead, you must set the example for others so that they can see that even when you take a risk and fail, you have moved forward and began progress in a direction that would have otherwise been stunted. If you believe you cannot succeed, you may be right. But if you believe you can, you are halfway there.

Do not worry about those who may find fault with what you do or attempt to do. As Theodore Roosevelt wrote in "The Man in the Arena":[1]

> "It is not the critic who counts; not the man who points out how the strong man stumbles, or where the doer of deeds could have done them better. The credit belongs to the man who is actually in the arena, whose face is marred by dust and sweat and blood; who strives valiantly; who errs, who comes short again and again, because there is no effort without error and shortcoming; but who does actually strive to do the deeds; who knows great enthusiasms, the great devotions; who spends himself in a worthy cause; who at the best knows in the end the triumph of high achievement, and who at the worst, if he fails, at least fails while daring greatly, so that his place shall never be with those cold and timid souls who neither know victory nor defeat."

When was the last time you took a risk to experience something that has been calling you — something that you know in your heart is for your highest good (and that of others as well)? What happened when you did? What did you learn? And how have you grown as a result?

---

[1] *"The Man in the Arena,"* speech by Theodore Roosevelt at the Sorbonne, Paris, France, April 23, 1910.

What is calling to you now? And what small, sweet step can you take to bring you closer to experiencing the exhilaration of moving bravely in a direction that might just take you and others around you to a new level of mastery?

We are all capable of so much more than we realize.
Now, not "someday," is the time to stand taller, reach higher,
and be willing to allow our greatest work to emerge.

Do not be fooled into thinking that going outside your comfort zone is merely a self-serving exercise that can wait until you have more confidence or time. In fact, there is no better way to increase your confidence than by taking this kind of determined action despite your fear and discomfort. This kind of courageous exploration enriches not only yourself, but everyone around you who will surely benefit from the gifts you uncover and give form to. When we shrink, we cheat more than just ourselves. When we expand, we allow ourselves to truly lead — in whatever form that leadership will take.

What you can do, or dream you can do, begin it; boldness has genius, power and magic in it.

~ Johann Wolfgang von Goethe, German author and polymath

Life's Sudden Storms

Many times our invitations and opportunities to rise up and play a greater part come in ways that are difficult to handle, such as sudden change or loss, as it did for Bill, who was suddenly asked to leave the company where he had worked for more than twenty years. Most of us prefer to be the ones doing the changing — it brings newness along with a sense of control; we are at the helm, steadfastly steering our ship. But imagine, if you will, that a massive wave summoned by a hurricane has ripped the captain's wheel right off the ship and you are left clinging to something that no longer has any power. The more tightly you grip it, the less energy you have to deal with your circumstances in a way that will truly serve you (and everyone around you as well.)

At times like these, we often pray for the storm to pass — for things to revert back to the way they were — or for a specific course of events that we believe would be life's perfect solution. These solutions are based on what we think we know — which is largely a product of what we have already seen and experienced. And relying upon the patterns and strategies that worked for us in the past is often inadequate for our present and emerging challenges.

The world is changing and so are we.

We tend to strive for comfort and familiarity, even when what's comfortable isn't necessarily effective or even satisfying anymore. We may wish and pray that the chaos be removed and order be restored. But often life's little disturbances are exactly what we need to reach our true potential and escape complacency. Stormy seas (and life's sudden surprises) have a way of testing our resolve and our resiliency. Pressure brings out our extremes — for better or worse. And fear does funny things to people. At its worst, it produces panic — a physical state that literally disables the brain's ability to think clearly. At one extreme a person is frozen by fear and at the other he will thrash about like a drowning victim who pulls his rescuers under the water with him. The key to surviving a seeming assault of this kind is learning to relax and stay calmly aware of our surroundings so that we can identify and creatively utilize the resources at our disposal.

> *To be thrown upon one's own resources, is to be cast into the very lap of fortune; for our faculties then undergo a development and display an energy of which they were previously unsusceptible.*
>
> *~ Benjamin Franklin, American founding father, author, political theorist, scientist and inventor (1706-1790)*

One of the most critical resources in our control when all else seems beyond it is our perspective. The way we view things determines the story we tell ourselves about what's happening, which directly influences the responses we will have. If we believe we are helpless victims at the mercy of something that seeks to destroy us, we will become bitter, resentful and apathetic. In this state our true power remains dormant. We collude with our view of reality to create a condition that validates our doomsday stories and sink even more deeply into the abyss. Those who try to rescue us from our self-imposed paralysis risk being dragged beneath the current created by our own negativity.

> *The greatest discovery of my generation is that a human being can alter his life by altering his attitude.*
>
> ~ William James, American psychologist and philosopher (1842-1910)

Hand in hand with perspective comes responsibility — or our ability to choose our response. When we react to things with fear, we end up amplifying what we are afraid of and adding to the anxiety. Our fears drive us to act in ways that keep us from accessing our intuition and finding answers that truly serve us. Sometimes, we end up behaving in ways that make our fictional stories become real.

As an example, when you tell yourself a story about what is happening that leaves you feeling threatened, you may find yourself closing up and treating others with suspicion and mistrust. The way you are behaving toward people may well provoke a response in them that appears to validate your fearful story. However, in this scenario, it is very likely that their behavior is more of a reaction to the actions your story led you to take than anything else.

Our fearful stories are like the viruses we protect our computers from. These nasty viruses are often embedded in emails that pique our curiosity or rouse our fear. When we unwittingly activate them, they can spread uncontrollably. We then risk contaminating the computers of our friends, associates and countless others. The viruses corrupt our systems until they no longer function effectively.

Like computer viruses, our stories have a way of spinning us out of control and interfering with our ability to rise up to our challenges and find the opportunity always there waiting for us to discover and leverage it.

If, however, like Pinocchio we view our predicaments as adventures and see them as opportunities to give all we've got, we reach deeply within ourselves and tap reserves of courage, wisdom and ingenuity we never realized we had. In the proverbial belly of the whale we find our inner grit and creatively rise up to life's challenges in ways that transform us — and everyone around us as well. We become the heroes of our own stories.

Beyond the Mind

Our rational minds want answers and security. They need to figure everything out and almost automatically occupy themselves with trying to sort through data to arrive at conclusions. There is nothing wrong with answers or security. The problem is that our minds plug imaginary variables into the equation that end up further exacerbating the anxiety we are already experiencing. When they are done with one variable, they plug in another and the churning continues, leaving us with uneasiness that keeps us on edge.

In the grip of this madness, sometimes the best thing you can do is indulge your mind with a variable that will allow it to do its thing. Go ahead and plug in the worst-case scenario. If the worst possible thing happened, what would you do? Allow yourself to sit with that question for awhile. Let the fear move through you and keep asking the question, what could I do that would allow everything to be okay? If you sit long enough with your question, you will arrive at some workable alternatives and reconnect with that part of yourself that is strong, resourceful and resilient.

Armed with the knowledge that you will be okay, even if the worst possible thing happens, you can come back into the present and recognize your fearful thoughts for what they are — fearful thoughts.

**One of the best pieces of advice I ever got is:
Don't believe everything you think.**

In the present moment, devoid of your stories about variables that are truly unknown, you are okay. And when new events begin to unfold, if you stay in the moment and access your inner wisdom, you will know exactly what you need to do — or not do — to be okay then, too. And as you go about your daily life in this way, your calm resolve will permeate your interactions with others and through your example, you will help others rise up to their challenges in ways that unearth the greatness in themselves as well.

A Space for Transformation

We can also look at the belly of the whale as a metaphor for the space where transformation takes place. Monstro the Whale is the last place Pinocchio seeks out before he is granted his wish to become real again. His desire to save Geppetto takes him beyond his own interests to serve those of another. This desire is greater than his fear, which allows him to bravely venture into the unknown, risking everything.

As each of us begins to hear and answer the beckoning of our own animating genius to unearth our individual greatness, we will be led to a space that is somewhere between the known and unknown. We have been there many times before, whenever we rode the wave of change in our lives that moved us beyond what was once predictable and somewhat effortless into a new challenge or opportunity that may have felt daunting, overwhelming and mysteriously promising. Maybe it was moving to a new neighborhood, beginning another leg of education, starting a new job, taking on a challenging project, or becoming a parent or an entrepreneur. I like to call this place limbo land.

Limbo land is akin to chaos. *Merriam-Webster* defines chaos as "a state of things in which chance is supreme; the confused unorganized state of primordial matter before the creation of distinct forms." I suppose it is what the caterpillar experiences in the cocoon as everything it has once been completely dissolves to become something entirely new. As we enter the bellies of our own whales, we begin a dance with uncertainty that requires us to trust in life's mystery. Much of the fear we encounter in there is about not knowing — not knowing what is coming next and whether we will know what to do — or even if we have the skills to be able to do it. The fear is also about not being able to control what happens. Limbo land is sacred ground. It requires us to let go of our puppet's need to have everything figured out and to trust that we will rise to the occasion — and that perhaps the occasion will also rise to us.

The knowledge, skills and experience we have gained that helped us get to these pivotal points are helpful, but they are not enough in and of themselves. The transformations before us require that we go beyond our heads to access our hearts — to trust in the wisdom of animating genius, which is connected to all things. This is the same inherent knowledge that leads birds to migrate in the winter, that tells a new mother how to nurse her child, that informs the caterpillar of when to build a cocoon and how to emerge from it. It is inherent in each of us. And to access it, we must find peace in the midst of chaos.

Trusting in the Moment

A few years ago while on a skiing trip I had an experience that taught me a lot about letting go and transcending the clamor of my mind. It had been a long time since I last skied and I was very rusty. But after an hour or so, the years that had since passed no longer seemed significant and my adventurous side led me to a very difficult black run, full of moguls and steep angles. Once I embarked upon the run, I realized I was in way over my head. At that moment the temperature dropped suddenly and a fog rolled in that was so thick that I could not see more than three feet ahead of me. I began to panic. I wanted more than ever to reach the bottom of the slope and became more fixated on having the run behind me than on the thrill of the experience itself.

As soon as my attention and focus went from the snow in front of me to the bottom of the steep slope, I lost control and came crashing to the ground, losing my skis and feeling the slap of the hard cold ground beneath me. I managed to somehow to get up and put my skis back on, but before long my focus would shift and the same thing would happen again.

It was only when I resigned myself to forget about finishing the run and pay attention to what was right in front of me that my body knew how to navigate each mogul. When I let go of having to know exactly how I would get down that mountain and trust that I could make it a few feet at a time, I had everything I needed to succeed.

Sometimes conditions aren't right for us to proceed full speed ahead, and circumstances take a turn that feels frustrating. Often the skills we need are those that can only be developed through a series of challenges that require us to move out of our comfort zones. We may see these events as setbacks and annoying diversions without realizing their perfect place in the larger orchestration of a course of events we are engaged in that has much greater implications than what we originally envisioned.

We will always be faced with challenges and opportunities. Some of them may feel daunting. They will push us to our edges and summon every last bit of strength, faith and fortitude we can muster. And we may find ourselves on the ground (literally or figuratively), feeling defeated and fatigued. In those moments, when we look inside ourselves, we will find the courage we didn't think we had — even if only to stand up and fall down again. Each time we rise to our challenges we learn a bit more about how to handle the next one.

Having been in the grip of our own fear
and experienced the disorienting confusion that panic and
adrenaline brings,
we can learn to be in the midst of chaos —
and still find our calm.

Inspiring and Motivating Others

As leaders, we cannot expect others to stretch themselves if we are not willing to do it too. When we allow ourselves to be humbled and vulnerable, we can identify with and understand the experiences we ask others to participate in. Remembering what it feels like to stretch beyond our own comfort zones, we can be patient with and supportive of others as they encounter and work through their forms of resistance, fear, frustration and doubt. We must resist the inclination to judge others for what they have done (or failed to do) up to this point and instead find ways to help them envision a future for themselves that generates enough desire and passion to rival their fear.

Leadership is not magnetic personality – that can just as well be a glib tongue. It is not making friends and influencing people – that is flattery. Leadership is lifting a person's vision to higher sights, the raising of a person's performance to a higher standard, the building of a personality beyond its normal limitations.

~ Peter Drucker, author, management consultant and social ecologist (1909-2005)

This requires that we learn more about the people we have the opportunity and privilege to lead — what their hopes and dreams are, what they value and care deeply about, and what their strengths and abilities are. It also requires that we look upon them with eyes that reveal possibility rather than limitation, so that they can learn to do the same for themselves and others. As we focus on people's true potential and treat them as though they are capable of achieving it, they will prove us right — often surprising and delighting themselves in the process. The ability to do this is one of the true marks of a leader.

Getting people to focus on possibilities and believe in themselves is a huge part of exercising inspired leadership, but it won't get you all the way there. To leverage people's strengths and make the most of emerging opportunities, inspiration must at some point turn into action. And that is when the puppet often steals the show, bringing with it doubt, skepticism and anxiety over the potential for failure.

This is where motivation becomes vital. Motivation is about getting people to move. And sometimes you have to remove barriers that are in front of people before they can do that. Obstacles can be physical, organizational or mental. Good leaders are instrumental in detecting and removing them, whether they are in the form of skill deficiency, inadequate equipment or resources, or a lack of confidence. You can soothe the clamors of the puppet/ego by mitigating risk, increasing the odds of success, and helping others to recognize what they have to gain as a result of exerting the effort necessary to succeed. With the parking brake removed, action and results can begin to accelerate.

> *Vision is not enough; it must be combined with venture. It is not enough to stare up the steps; we must step up the stairs.*
>
> *~ Vaclav Havel, former president of Czechoslovakia, playwright and essayist*

Sometimes despite your best attempts with both inspiration and motivation, people will choose to remain complacent. A leader has done due diligence when she has made performance a matter of choice, when people understand what will be gained if they perform and what is at stake if they do not — both for themselves and the organization — and every effort has been made to give them the tools necessary to rise up to the challenges and opportunities before them. When people decide to stay behind, sometimes the kindest thing a leader can do is release them from the organization.

No one likes to be fired, and most people do not like to have to terminate the employment of others. But in cases where people have stayed in jobs to play it safe, and have become stagnant in such a way that they are not only cheating themselves of growth but also having a negative impact on others, a forced separation can be the best-case scenario.

A Shakeup Can Be Good

The other day I had a conversation with a colleague who had held a leadership position in a large firm several years ago and had the difficult responsibility of terminating a large number of people. Recently, one of the women she had let go saw her name and contact information on the Internet and decided to call her. Much to my colleague's surprise, this woman was phoning to express her thanks for being given the wakeup call she needed to move on to other opportunities that had a profound impact on her life.

Often our greatest attributes, talents and strengths lie dormant inside of us until something happens that requires we summon them up.

The belly of the whale is a powerful, mysterious place that allows us to run smack into our fears and discover ourselves to be stronger than we ever realized. When we are courageous enough to venture into our fear, we begin to realize just how much of it is an illusion and instead identify with what is real — the resilience, creativity, determination and unique potential within each of us. The puppet's hold on us is broken and we are free to dream and create to our heart's desire. Then we are ready to explore the magic of creation we all possess and learn to harness and apply that power in extraordinary ways.

It is only in adventure that some people succeed in knowing themselves — in finding themselves.

~ André Gide, French Nobel Prize-winning author (1869-1951)

Chapter 10

The Fairy's Wand

After reaching the shore, Geppetto regains consciousness and carries Pinocchio home to bed. He sees Pinocchio's donkey ears and thinks of how brave he was. Suddenly, the room turns blue, and the Fairy appears and addresses Pinocchio. "Pinocchio, you have been brave, truthful, and unselfish," she tells him. He sits up and opens his eyes saying, "Father, I'm alive!" Upon examining his hands, he says, "And I'm real! A real boy!" Geppetto and Pinocchio hug. On Jiminy's breast appears a badge that says "Official Conscience," and when the cricket goes to thank the Fairy, all he sees is a brilliant star winking at him. The scene closes with Jiminy singing, "When you wish upon a star, your dream comes true."

The Fairy's wand represents power that is within each of us to create what we most desire. It is not a magic pill, or some kind of sorcery. Rather than being something we must rely on others for, it is something we are all born with that we gradually learn to utilize, as we become more and more aligned with what is most true within us.

The power of the Fairy's wand, which we all innately possess, is quite simply the strength of the feeling we generate when we identify with something so completely that we take it to be real. With sustained and unwavering belief, whatever we hold in our minds and our hearts in this way becomes our reality. The irony is that most of us learn to tap into this power and unintentionally use it in a way that brings us more of what we don't want, before we understand exactly what it is and how it can be used far more constructively.

There are powers inside of you which, if you could discover and use, would make of you everything you ever dreamed or imagined you could become.

~ Orison Swett Marden, American author (1850-1924)

The Power of Thought

We, too, tend to identify more with our limitations, doubts and what we feel we are lacking for a good part of our lives, without recognizing that by identifying and focusing on these things, we actually make them bigger and exacerbate the separation between our puppets and animating geniuses.

Have you ever noticed that the quality of your life tends to mirror your thought?

Think back to the last time you had "one of those days." You know, where nothing happened quite the way you would have liked and even the best-laid plans seemed to go awry. You may have found yourself becoming irritated or annoyed, and before long felt surrounded by people or things that were equally irritating and annoying which only served to intensify your frustration. Resigning yourself to being a victim of unfortunate circumstances, you may have thrown up your hands and given in to self-pity, feeling it well up inside you like a toilet about to overflow.

A Day of the Domino Effect

I can recall a day that had me in a very similar state. I may have even woken up in a bad mood, feeling resentful at having to do one thing or another and finding that nothing, from my kids to my coffee maker, was cooperating with me. At five years old, my youngest son, who had recently become quite proud of the large bowel movements he was having, was reluctant to flush the toilet. Our new Golden Retriever, apparently unsatisfied with her puppy chow, decided that the contents of the toilet were an appetizing alternative. Several minutes later, she threw up on the carpet and I found myself on my knees cleaning up regurgitated feces. It was all I could do not to add my own vomit to the pile.

This unwelcome deviation from my morning routine threw me behind schedule and increased the level of urgency with which I corralled my young children into the car. Reacting to the heightened volume and pitch of my voice, my daughter, who had just turned three, began to scream and cry. My oldest son, then eight years old, realizing that he would be late to school, began to reprimand his younger brother for his role in creating the offending mess that caused the delay. Eager to escape the rising crescendo of screaming, whining and yelling, I ran into the kitchen to fill my travel cup with the one and only beverage that seemed to have a way of making everything right, only to find that the coffee maker had malfunctioned, spewing hot water and coffee grounds all over the counter.

After reaching the daycare parking lot, I managed to slam my skirt in the car door and rip a large hole in it as I attempted to walk away. By the time I reached the parking garage at work, the only space I could find in the garage was between an oversized truck and a large concrete pillar, which took the side mirror clean off my car as I pulled in. The space was so tight that I had to crawl out the passenger side of my minivan to exit. I walked all the way to the office to realize I had left my security badge in the car.

On my lunch hour I drove to the bank as the side mirror flapped in the wind, clanging loudly against the side of the car, held loosely in place by a couple of cables. Pulling into the parking lot, I drove toward a car coming from the opposite direction and realized we were both headed for the one parking spot that was in close proximity to the building. We both stopped our cars for a moment. Staring back at me from the opposite windshield was a woman whose face was scrunched into a ball, mouth contorted into a tight grimace and shoulders up to her ears. She yanked the steering wheel quickly to the right, punched her gas pedal and darted into the open parking spot.

But before she did, I couldn't help but realize this woman was a perfect reflection of myself — my mood, my demeanor, and most likely my expression and posture as well. And though one could say she stole my parking space, I suddenly felt a kinship with her and recognized that she had come along at the perfect moment to jolt me back into a state of awareness and empowerment. As I reflected on the morning's events, it occurred to me that the frustrated, anxiety-ridden state I was in had been wholly and completely a matter of choice for me. Having totally given myself to it, perhaps I colluded in such a way as to attract all manner of events and people that would allow this state of being to perpetuate itself.

Perhaps if I redirected my attention to something more aligned with the state of mind I would rather be in, things would change. I drove to the edge of the lot and parked under a tree. Turning my car off, I took a deep breath and looked around. It was a beautiful day. The sun was shining and the spring air was fresh and cool. I walked to the bank listening to the sweet sound of birds singing.

As I entered, I noticed a woman with two small children who were completely out of control. We both stepped into the long line while her children ran around the room yelling and screaming. She feebly attempted to control them with a stern word, which neither child seemed to hear. As I looked at the lines on her face, I recognized her from the parking lot. A few minutes ago, I would have been annoyed with the disruption, but now I found myself empathetic and somewhat amused. In the corner of the bank, sitting hunched over on a red microfiber love seat with a cane in one hand was a frail old man who grinned from ear to ear as he watched the children chase each other around.

At the front of the line a woman fumbled through her purse as papers flew to the ground. She hadn't completed the forms the rest of us had finished before we got in line, and was attempting to furiously scribble down figures while the rest of us waited. The people behind her anxiously shifted from one foot to another, and I felt a slight irritation welling up within me as well. Then I thought of the way I'd rather be feeling and pulled an article from my bag that I'd wanted to read.

When I got back into my car and turned the key in the ignition, a song came on the radio that I didn't particularly care for. I promptly pushed a button on the console that brought different music into the car. And then I realized that my ability to change the station wasn't limited to the radio.

You and I are essentially infinite choice-makers. In every moment of our existence, we are in that field of all possibilities where we have access to an infinity of choices.

~ Deepak Chopra, Indian-American physician, speaker and author

At any given moment, we all tune into frequencies that, from a myriad of possibilities, determine which we will pursue at the exclusion of all the others. They radiate around us like a magnetic force, attracting more of the same into our paths, and sometimes setting the tone for those who surround us. But if we don't like what we are seeing, perhaps upon becoming aware of it we can simply select a different channel.

Maggie's Altered Perspective

Maggie, one of my clients, felt certain that she had been passed over for promotion and was hurt by the apparent lack of consideration she was given for a leadership position she felt she was qualified for. Over the course of the next several weeks, she continued to interpret the remarks and actions of others (or lack thereof) as further evidence that she was unworthy and unappreciated. She became resentful, sullen and somewhat apathetic toward her work. What was strange to me was that in our coaching meetings, Maggie had told me several times that she didn't really have much interest in climbing the corporate ladder. She liked the position she had and enjoyed the people and activities it allowed her to interface with.

When she was honest with herself, Maggie realized that if she had really wanted the promotion, there were a number of things she could have done to merit more attention. Once she shifted her focus from a belief that she was somehow inferior, to recognize that she was choosing a path that gave her much more personal fulfillment, she began to show up differently. She took greater interest in the people and activities around her, her health and appearance, and her own passions and hobbies as well. She used the next couple of years to finish projects she felt passionate about and to help develop leaders she believed in and then happily retired to pursue the next leg of her personal adventure. At her retirement party, several people told moving stories of how she had touched their lives with her warmth, support and encouragement. Others conveyed appreciation for the many ways in which she had contributed to the organization's success.

Mark's State of Mind

Mark wanted to become a CEO someday. He was passionate about his personal and career development, as well as that of others. Like many ambitious professionals, he felt things just weren't happening fast enough for him. He wanted bigger projects with more exposure and significance. He longed for more responsibility and the ability to impact a larger portion of the organization. He sought out executive coaching in the hope of learning to employ strategies that would help him reach his goal faster.

Gradually, Mark began to shift his focus from frustration over what had not yet happened to envisioning what life would be like when it would, and living as though it already had. He wrote himself a letter, dated five years in the future, describing in present tense the state of his life, how he felt about his career, and what he had been able to accomplish as a result of his personal and professional endeavors. In it, he expressed gratitude for all he had experienced which perfectly prepared him for the challenges and opportunities he had gone on to tackle that led him to realizing his ultimate vision. Mark read that letter periodically, and added to it whenever he felt inspired. As a result, he began to identify with the state of mind of a rising star. In less than a year, he was promoted from his manager position to become a director, and within two years of that was interviewing for a C-level (high corporate) position in his company.

Both Maggie and Mark were experiencing the perfect manifestation of what they were thinking about at the time. Though Maggie may have enjoyed the attention and affirmation a promotion would bring, what she identified with and considered real was her current position. She never had a great deal of desire for the new position and didn't have any occasion to envision what it would have been like if she had attained it. Her energy was more aligned with the position she had held for many years.

Mark's state of increased frustration with the lack of momentum of his career path was also perfectly reflected in his ongoing reality — until he changed what he identified with, to be more aligned with what he really wanted. Once he began to see himself through the eyes of someone who had already arrived at his goal and trust that in time it would come to fruition, his identification with having to endure an endless wait gave way to being a man on his way to success. And now his path was allowing him to have the perfect combination of experiences that would prepare him for what was coming next.

Private victories precede public victories. You can't invert that process any more than you can harvest a crop before you plant it.

~ Stephen Covey, American author, speaker, professor, consultant and management expert

A State of Grateful Certainty

As a teenager I began to read a lot about the power of positive thinking and visualization. I was enthralled by stories of athletes who would spend time imagining sinking those critical shots at game time and performing exactly as they had rehearsed in their minds. I utilized affirmations of positive intent around the person I was becoming and the wonderful things that were coming into my life. I played with creating vision boards for myself, made from large poster paper with various pictures of things I wanted to have or symbols that represented experiences I longed for glued onto it. I created movies in my head that featured me performing — powerfully and passionately — anything from sports to public speaking with great success. Many of these visions and dreams have come true over the years. And many have not.

I have reflected at length on what it might be that differentiated the dreams and visions that came to fruition from those that didn't. And I have come to the conclusion that there are three significant factors.

Alignment with True Purpose. One is quite simply that some of the things my mind (and puppet) believed I needed to have were not in the best interests of my spirit (animating genius), aligned with my true purpose, or in service to something greater than myself. Believe me, I have had many occasions to thank God for unanswered prayers that I initially believed would have been the best thing I could have imagined for myself.

> *Life is full of miracles,*
> *but they're not always*
> *the ones we pray for.*
>
> *~ Eve Arden,*
> *American actress*
> *(1908-1990)*

Attachment to Details. The second factor often present when things didn't quite play out the way I had envisioned was my fervent attachment to having something happen in just the way (or at just the time) I thought it should. While it is true that we need to be passionate about our visions and dreams, we must also remain somewhat willing to let go of the details and trust in something bigger than ourselves to step in and collaborate with us. This higher intelligence, to which our animated genius is innately connected and from which we all originate, is capable of orchestrating things far more magnificently than we could ever attempt to do. Though it is important that we are willing, if we step over the line and become too willful, our thoughts and actions have a way of throwing a monkey wrench in things.

The urgency with which we desire things can have us acting not out of trust but desperation. As a result, instead of identifying with what we most want, we embody the state of not having it and trying fervently to do whatever we can to change things. Taking our current state to be more real than what we truly desire, the Fairy's wand

> *Destiny grants us our*
> *wishes, but in its own way,*
> *in order to give us something*
> *beyond our wishes.*
>
> *~ Johann*
> *Wolfgang von Goethe,*
> *German author and polymath*
> *(1749-1832)*

works perfectly to deliver to us exactly what our thoughts have been fixated on — leaving us in a state of want, working madly to make everything happen the way we think it should. We must learn to give ourselves over to our visions and dreams while allowing for divine timing, unforeseen incidents and the hand of providence, which often enables things to happen in ways that exceed our wildest expectations. I like to call this state "passionate detachment."

Anticipation, Gratitude and Faith. The third dynamic that can keep our manifestations at bay is that visioning or imagining something in and of itself is not enough. I can dream great dreams, but if they are devoid of feeling and passion, they fall as flat as the set of a three-act play after the audience has left the final performance. To unleash the full power of the Fairy's wand we have to go beyond simply watching the movies we create in our minds that have us sinking that shot, mesmerizing that audience, or jumping for joy at our victories. Rather than seeing ourselves up there on the screen of our minds, we must see *from the eyes of the person in the movie*. We must experience in our minds and our bodies the *feelings* associated with that which we desire most — the exhilaration of victory, the soothing relief of having completed something we were unsure or afraid of, and the sweet satisfaction and joy that accompanies success.

> *To succeed you have to believe in something with such a passion that it becomes a reality.*
>
> ~ *Dame Anita Roddick, Founder, The Body Shop®*

Similarly, it is not enough to create a visual wish list or a series of affirmations or declarations about the things we would like to own, achieve or experience. We must look upon these things as what we have already been gifted with, and feel the gratitude welling up in our hearts for having received them.

The state of grateful certainty we need to give ourselves to is not unlike the way you may feel after ordering something off the Internet. After clicking the purchase button and entering your shipping address and credit card information, you can have reasonable certainty that what you ordered is on its way. With this assurance, you identify with the state of already having owned what you just bought — even though you do not yet physically possess it. It is this same state of graceful anticipation, gratitude, and faith that those, who seem to magically attract exactly what they want into their lives, have learned to enter into time and time again.

Claire Creates the Change She Wants

Claire was ready for a change. She wasn't sure exactly what she wanted to do. She longed for more excitement in her work and was eager to explore new and different areas of the organization, but felt certain there were no openings in any of the areas she was interested in. In our coaching meetings, Claire expressed frustration over her perception that there didn't seem to be any opportunities that would allow her to branch out. Though she wasn't clear on the specific job she wanted or what her title might be, she did have some solid ideas about what she wanted to do. So she began to make a list.

In the process of thinking about what she wanted from her ideal job, she considered the kind of boss she wanted to work for, the degree of autonomy and flexibility she desired, the type of team she might like to lead, and the nature of the work. She wrote down the qualities and attributes of her desired position, as well as the talents and skills she wanted to bring into it and added to the page as new things occurred to her. Every so often, she opened the drawer in which she kept her list and read it as though she had rediscovered it a year in the future and was looking back on it with amazement that all the items she specified had come to fruition. She allowed herself to feel the excitement and thrill over having realized that her dreams were coming true.

As Claire gained clarity on the specific area of the organization she wanted to work in, she began to learn more about it and get to know the people there and the challenges they faced. She realized that she had skills and experience that would bring a new perspective to meeting those challenges and solve some of the problems that had not yet been addressed. Within six months of creating her list, Claire was approached by executives from the area in which she wanted to work. They proposed to create a special position that would allow her to utilize her expertise and insights to help them seize emerging opportunities and wanted her input on how that job should look.

The Reality of Imagination

It may be somewhat difficult to get your head around the notion of experiencing and acting as if something you long for has already happened. But our children do it every day using the gift of imagination we were all born with. If you are out of touch with it, treat yourself to a quality children's movie and allow yourself to become enthralled with images and stories that suggest that if you can believe in something long and hard enough, it will come to be.

Imagination is everything. It is the preview of life's coming attractions.

~ Albert Einstein, German Nobel Prize-winning physicist, philosopher and author (1879-1955)

It is only as adults who have been hardened by "reality" that these notions begin to seem strange to us. The reality we sometimes buy into that seems to dampen our dreams is often more a product of our own doubts than anything else.

The sooner we realize and understand that through our thoughts we have a hand in creating the reality we experience, the more we harness the power of the Fairy's wand to work its magic in ways that bring us our heart's desires.

We can practice utilizing this power in the simplest of moments, applying it to everyday challenges, such as having a critical conversation or anything that requires us to step into our fear or anxiety and perform in spite of it.

Early in my career I taught many classes and workshops designed to give people a step-by-step process for engaging in difficult conversations — perhaps to provide feedback, resolve conflict, or simply raise a point. I can recall one of the formulas often taught with regard to conflict resolution: "When you (do what you just did)... I feel (hurt, angry, overlooked, sad, etc.)... In the future (I would appreciate it if you)..." The classes often provided participants an opportunity to practice by role-playing with others. They were given a few minutes to reflect on a real challenge they were having with another person, organize their thoughts, and then spend two to three minutes practicing dialogues with their partners using the techniques they had learned.

Some people would spend a great deal of time scripting what they wanted to say and refer often to their notes. Others wrote down bullets and tried to incorporate the major points into the conversation. And of course there were always some who hated the whole exercise so much they didn't do anything at all and would just wing it when their turns came.

In the debriefing that followed the activity, it was not uncommon to hear people talk about how they got so wrapped up in trying to remember the techniques, and what they wanted to say, or referring to their notes, that they felt awkward and stiff during the conversations, unable to connect with their partners. Many felt the whole process was unnatural and unrealistic as most conflicts and uncomfortable conversations take people by surprise and often create so much anxiety that even the most well rehearsed monologue simply goes out the window. And monologues rarely achieve the goal of collaborative, open-ended conversation anyway.

What I learned over the years, through my own experiences as well as that of working with others, is that the best way to prepare for such an engagement is to focus on the intention we have for what we hope will happen as a result, and elevate it to the highest good. During times of stress and anxiety, our puppet does whatever it can to ensure that the mission at hand is to protect oneself, be right and win at all costs. But upon further examination, these ends rarely lead us to what we really want and often create more problems for us than they solve.

Norm and Sheila

One of my clients, Norm, was irritated with Sheila because he felt she had been disrespectful to him in front of their mutual client. This wasn't the first time she had behaved that way, he told me. He wanted to confront her to express his indignation and disappointment over the way she had been handling things. When I asked Norm what his goal was for the conversation, he said it was to prevent the situation from happening again. As we discussed how he might go about initiating the conversation, it became clear that Norm wanted Sheila to see that her behavior was inappropriate and unprofessional.

But upon further examination Norm realized that what he really wanted went much deeper than just preventing another outburst from occurring. His true desire was to be able to ultimately partner with Sheila in such a way that demonstrated mutual respect and collaboration. He realized that there were things each one of them was frustrated about, with the other, and he wanted to clear the air and lay the ground for more constructive interactions in the future. In order to achieve this objective, Norm had to move from identifying with being a man trapped in a lousy situation with a woman who would never respect him, to embodying the state of a man who had created a strong working relationship with his colleague and was reliving the moments and experiences that led up to it.

Working from this orientation, Norm saw Sheila in a whole new way — himself as well. He initiated the conversation by acknowledging that he wasn't pleased with the way the two of them had been working together and expressed his desire that they take the time to explore what each could do to more effectively work as a team. With this as their guiding intention, Norm didn't need a script to be able to effectively continue the conversation. Guided by an overarching intention that was mutually desirable and his faith that the two of them could come to a mutual understanding, the words he needed found him. Norm admitted that there were times when he felt compelled to defend himself and even attack Sheila for things she had said or done in the past, but kept returning to the higher ground he really wanted to reach. In this way, his animating genius was able to take the driver's seat and allow Norm to access his inner wisdom and creativity.

> It isn't common ground that bonds people together, it's higher ground.
>
> ~ Tom Brown, American author

Norm drove to work the day of his meeting with Sheila envisioning how he would feel sitting in the same seat, hands on the same steering wheel, driving home after the conversation had taken place. He imagined feeling the relief of having been able to calmly express himself and remain open to whatever might happen next. He remembered the way he felt the last time something he was nervous about turned out better than he could have hoped and allowed himself to replicate that feeling of fulfillment with regard to his conversation with Sheila and their relationship as a whole. He gave thanks for the experience and the positive result it yielded, reliving the way he felt during the conversation and in the moments that followed, as though it were a happy memory. And when Norm actually did drive home that day, he felt the same gratitude for having a successful interaction that he did when he drove into work, only this time after having actually come to a gratifying resolution with Sheila.

Honoring Unforeseen Circumstances

The dynamics of the Fairy's wand are at work during every second of our lives, delivering to us the reflection of what we identify with and take to be real in each moment. This is not to say that if you find yourself in dire circumstances or experiencing an illness or some kind of injury that you are to blame for bringing tragedy upon yourself or your loved ones. As discussed in Chapter 4, over the course of our lives we will undoubtedly face many challenges and obstacles that will test our faith and resolve, and serve to strengthen and prepare us for our unique purposes in the world. Many times the paths we walk will not be those we would have consciously chosen for ourselves, but they are extremely essential nonetheless.

However, we have a role in determining whether the roads we walk upon will be treacherous and exhausting or whether they will awaken the warrior within, allowing us to use our creative powers even during the lowest and darkest moments of our lives to generate brightness and beauty for ourselves and others. And nothing serves to better put us in touch with our innermost self, at its rawest and purest forms, than what seems to cut us to our core. The key test in these moments is to find our faith and summon it up — to remember that even on the verge of death we still have some life left within us, and to identify with that. Even at our poorest we still have the means with which to give bountifully, if only through our love and attention. And even at the times when it seems all has been taken from us, we can still find *something* to be grateful for, and build on that.

The seeming randomness with which things often occur can lead us to doubt that everything is unfolding in a manner that is in our highest interest. Unpleasant and unforeseen circumstances try both our patience and our faith. But it is more important than ever at times like these that we trust in life's beautiful mystery.

Have you ever walked by a building under construction and been curious about what was being built? Perhaps there were people working diligently, all focusing on their own specific task. Maybe there were steel girders, half-constructed walls, and unidentifiable objects at some stage of completion. At first glance, it may appear chaotic and messy. But amidst the sawdust and cement blocks there is something that pulls it all together.

Though we may not know exactly what is being built, over time the construction begins to take shape and we start to recognize a room here, and another there. And then we may begin to surmise the purpose and function of each room. As the walls are plastered and the paint is applied, the appearance becomes neater — something real and useful, perhaps even beautiful. And suddenly, it is completed in all its glory — a stunning compilation of raw materials, sweat, and focused action.

Perhaps we, too, build things in this way. We can envision what we want to create and experience it as though it has already happened, reveling in the fulfillment of having realized the dream. But sometimes the vision we have created is a part of something bigger, the magnitude of which we cannot easily discern. When we aren't sure exactly what that is, things may feel chaotic, disconnected and random. We have some experiences that uplift us, and others that disappoint. We might find ourselves without an explanation of why certain events and experiences are taking place. But underneath it all, there may be a larger plan at work — one that will reveal itself over time. As we undertake each new experience, another wall is constructed and a new room is being built.

A rock pile ceases to be a rock pile the moment a single man contemplates it, bearing within him the image of a cathedral.

~ Antoine de Saint-Exupery, French author and aviator (1900-1944)

What if we were willing to experience our lives with the same wonder and curiosity with which we look upon that building that is under construction? And what if we were able to engender that same enthusiasm and optimism in everyone around us?

Perhaps the whispers of our heart and the calls to greatness that we feel within our souls are essential components of a larger, collective plan that we each play a vital part in.

As we rise up to play these parts fully and wholeheartedly, we can revel in the splendor of its mysterious unfolding. In the process, we will discover ourselves to be greater than we thought we were and use each moment of our lives to create something extraordinary — for ourselves as well as others.

The Law of Attraction and Living the Dream

Whatever you focus on will expand. Like attracts like. It is one of the tenets of physics, often referred to as the law of attraction. Quantum physics tells us that everything consists of information and energy. When taken down to its most basic elements, nothing has any solidity. One of the first lessons taught in science is that every solid object is made up of molecules, and molecules are made up of even smaller units called atoms. Atoms are made up of subatomic particles, which have no solidity at all. They are packets or waves of information and energy that vibrate at different frequencies. At high frequencies are waves, such as thought and radio waves, not visible to the eye. Physical objects vibrate at much lower frequencies.

Nothing happens unless first a dream.

~ Carl Sandburg, American Pulitzer Prize-winning author and editor (1878-1967)

In the 1920s, Albert Einstein was conducting his now famous experiments in photoelectric effect and discovered that light, which had been understood to be a wave, could also show up as a particle (the photon). This was baffling, because in classical terms, waves and particles are mutually exclusive. Particles behave more or less like physical objects while waves are fluid, more of an activity than an object. You could call them possibilities. What Einstein discovered was that whether light showed up as a particle or a wave depended on the *intention* of the experimenter.

Some years later another physicist, Louis de Broglie, expanded Einstein's findings to include all microphysical particles — so it wasn't just light, but every electron and every quantum that had the same twofold nature. It is not unlike the frequencies that are broadcast over the airwaves. Every radio station exists, but we hear the one we tune into — it becomes real to us as we listen to it. This suggests that perhaps we can determine the reality (radio station) we want, and that the simple act of tuning into it collapses the wave of possibility into a particle that matches our frequency, thought or intention.

Look around and recognize that every human creation you see — the cars we drive, the buildings we inhabit, the computers and gadgets we operate, the music we listen to, the books we read, television and movies we watch, the resorts, monuments and theme parks we travel to — each of these things once existed merely as a thought in the mind of a human being. Bridging the gap from thought to reality requires many things, not the least of which is effort, money and other resources. But first, there must be a vision or a dream — something compelling enough to mobilize the minds, hearts and hands of others. And the power of these dreams is amplified when the dreams themselves serve a greater good.

In organizations and communities, we can harness the power of the Fairy's wand to collectively create things that truly benefit humanity. This power proliferates when shared by those

> *When you are inspired by some great purpose, some extraordinary project, all of your thoughts break their bonds; your mind transcends limitations, your consciousness expands in every direction and you find yourself in a new, great, and wonderful world. Dormant forces, faculties and talents become alive and you discover yourself to be a greater person than you ever dreamed yourself to be.*
>
> *~ Patanjali,*
> *Indian philosopher,*
> *compiler of the Yoga Sutra*
> *(circa 150 AD)*

> *"Leadership is the wise use of power. Power is the capacity to translate intention into reality and sustain it.*
>
> *~ Warren Bennis,*
> *American scholar,*
> *organizational consultant*
> *and author*

who hold in their hearts a common vision and dream. It must go beyond clever platitudes or vision and mission statements hanging on walls or printed on laminated cards to truly engage and create meaning in those who will play a part in its realization. Images of shared significance that lead people to identify with a future state as though it is already unfolding will allow individuals to activate the power of the Fairy's wand and harness it with others to realize their collective vision.

It isn't where we came from; it's where we're going that counts.

~ Ella Fitzgerald, American jazz and song vocalist (1917-1996)

Over the history of time, there have been among us people who dared to dream big and ended up creating something magnificent as a result. What they had in common was not their station in life, their family inheritance or even necessarily a solid education. Many rose up despite odds that would suggest their lives would be quite ordinary, or insignificant, perhaps growing up amidst gangs and violence and poverty to become leaders whose life stories would inspire millions of others from all backgrounds and circumstances.

People who do amazing things in the world have in common glorious dreams that they lovingly nurture and protect. From somewhere in the depths of their being, they know they are capable of greatness — not because they were born into it or are particularly more gifted than everyone else, but simply because it is their birthright — as it is for all of us. Each one of us has the ability to create something extraordinary. We all have different talents and strengths, diverse styles and passions — along with a unique combination of experiences (for better or worse) that allows us to discover and apply our gifts to create something bigger than ourselves. We may not know exactly what form it will take, but if we pay attention to the whispers and yearnings of our hearts, we begin to make out the shape of something that beckons to us.

As children, most of us receive mixed messages. We are often encouraged to follow our hearts and give life to our dreams, in addition to being conditioned to be practical, hedge our bets and take the safest route. Over time, many of us have allowed the roar of public opinion — that often tells us our dreams are frivolous, selfish and unlikely to come to fruition — to silence that small still voice within. But those among us who have risen against their odds have learned to reverse that process and believe in themselves and their dreams despite the overwhelming evidence around them that would suggest that success is improbable.

Every new day brings with it the question of what we will focus our time, energy and resources into accomplishing. It is essential that we reacquaint ourselves with our dreams and visions, our purpose and values, and the question of how we can become living examples of what we most admire.

You may be quite sure of what it is you would like to create, do, have or become. Or perhaps you have only small pieces of a bigger puzzle that have not yet come together. The power of your dream will be bolstered by the degree to which your vision expands beyond your own interests to those of others around you. Spend some time contemplating where you feel most drawn — and why. When you land on something that will allow your gifts to align with those of others to accomplish complementary goals, you will join forces with something much greater than yourself. It will lift you up when your energy is low and sustain you through moments of doubt and fear.

For many, dreaming is the easy part. Finding a way to bring those dreams to life can be challenging and somewhat daunting. For years, I was convinced that having a vision and goals meant perceiving a clear and specific picture of what was to come and creating a plan that would ensure that certain milestones were met at designated intervals. I was taught that goals had to be specific, measurable,

Establishing goals is all right, as long as you don't let them deprive you of interesting detours.

~ Doug Larson,
American author

and time bound (and spent a good part of my career teaching others the same). I would spend a significant amount of time "wordsmithing" these goals and creating something similar to a detailed project plan as though I could bend reality to my will.

Then life would happen and I'd get exceedingly frustrated when things didn't happen the way I had planned.

Our Inner Leader

The puppet wants to identify a course of action that mitigates risk and controls all the variables. It is akin to a manager, whose responsibility is to plan, organize, control and measure. The challenge is that preconceived ideas of what must be and all that has to happen to bring it to fruition can never take into account all the unexpected twists and turns that each day throws at us. So the manager in each of us needs to take its orders from a higher authority.

This higher authority, our animating genius and inner leader:

- Lives in the present, takes its cues from its inner and outer environment, and speaks to the hearts as well as the heads of its people;

- Is often that part of us that rises up and recognizes that we must make a change in course in order to realize our greater visions; and

- Blends concrete data with intuitive hunches and moves much more fluidly.

Live out of your imagination, not your history.

~ Stephen Covey,
American author, speaker,
professor, consultant and
management expert

The puppet/manager in each of us often wants to fix things and tends to place more attention on what is wrong than on what is right. It is so concerned with problems that it has a way of identifying with them and unwittingly propagating them. The puppet would have us set goals about the behaviors we want to stop, and the things about ourselves that aren't good enough. These goals almost always fail because they lead us to identify with the very state we wish to rise above. We enter into them from a state of lack, and though our behaviors may temporarily change in accordance with detailed plans we have outlined for ourselves, our thoughts about who we are and what's wrong keep us tethered and ultimately lead us to act in ways that reinforce old habits and patterns.

The animating genius/leader focuses on possibilities and speaks to that part of us that has the capability and potential to achieve it. It sees through the eyes of someone who has already realized his or her goals and visions rather than identifying with the experience of not having been able to do something in the past. The leader in each of us knows that action follows thought and invests time in identifying limiting beliefs and trading them for something more empowering.

Rather than moving away from an undesirable place, the leader in us focuses on moving toward what it desires to create.

With animating genius in charge, the puppet's willfulness is balanced with willingness — willingness to change and adapt even the best-laid plans, to reach higher, and to trust in what is not easily explained or understood. It allows us to move from the rational mind to the collective mind — a higher intelligence that operates at such a high frequency that the human mind cannot understand and process it without significantly slowing it down. Rather than getting hung up on trying to figure everything out, animating genius simply trusts and allows this higher intelligence to inform and guide the way.

When it comes right down to it, those who achieve and sustain the greatest success in life — whether in a corporation, school, team, community, or family — get through their most challenging times with faith and trust. This faith might be in those around them who share their dreams and visions as well as the belief that they will come to fruition. It might be faith of a spiritual nature. And it could also be faith in life itself.

As we look back over the course of our lives, no doubt there will be both positive as well as less than pleasurable events that we will recall.

**When things take a turn that we didn't anticipate,
in retrospect we can often appreciate the ways
these little deviations strengthened us,
helped us get where we needed to ultimately go,
or in some way prepared us for what was yet to come.**

Navigating the Course

As we entertain dreams, visions and goals that seem so large that they become daunting, we must not be intimidated by the seeming length or difficulty of the journey ahead of us.

Faith is taking the first step even when you don't see the whole staircase.

~ Martin Luther King, Jr., American Nobel Prize-winning clergyman, activist, and civil rights leader

When we feel dismayed at not having everything figured out right off the bat, we can ask ourselves what we can do right now that will move us closer to our goals and trust that we will be given exactly what we need to continue our journey right when we need it. The very process of asking a question invokes the power of the Fairy's wand.

**It has been said that you cannot ask a question
without having access to the answer.**

It's as though the action of asking directs your focus and identification to what you are inquiring about and attracts the answer to you in ways that you can intuit using many of the navigational tools discussed in Chapter 5. In his intriguing book *Power vs. Force,*[1] Dr. David Hawkins writes:

"The process of animating genius most

[1]Dr. David Hawkins, *Power vs. Force: The Hidden Determinants of Human Behavior* (Carlsbad, CA, Hay House, Inc., 1995).

commonly involves first formulating a question, then waiting an indefinite interval for consciousness to work with the problem — until suddenly, the answer appears in a flash, in a form that's c h a r a c t e r i s t i c a l l y nonverbal. For example, great musicians throughout history have stated that they didn't plan their music, but simply wrote down what they heard within their own minds. The father of organic chemistry, F.A. Kekule, saw the molecular structure that he based the ring theory on in a dream. And in an illuminated moment, Albert Einstein had the revolutionary insight that then took him years to translate into provable mathematics."

> *If I had an hour to solve a problem and my life depended on the solution, I would spend the first fifty-five minutes determining the proper question to ask, for once I know the proper question, I could solve the problem in less than five minutes.*
>
> ~ *Albert Einstein, German-Swiss Nobel Prize-winning physicist, philosopher and author (1879-1955)*

We need to remember to phrase our questions in such a way that the answers will bring us up rather than down. Asking "Why does this always happen to me?" "What is wrong with me?" or "Why can't I ever get what I want?" may reveal answers, but most likely they will not be of the nature that will inspire and empower. Instead, we can ask:

- "What is the purpose behind this and what can I learn?"

- "What can I do to make the most of this situation?"

- "How can I reframe what I am seeing so that I can get the bigger picture?"

When we ponder questions such as these, our subconscious minds occupy themselves with finding solutions for us, and the answers we seek can show up in surprising ways — often when we least expect them. It is not uncommon for these answers to reveal themselves when we relax our minds and let go of our attachment or need to find the answers. Perhaps an enticing idea will occur to you when you are in the shower, driving home from work, or tossing a ball around with your kids. You may have dreams that suggest interesting possibilities, or you could find yourself doodling pictures that spark something inside you. Certain pictures, images and even words may take on increased significance. As discussed in Chapter 5, these are all ways that our animating genius communicates to us via our intuition to deliver to us the answers we seek.

We shall not cease from exploration, and the end of all our exploring will be to arrive where we started and know the place for the first time.

~ T.S. Eliot, American-British Nobel Prize-winning poet, playwright and literary critic (1888-1965)

Pinocchio's Dream Come True

Though Pinocchio's journey initially took him away from himself, in the end his dream of becoming real prevailed. It allowed him to exercise the courage to face his fear and identify with something within him that was far truer than the illusion of limiting beliefs created by his puppet, and ultimately become of service to another human being. Having faced his fear in the belly of the whale and victoriously emerged, he satisfied the Fairy's three requirements for realizing his dream: to be truthful, brave and unselfish.

Pinocchio became real not as a result of what he did to prove himself brave, truthful and unselfish, but when he learned to identify with that part of himself that already embodied those qualities. I believe the same is true for each of us. In his beautiful book *As a Man Thinketh*,[2] first published in 1901, James Allen writes: "Dream lofty dreams, and as you dream, so shall you become. Your vision is the promise of what you shall one day be; your ideal is the prophecy of what you shall at last unveil."

Henry David Thoreau[3] writes: "If one advances confidently in the direction of his dreams, and endeavors to live the life which he has imagined, he will meet with success unexpected in common hours." And Napoleon Hill affirms, "What the mind of man can conceive and believe, it can achieve."[4]

When we give merit to our greatest dreams and visions, we begin the process of breathing life into them. Our desire and enthusiasm for what is possible allow us to enter a realm of possibilities where anything can happen. The ironic thing about possibilities is that though we may like to believe they live in the future, they actually exist in the now — they are unmanifested reality that exists just as the baby who has not yet been born is alive and kicking.

> *It's time to start living the life you've imagined.*
>
> *~ Henry James,*
> *American-English*
> *author (1843-1916)*

We must embrace our precious dreams and visions,
nurture them and allow them to grow and prosper,
and inspire others to do the same,
for they are divine whispers of a unifying Spirit
that longs to create through each of us.

Do you have some secret dream of becoming more than you currently are? Of tapping into the vast field of potential that lies waiting for you to discover it? See if you can envision what it would be like to have already achieved that dream. What would

---

[2]James Allen, *As A Man Thinketh* (Ilfracome, England, 1901).

[3]Henry David Thoreau, *Walden* (conclusion chapter, 1854).

[4]Napoleon Hill, *Think and Grow Rich* (1937).

your life be like through the eyes of someone who has already arrived? Get into it. Play with it. Become it – if only in your mind.

Now, with that state of mind:

- What would you do differently in the face of all the challenges you have today?

- Would you find ways to minimize the time you spend on trivial things so that you could pour more of yourself into what really matters?

- Would you show up differently in those meetings, projects and tasks?

- Would you get started on that project/venture/creation that has been quietly and persistently beckoning to you?

- Would you bring more of yourself to what you are doing?

- Connect more deeply with others?

- Be more present?

- Could you find a way to transform your conflicts into opportunities for collaboration?

Sometimes the roar of activity and busyness that occupy so much of our lives obscure our greatest dreams and visions. It is easy to become so absorbed in playing the game that we lose sight of the larger goal and even the fun of playing it. At times like these, it is important to refresh and revitalize ourselves, take the time to reconnect to our animating genius and come home. This is the subject of the next as well as the final chapter.

As for the future, your task is not to foresee, but to enable it.

~ Antoine Saint Exupery, French author and aviator (1900-1944)

Chapter 11

Finding Geppetto

After escaping from Pleasure Island, Pinocchio returns home to discover that Geppetto has gone searching for Pinocchio. When he learns that Geppetto was swallowed by a whale, Pinocchio immediately sets off to find him, regardless of the impending peril.

Pinocchio's unwavering determination to reunite with Geppetto is analogous to our desire to return to our roots, to remember why we are here, and to experience the unity of unconditional love. Geppetto's search for Pinocchio and his role in bringing Pinocchio to the belly of the whale is also significant. In addition to providing Pinocchio the opportunity to face his fears and emerge victorious, the experience allows him to insulate himself from the distractions that keep him focused on his dream and reconnect with his true purpose.

Like Pinocchio we, too, may wander far and fill our lives with a great deal of commotion before we finally allow ourselves to return to our inner sanctuaries — which are always calling softly to us. One of the major reasons we continue to wander off into the world of chaos is that we tend to think the commotion serves us. Most of us have been brought up to believe that the harder we work, the more we will accomplish and that the busier we are, the more important we must be. We are conditioned to see inactivity as laziness and the need for rest and relaxation as a sign of weakness. And our puppets perpetuate these beliefs.

You have to put in the clutch to shift gears. You have to let go to re-engage at another, more high-leveraged ratio. And when you least feel like slowing down may be the most critical time to do it.

~ David Allen, American productivity author and speaker

Additionally, the daily grind has a way of keeping us tethered, feeling as though our best is just around the corner, if only we can get through what's in front of us, which is often an accumulation of projects, events and other commitments that ends up growing far faster than it shrinks. Every once in a while, it becomes apparent that something's got to give.

Making Time for What's Important

But who has time to slow down when there is so much more to get done? The fantasy many of us have bought into is that if we just work longer and harder, we will get there. And despite our longing to find balance and the sweet spot that will

When you find yourself in a hole, stop digging.

~ Will Rogers, American humorist, social commentator, actor and vaudeville entertainer (1879-1935)

finally allow us to relax and be more effective, we often act in ways that bring greater levels of anxiety and toil. As leaders, we also unwittingly influence those around us — in our communities, organizations and even our families — to emulate our frenetic behavior in the name of getting ahead.

**The hamster in the wheel doesn't realize
he isn't getting anywhere.
And before he can, he must realize that
he is, in fact, in a wheel.**

Our wheels are much more sophisticated and deceiving than those of the hamster. Initially, our wheels do get us somewhere. It's just that over time, they lose traction and become stuck in comfortable ruts. And we don't realize when we're stuck, because it doesn't seem possible to be standing still when you are running as fast as you can.

Clay's Conundrum

Clay was a director with about forty-five people reporting to him. He left the office each night at about seven o'clock loaded down with an overstuffed briefcase and a satchel of documents that he would go home to review after (and often during) a quick supper. Before going to bed, Clay would spend at least an hour checking and responding to email.

The next morning he was back in the office by six and on his fourth cup of coffee, which he proceeded to refill throughout the day. Though he was in a position to oversee creative endeavors within his division of the company, it was all Clay could do to put fires out and respond to an overwhelming number of requests throughout each day. There was no sparkle in his eyes, no lightness in his step. His posture looked like that of someone carrying a couple hundred-pound weights on his shoulders. Life had become, in Clay's words, "one damn thing after another."

Clay decided to work with a coach because he wanted to improve the quality of his life and his leadership. He felt he was working like mad, but not getting much done. He longed to inspire the people in his organization to create something they could be proud of, but could never seem to find the time or the energy to figure out how to do it.

My first assignment for Clay led him to question whether I was the right coach for him. The challenge was simple — leave work empty-handed for one night. Go home and enjoy your evening with your family and see what happens. Because he was committed to his goal and felt that anything was worth trying once, he did as I asked.

To Clay's surprise, the experience was quite satisfying — so much so that he incorporated it as an ongoing challenge for himself, and started keeping a log to see how often he was able to repeat it. To keep himself from feeling the burden of work that would be waiting for him when he returned, he began to exercise greater scrutiny around what absolutely had to get done, what could wait, and what he could delegate to others.

Upon reflection, Clay realized that the source of energy he needed to achieve his goals was in low reserve because he had not been making adequate time for himself. He began keeping a journal to capture additional insights he would receive throughout the course of each day. A writer, musician and poet at heart, he also designated time during his week and weekends to pull out and play the guitar that had sat in its dusty case at the back of his closet for many years. Beginning a regular exercise routine allowed Clay to increase his energy levels and clear his mind. As a result, he was able to make better decisions more quickly and think better on his feet.

Clay found that some of his greatest inspirations and ideas for taking the people in his division to a new level of excellence came when he was immersed in creative endeavors and not forcing his mind to generate solutions.

People in Clay's organization began to notice changes that were taking place in him, commenting that he looked a lot healthier and was far more fun to be around. As Clay learned to better prioritize and focus on what was most important to the organization's success, he spent more time developing and supporting the leaders who reported to him and challenged them to do the same for their teams. He injected enjoyable activities into the workplace that helped unlock the creativity of his people and give them opportunities to collectively dialogue about upcoming challenges and opportunities.

Within the course of the year, senior management recognized Clay's division for excellent service to the organization, and Clay received an increase in pay.

Leadership and life itself require energy, enthusiasm, creativity, insight and wisdom. These things need to be replenished from time to time. And the way to replenish them is to engage in

> *Dig the well before you are thirsty.*
>
> *~ Chinese proverb*

activity that feeds the soul. When we do not create time in our lives for this to happen, we may find that our bodies (or our souls) create them for us through illness or some other experience that requires that we slow down for a while.

Pay attention to the signals you get that tell you your energy is running low. When your focus is scattered and you start to feel like you are on a treadmill, you need to plan activities in your days that will nourish you back to life. Until you do, you will not have the ability to impact, influence and inspire others in quite the same way.

> *For fast-acting relief, try slowing down.*
>
> *~ Lily Tomlin, American actress, comedienne, author and producer*

Additionally, running from one thing to another without stopping to reflect and check in with ourselves keeps us disconnected from our intuition and animating genius. As a result, we can travel long distances upon roads that actually lead us further from ourselves. Have you ever set a goal that left you feeling less than fulfilled when you actually achieved it? Maybe it was a target you wanted to meet, a possession you longed to acquire, or a promotion you were hoping to receive. You kept your eye on the ball and hunkered down to do whatever it took to get there. When obstacles presented themselves, you busted through them and may have felt as though you were repeatedly banging your head against a wall. "The reward for your exhaustion would be the sweet taste of victory in the end," you may have told yourself.

I did. And when I got to the top of the hill I was climbing I realized the mountain I was scaling was not mine, but someone else's.

A Meandering Path

The irony of my divergence is that initially I was looking to find better balance and create more time for my family and personal life. Like many entrepreneurs, I had envisioned that owning my own business would allow me far more flexibility and downtime than being someone's employee. While that would ultimately prove to be true, initially I was overwhelmed with the many administrative and marketing tasks that were required to incorporate and launch my business. I felt like I had jumped into a deep pool, and remained submerged for a couple of years before I finally learned to get my head above water and breathe.

Looking for a way to gain leverage, I began to attend seminars and conferences to learn to market myself and do business over the Internet. I became excited about the possibility that I could create something that would allow me to reach larger audiences without significantly increasing my workload. The idea that I might ultimately be able to automate my work in some way was also enticing. I dreamed and schemed of potential programs and offerings that I could create and sell, and then went to work on a design.

The web-based leadership development program I ended up creating combined elements of coaching and lecturing along with monthly interviews of exemplary leaders and feature articles on various leadership challenges. I contracted with some colleagues to serve as coaches who would be available to complement each participant's web-based experience with one-on-one coaching. For months, I consumed myself with writing lesson plans, articles, case studies, and creating PowerPoint presentations and participant materials to accompany them. All of this was in addition to continuing my work with seventeen regular coaching clients and trying desperately not to neglect the needs of my husband and three young children.

I was fortunate to have a major client company enroll forty-five of their leaders in my new program not long after I pitched it to them. But the next few months completely exhausted me. My husband was understandably perplexed by my actions. What began as an effort to simplify and streamline my work to allow for more balance and attention to the family ended up tripling it and kept me so preoccupied that even when I was with my husband and children, I wasn't really present.

Intoxicated by the success the program was having and the possibilities for expanding it, I began to envision what another phase would look like, opened up for public enrollment. Unlike what I had already created, this would require a significant amount of marketing — something that was not one of my strong areas. I hired a number of coaches and consultants to help me create a strategy that would allow me to reach beyond my current networks. I wrote copy, redesigned my website, created fancy flyers and direct marketing materials and hosted free preview webinars. At the recommendation of my various advisors, I sent and resent email after email to people who likely got tired of hearing from me (as I do when barraged by emails and special offers). When people I respected expressed concern over the methods I was using or asked to be removed from my mailing list, some of the experts I was working with told me that comments like those were part of the process and that I needed to get used to them. With every new email blast and promo webinar I did, I felt a growing sense of incongruence that I just couldn't shake.

It wasn't that the methods I was being taught were wrong or suspect in any way. They just weren't aligned with who I am and didn't feel authentic to me. At the end of a promotional webinar, where I had almost lost my voice, I recall my assistant remarking that it seemed I had been sick a lot lately and encouraging me to get some rest. My exhaustion and desire to keep forging ahead led me to disregard the signs that told me I was headed in a direction that wasn't serving me. In addition to promoting the second phase of the program, I decided to offer the first phase again in tandem with it.

About two weeks before the new programs were due to launch, the fact that my enrollment was drastically lower than I had hoped finally hit me. To add to the frustration, those who did register were people I already knew, some of whom confided that they did so *despite* the marketing strategies I had used. Coming to grips with the reality that things were not happening the way I envisioned required me to acknowledge both my disappointment and exhaustion.

One day when I was out running, I decided to sit awhile under the willowy umbrella of an old eucalyptus tree. I recall folding myself into a ball, resting my chin on my knees, and finally allowing all the emotions that I had held at bay enter in. As tears streamed down my face, I realized that I had completely lost touch with myself.

The disappointment of not having filled the programs eventually gave way to relief as I realized that keeping up the pace I was already struggling to maintain would likely have completely broken me. I felt I had let my whole family down and all but forgotten my initial intention of creating a work/life balance that would allow me to enjoy the best of both worlds in such a way that one would breathe life into the other. In contrast, what I had created drove a division between the two and pit them against each other. I finally realized how miserable things had become and committed to making it all right.

The key thing to remember is not that we need to be fast but that we are running a race that has no finish line. So the fuel that drives us needs to be made of something substantial — something for the heart that the head can also follow.

~ Vincent Kralyevich, American film producer, director, author, art director and composer

Doing so would require that I make some tough decisions and even tougher phone calls. I scaled down phase one of the program and completely pulled the plug on phase two, which would have necessitated that I continue to create original content — requiring creative juices that had temporarily run dry. I heard the voice of my puppet loud and clear, contending that I had failed miserably and let everyone down as a result. It alleged that I had gone too far, flown too close to the sun and would surely pay for my recklessness. But the wiser part of me knew that my misstep was not in dreaming too big, but rather in neglecting to ensure that the well I would be drinking from was full enough to replenish and sustain me along the way.

When I take on new clients, they are often in a state similar to the one I found myself in. They have worked hard to get somewhere, but they know in their hearts there is something greater available to them. Perhaps they haven't been getting the results they wanted, have been experiencing a great deal of stress or even burnout, or are just ready for a change. During times like

these often the best thing is to not speed up, but slow down —
way down.

**If the path you're running on isn't getting you where you want
to go, moving faster won't do you any favors.**

Marking Passages to New Doors

Life can come at us so fast that if we don't take the time
to stop and reflect, we do not fully receive and integrate its many
gifts. As a result, our experiences can seem disjointed, frustrating,
and somewhat overwhelming. But upon further examination,
there may be a perfect order beneath what seems like random
chaos. And the moments that may feel the most uncomfortable or
unpleasant are often quite pivotal in our lives, despite what we may
believe at the time they are happening. Often we underestimate
the amount of growth we have achieved until we take some time
to reflect on the unique combination of experiences we have had
that led to both successes and disappointments and what we have
learned from them.

In workshops, I often ask participants to write about their
defining moments. We all have them. Sometimes while they are
occurring, we feel as though everything is coming apart. They
can be painful experiences that we end up gaining a lot from
but would rather never repeat. Pleasant or unpleasant, they are
critical to our growth as they mark the passages that lead us to
close one door and open another. They may be dramatic changes
that end up altering our jobs, environments or careers or they
could simply be significant shifts in the way we view ourselves,
and the world around us. As we look back upon the various
defining moments of our lives, we can begin to appreciate the gifts
they have brought us and better leverage those gifts in whatever
situation we currently find ourselves.

**There is a sense of peace that comes with the realization
that nothing we experience is ever without
meaning and significance.**

One Door Closes, Another Opens

One of my defining moments came after working for about a year at an advertising agency right after college. Having yet to arrive at the realization of what I wanted to do with my life, I took the job because it had elements of what I studied in college: English, business and communication — and because it sounded enjoyable and interesting. I started as an administrative assistant with the promise that it wouldn't be long before I would be promoted into something a bit more substantive.

Turns out that advertising just wasn't my thing. The work itself didn't pique much interest in me, but I was intrigued with the organization and the people in it. Turnover was high, morale was low, and the customer was an afterthought. I knew that all that could be changed — that something could be done to allow people to feel more alive in their jobs, to ensure that the customer was happy, that the company was growing and profitable. So I got to work talking with people.

I interviewed smart, ambitious entry-level personnel, who felt discouraged and overlooked when the jobs they had been working toward were filled by people from outside the company. I talked to new creative staff and account executives who came in and hit the ground running, knowing little about the agency or its customer. I spoke with seasoned executives who lamented that no one seemed to care about what was most important anymore. I integrated all their insights, ideas and suggestions with my own observations and created a proposal to implement a program that would allow seasoned people to train and mentor newer folks, better integrate with the customer, and grow the business from within.

Knowing little about corporate politics, I went straight to the VP of Operations with my proposal to create the program and allow me to run it. He listened intently, asked several questions, and arranged subsequent meetings with others in the company. It wasn't long before a position was created. My boss at the time — who wasn't impressed with my lack of passion for being an administrative assistant or the fact that I went over her head with my proposal (which I never even told her I was working on) — was outraged. She called upon her networks to put a stop to things. A few days later I was told that while the company was going to create the position and launch the program I proposed, because of all the controversy, they could not allow me to head it up.

I was crushed. I remember walking across the agency's glossy floors and out the tall glass double doors of the building to sit on a park bench. I was burning with animosity, rage, and frustration at the seeming injustice of it all. Sitting on that bench writing my letter of resignation with a shaky hand, the wave of anxiety eventually released me from its grip and I was overcome with a sense of calm clarity. I was onto something here. Maybe there was a way that I could work with corporations, organizations and people themselves to bring out their latent talent and harness it in a way that could contribute to a common goal.

That defining moment led me on a search that would allow me to find ways to do more of the work that beckoned to me. It launched a chain of events that has led me to learn more about myself and make the most of experiences that would further prepare me for the work that I do now. And I am grateful — so completely and utterly grateful — that it happened, though at the time I thought it was the worst possible thing.

See if you can identify some of your defining moments. What have they prepared you for? As you look back, what have they taught you about yourself? Perhaps you are experiencing a defining moment right now. If as you read these words you are feeling disoriented, fearful, or even plain confused about a course of events that doesn't seem to have any purpose other than to make life miserable, chances are you may be in the midst of one. If you have not yet found the gift in the experience, rest assured that you soon will — if that is what you desire. Chances are it will lead you to new frontiers that will allow you to breathe more life and love into everything you do.

Many people have a ritual that allows them to check in with themselves as each year comes to a close and a new one begins. Being at the threshold of a new year is like climbing to the top of a long staircase to find yourself on a landing, standing before a large glimmering door just waiting to be opened. As you look down, you realize how far you have climbed to get there. Yet you cannot help but wonder what lies behind the door.

I often work with people who feel they are ready for a change, but aren't sure what that change should be. They aren't necessarily miserable in their jobs or other areas of their lives — they just long for something that will fill them up in ways they haven't been fulfilled in the past. When I coach people who feel this way, they sometimes want me to tell them what the next best step is — give them the answer, or perhaps a step-by-step process that will lead them to find what they seek. Of course, no person has these answers for another. Our greatest challenge and opportunity is to find them for ourselves.

Each of our lives has a story with perfect order and meaning. As within a novel or a screenplay, each character has a specific relationship to the main character and every scene has some relevance to his growth and evolution. There will be victories and disappointments, as well as twists and turns that transition us from one to another and back again. We will have occasion to laugh, cry and experience a myriad of other emotions that are somewhere in between. And as a result of this perfect combination of events and mini-plots, we discover ourselves to be better people.

When we are reading a book or watching a movie, the perfect order is often easier for us to see than it is for the characters enmeshed in the stories we are watching. Yet the mystery and intrigue, the humor over each misstep and the courage we see the characters exude to find their way give substance to the story and allow us to leave the book or the theatre feeling moved or inspired in some way.

As you reflect upon your life, see if you can identify the most pivotal turns your story has taken:

- What did you learn from them?

- Think about your character sketch. What are the endearing qualities you have that make you unique and special?

- How can you leverage them to build on the previous events to create a story worth telling?

- Think also about the people that surround you. In what ways are they helping you grow?

- What are they teaching you about yourself — whether in joyful or painful ways?

- And what qualities do they possess that are similar to and different from yours?

- How do you complement each other, and what might it be that you can create together?

As you sit at the threshold of another chapter in your story, contemplate what you have already experienced and ask yourself how you might build upon it to create a bit of intrigue and adventure. Identify the ways that you could add a little lightness and humor. Think about the interplay between the characters and how you could spice things up a little. We have each been given the makings of a beautiful tale. Open your eyes and survey them the way you would the perfectly planned detail of your favorite movie or novel.

**Give yourself completely to the adventure,
the possibilities, and the humor in your life.
Then find a way to revel in the joy of living it.**

Silencing the Roar of Activity

Leadership is about taking ourselves — and others — to a higher place. But before we can go there, we must envision it and create it. We must pay attention to the ideas, thoughts and inspirations that land gently on us and beckon to be given a vehicle to enter the world. In order to do that, we need to take steps in our own lives to nurture them. Creativity and innovation bubble up in a mind that is unencumbered with frenetic activity.

**When we are relaxed, thoughtful, and open,
our greatest ideas land softly upon our shoulders.
They often start as small whispers that compete for our attention
among all the other things we think we need to be doing.**

Intuiting and discerning these insights requires that we quiet and center ourselves. And we cannot do this if we are running from one thing to another without some time to reflect. Though our frenzied pace may generate activity, if we don't pause from time to time to evaluate where we are going and where we have been, we may forget what all the activity is for. Philosopher and poet George Santayana said, "Fanaticism consists of redoubling your efforts when you have forgotten your aim." He also said, "Those who cannot learn from history are doomed to repeat it."

When we pause and silence the roar of activity that occupies our bodies and our minds, we are able not only to reflect upon our lives, but also to integrate our experiences in such a way that they become meaningful and holistic. These quiet moments are akin to the last five minutes of any yoga practice, called Shivasana. Yoga instructors often reiterate that these final moments of the class are the most important. During this time, the fifty to seventy minutes of engaging and stretching muscles give way to a period of lying flat on your back, letting go of everything and allowing your body to melt into the floor. It is during this time that all the benefits of the previous activity take root.

Just as many people have more trouble listening than they do talking, we also seem to be more challenged with receiving inspiration than acting on it.

And just as listening requires us to stop talking, becoming inspired requires us to stop doing – if only for a few moments.

In these moments, whether you are sitting at your desk, taking a stroll, enjoying lunch with a friend, listening to music or engaging in whatever allows you to relax and reflect, you have the opportunity to be truly strategic — to contemplate answers to the bigger questions of how, through your leadership, you can accomplish something truly remarkable, meaningful and satisfying for you, your family, and the organizations and communities you are a part of.

Men of lofty genius when they are doing the least work are the most active.

~ Leonardo da Vinci, Italian polymath, artist, architect, inventor and author (1452-1519)

We must create the time in our daily lives to process and learn from our experiences, honor and develop our dreams, and take care of ourselves in such a way that those dreams continue to come to us. It is important that we pay at least as much attention to the possibilities for change and improvement that exist all around us as we do trying to keep things running the way we think they should.

Becoming More Focused, Effective and Strategic

Though many agree that taking time to reflect and regenerate is important, few find it easy. "How can I take the time to sit and think if I can't even get through my 'to do' list?" I often hear people ask. I have felt this way myself. Over the years most of us have seen time management systems or productivity principles that promise to help us get the clutter out of our heads and organize our thoughts, goals and actions to accomplish more with each day. Creating a "to do" list capturing all the tasks and projects that might need attention doesn't necessitate that you actually have to *do* everything on the list. In fact, we will not break free of the delirium that keeps us from truly being effective and strategically focused until we realize that we will *never* finish all those things on our lists.

Think about your own "to do" list right now. Chances are that half of what's listed there are things that were taking up brain space, which you felt you needed to write down somewhere so that you wouldn't lose them. (This is a very good practice, by the way, because it allows you to let go of things that are distracting you and really focus on what you need to do.) My guess is that once you wrote those nagging tasks down, you could relax a little (until you happened to go back to that multi-page "to do" list and experienced a sinking feeling.) That sinking feeling is connected to a belief that you need to get it *all* done.

> *What lies in our power to do, lies in our power not to do.*
>
> ~ Aristotle,
> Greek philosopher and
> author (384 BC–322 BC)

What if you were free of that? I challenge you to look at your "to do" list with new eyes, and think of it as more of a "not to do" list, or perhaps a "maybe I'll do" list. Ask yourself, what on this list is truly aligned with what is most important right now? You will need to weigh these things against your own personal vision and values as well as the strategic direction of any larger context you are a part of. Then select the areas that will have the greatest impact.

> *The main thing is to keep the main thing the main thing.*
>
> ~ Stephen Covey,
> American author and
> management consultant

Business coach Melanie Strick[1] gave me the following advice early on in our work together: Identify three high payoff activities each day that must be done by the day's end. Then, filter

---

[1] Melanie Strick is President and Founder of Success Connections, Inc. For more information, visit: www. SuccessConnections.com

the remainder of your list by using these three classic questions:

1. What can I delegate?

2. What can I defer?

3. What can I dump?

Schedule blocks of time to do important things that require multiple steps. Another terrific resource for helping people focus their time and energy on what is most essential and break free from anything that gets in the way is David Allen's book *Getting Things Done*.[2] I highly recommend it.

> *It is always amazing how many of the things we do will never be missed. And nothing is less productive than to make more efficient what should not be done at all.*
>
> *~ Peter F. Drucker, American author, management consultant and social ecologist (1909-2005)*

One of the major obstacles that keeps us from doing what is most important is conditioning that compels us to immediately respond to emerging challenges without taking the time to think much about them. So often we engage in the grownup equivalent of "whack-a-mole." Remember that arcade game where you have 120 seconds to bop small rodents with a large hammer as they emerge from their holes? You can see this dynamic in play for yourself the next time you are near your computer and hear that little melodic alert that tells you you've got email. It has a way of perking up many people's ears the way Pavlov's bell got dogs to salivate and can completely divert them from whatever they were doing before. And it doesn't stop just at email.

We succumb to this enticement every time the phone rings. Did you ever stop to ask yourself the question of whether you actually have to answer it? At times you may not have a

---

[2]David Allen, *Getting Things Done: The Art of Stress-Free Productivity* (New York, NY, Penguin Group, 2001).

choice. But often we pick up the phone, without thinking, half-distracted and potentially annoyed at an interruption that took us from something we were really making headway on. As a result, we risk missing out on the opportunity to truly engage with the person calling, and also lose ground on something that truly merited our attention and focus in that particular moment.

The danger of this conditioned response is that it compels us to engage our time ineffectively. Rather than stopping to identify the level of urgency and importance each task or request has, we unthinkingly whip into action. We may get a lot done, and pat ourselves on the back for being able to handle so many tasks with agility, but it is often at the cost of things that merit our time far more than what we ended up filling it with. As a result, we end up feeling as though we are at the mercy of a frenetic pace that never seems to let up and we don't seem to be able to accomplish anything of any real importance.

Things which matter most should never be at the mercy of things which matter least.

~ Johann Wolfgang von Goethe, German author and polymath (1749-1832)

You will never be free of this until you realize what you are personally doing to contribute to this state and take action to deliberately and mindfully turn it around. You can start by paying attention to the way you handle emerging issues and challenges and ask yourself what you could do to be more focused, effective and strategic. Then, shift your patterns by acting on your insights and continuing to observe and make adjustments accordingly.

As an example, try setting a certain time (or times) of the day for looking at your email or returning phone calls and see if that boosts your productivity and effectiveness.

Time is a created thing. To say 'I don't have time,' is like saying, "I don't want to.'

~ Lao Tzu, ancient Chinese philosopher (6th Century BC)

Learning to Let Go

Using discernment to determine what truly merits our precious time, energy and talent is a critical leadership skill. There is comfort in engaging in tasks we are already good at which require little or no brain power. They give us the satisfaction of getting things done and doing them well. But they keep us engaged in tactical rather than strategic endeavors. And when leaders hang on to things that are better delegated to others, everyone is deprived of critical growth opportunities.

Leaders succeed by bringing out the best in others to accomplish something for a greater good, and they must start with themselves.

**We will not succeed in bringing out the best in others
if we insist on doing everything ourselves.
And we will not bring out the best in ourselves
if we continue to insist on doing things we are already good at.**

We must move out of our comfort zones and be willing to experience the exhilaration and anxiety of not knowing, once again. Many tasks leaders are really good at are things they did very well before they became leaders, which they should really be delegating to others. And I'm convinced that the primary reason people don't delegate is not that they don't know how, but rather that they are not willing to — because of this very dynamic. When you start to let go of having to do everything that you are good at, you will begin to build the capacity of others who will be instrumental in taking you and your creations, communities, and organizations to the next level.

And you will not be in a space to conceive of that next level until you free up the time to connect the dots between where you are and where you want to go, where what you are leading is, and where it needs to go, and what you can set into motion to bridge those gaps.

Though it is tempting to occupy ourselves with thoughts of what we need to do more of, perhaps what we really need to start with is what we need to do less of — what we need to let go of in order to create the space for something new to come in. We are constantly evolving as human beings — and as communities of human beings. It is so easy to look to the past to define who we are through the things we've already done — goals we've achieved, titles we've acquired, or creations we have built. Our previous experiences coagulate to form an identity that is easy to confuse with our true nature.

> *Besides the noble art of getting things done, there is the noble art of leaving things undone. The wisdom of life consists in the elimination of nonessentials.*
>
> *~ Lin Yutang,*
> *Chinese author and*
> *inventor (1895-1976)*

The fact of the matter is, you are not your accomplishments, your creations, or the sum total of the various roles you play in your life — manager, director, vice president, mother, father, friend, son, daughter. You are much, much more than that. Your potential is infinite.

And yet, we limit ourselves by these definitions. They filter the experiences we allow ourselves to have and compel us to define the form that our deepest longings should take. In order to be happy, we reason — we must get that promotion, achieve this or that particular goal, hit that target. So we continue to go through the motions, doing the kinds of things we've always done — on a sort of auto-pilot. Some of this may bring satisfaction, and some may bring a growing source of discontentment. We need to attune ourselves to what brings us the most of what we truly desire and open ourselves to the possibility that what we really want may need to come in a form that has previously been undefined for us. In short, we must allow ourselves

> *If success is not on your own terms, if it looks good to the world but does not feel good in your heart, it is not success at all.*
>
> *~ Anna Quindlen,*
> *American Pulitzer Prize-winning author and journalist*

to surrender what we think we know, to open up to the mystery that is unfolding in each of our lives.

Easier said than done, right? How exactly do you go about letting go of the known when it is all you know?

We can take our cues from nature. Snakes and other reptiles shed their skin, trees drop their leaves, and caterpillars create cocoons in which their forms entirely dissolve before recreating themselves in the form of butterflies. Even a fish in a bowl cannot stay in water that contains its excrement — the waste must either be emptied and replaced with new water, or absorbed by something else that will remove it from the fish's environment. Without engaging in these renewal processes, these creatures will die. And so it is with us. Many of us are already walking around encased in layers of old, dead stuff that needs to be released.

- What are you holding onto in your life that has run its course?

- What are the old outmoded ways of doing things that no longer bring you energy?

- What are the things you've acquired that you no longer need?

- What beliefs are you holding onto that are no longer true for you?

- Pay attention to the times that you feel constricted, anxious, or tired and in those moments ask what you can let go of.

Don't be afraid of the answer. Though it may frighten you because it introduces an element of the unknown, following these insights will always lead to freedom and liberation.

Your computer can handle only so much data. If you do not delete old email and get rid of files that have been accumulating over the years, and if you continue to add new programs without deleting old ones, you will find that it becomes sluggish and unresponsive. Just as freeing up space allows your computer to process things more quickly, so will clearing your own personal space (whether of things or thoughts) allow you to access new levels of clarity and creativity. You will breathe easier, be more present in every action and interaction you partake of, and bring more of who you really are to what you do. And you will open the space of possibility that will allow something to come in that may surprise and delight you. Rather than being something you slave away for, it will simply emerge and reveal itself to you.

> *"There are far, far better things ahead than any we leave behind."*
>
> *~ C. S. Lewis, Irish-born British author, literary critic and essayist (1898-1963)*

Clearing the Clutter

When I got over my initial disappointment and frustration over not being able to move full speed ahead with my web-based programs, I began to become increasingly aware that it was time for me to simplify in other areas of my life as well. I felt an overwhelming desire to begin cleaning things out — closets, drawers, cabinets, files. What began as an attempt to clear clutter and create some order turned into a full-out purging. I found myself chucking binders of course materials (some that I had participated in and others that I had created) into the recycling bin and noticed a feeling of liberation that snuck through the initial shock at behavior that is pretty uncharacteristic of me (I've always been someone who carefully saved and catalogued just about anything in case I might need it later). I boxed up more clothing and household gadgets than I had realized I even had and donated them to charitable organizations. I got to the point that I could stand in front of something and detect whether it was giving me energy or sucking it from me. Anything that fell into that second category had to leave.

As the clutter in my surroundings cleared, I found my inner state gradually coming to match my outer one.

The thoughts that previously swirled around in my head now had somewhere to land. I resisted the urge to fill the time I had been spending working on my old programs with more work. Instead, I learned to sit still and enjoy the silent spaces. Without all the craziness involved in the program design, maintaining my coaching practice seemed like a cinch. I was able to be more present than ever before, both with my clients as well as friends and family. Though I intuitively felt that this newfound state of being was well appreciated by those around me, I knew that I was the biggest beneficiary.

The Gift of Presence

The word present derives from the Latin past participle *praesse* meaning "to be before one," from the roots *pra – pre + esse* – to be. I believe presence is a state of being achieved when we are truly in the moment, allowing it to unfold without judging it, labeling it, or getting lost in our thoughts about what it means or what we believe should be happening next, or instead. Presence allows us to cut through the clamor of our preoccupations, worries and fears so that our true selves can emerge. It is a gateway through which our intuition and inner wisdom enters and expresses itself. A moment of presence is a state of grace that can produce great insights that help us truly learn from our experiences, make the most of our opportunities and rise up to our challenges in creative ways. In these moments of presence, we know who we really are and what we are truly capable of.

Real generosity towards the future lies in giving all to the present.

~ Albert Camus, French-Algerian Nobel Prize-winning author, philosopher and journalist (1913-1960)

Have you ever noticed that people tend to match each other's intensity and tone when they are together? Comments about trivial matters are often matched with similar banter. Expressions of fear or dread often elicit responses that are equally charged, and expressions of anger have a way of provoking reactions that people later regret. In a similar manner, moments of presence when shared with others can evoke powerful responses that can be revealing and transformational. This is because when you are truly present with another human being you create a space that allows that person's true self to come out as well. This is why the best leaders have learned to become comfortable with silence, to listen more than they talk, and to allow themselves to become instruments that help others recognize their own greatness — not necessarily through anything they say or do, but rather through moments of presence that are created and shared with others.

So how does one cultivate a moment of presence? It is really rather simple, though far easier said than done.

The first step is to be still. That's right. Sit still. I know it goes against everything you were probably taught about getting things done and being useful. But do it anyway. You can practice now, while you read this. Become aware of your breathing, of the space you are sitting in, of the weight of your body and how it feels in this moment. Feel the life inside you and trace it to each part of your body. Listen to the sounds around you. Take a deep breath. Let it out slowly.

Become aware of your thoughts. Observe the activity of your mind as it continues to process whatever is there — thoughts such as, "This is silly, really — I have way too much to do to be sitting here, doing this..." and "I have to remember to call so-and-so back today," and "What did my [boss, colleague, friend] mean when she said...." Recognize that you are not your thoughts, but rather the thinker of your thoughts. Simply watch them parade around, without getting sucked into them. Feel how much bigger you are than all of that. Continue to breathe it in.

Simply continue to repeat steps one and two, immersing yourself more deeply into the experience with each breath. You don't need to do this for an extended period of time, unless you want to. Often even a couple of minutes are sufficient to bring you to a more intense state of awareness and aliveness.

In these moments of presence, you will experience things on a different level — one that allows you to respond from a deeper, wiser part of yourself. And when you are with others, you will bring out that deeper, wiser part of them as well. Presence is incredibly powerful to practice with others. The process is the same, except that you expand your awareness to take in the other person as well. Look into that person's eyes, and listen to what he or she is saying. But listen to what he or she is not saying as well. Presence is more about being than doing. So allow yourself to truly BE with another, devoid of judgments, labels, and agendas. When you listen from this place, you are like water to a thirsty plant, allowing others to open up and soak in needed nutrients. And in this space, they may just find the answers they seek as well — not because you are giving them, but because you have created a space that is illuminating for everyone.

Creating this space for myself became one of my highest priorities. I arranged my coaching meetings to allow for large chunks of unscheduled time, during which I went for long walks and runs, wrote in my journal and worked in the garden. As I pulled the weeds from the neglected planters in our yard, I couldn't help but think of the parallels to what I was doing with my own life. Getting my hands dirty as I plunged them into the warm, musty earth allowed me to feel the connection to something bigger than myself once again. I completely lost track of time and space and became one with my surroundings. After clearing and amending the soil, I planted petunias, snapdragons, and geraniums next to my front patio. They reached for the sun and warmly welcomed anyone who came to the door. In the back yard, for the first time ever, I tried my hand at a vegetable garden. I planted tomatoes, corn, sweet basil, sage, eggplant and peppers. Some of the seedlings flourished and others did not. Again, the similarities to my recent experiences continued to intrigue me.

Among the many seeds I had planted over the years in my personal and professional garden, one that had been neglected for some time broke through the surface and begged for my attention. Sequestered in a file in the bottom drawer of my filing cabinet was the manuscript for the book you are now reading, which I had begun more than three years prior. As I flipped through the pages, I recalled how excited I was at the thought of using Pinocchio as a metaphor for personal growth. I had written earnestly for several months and then realized that before it would take the form of a book, Pinocchio's story would be incorporated into an intimate workshop that I offered regularly for the next few years. Periodically, I had felt compelled to revisit my manuscript, and even tried to force myself to spend time on it — feeling as though it deserved my energy and attention. And then one day I realized I had hit a wall. My writing felt flat and forced and needed a rest. So the document sat dormant for many months, waiting until the time was right to come alive again.

After clearing the debris that kept it underground, the manuscript had begun to emerge once again and beckon encouragingly. Upon reading the pages I had written so long ago, I realized that they were devoid of the energy that was now pulsing through me. Instead of picking up where I left off, I rewrote much of what was there. It was as though Pinocchio himself was behind it all, smiling and enthusiastically cheering me on. In my silent moments, I knew this was the seedling that deserved the energy that had been newly revived within me. The act of writing further renewed me and helped me better understand my own personal journey.

**When we take the time
to reconnect with ourselves and what gives us life —
to find Geppetto in whatever form he takes for us —
we reignite the spark of animating genius.**

In the midst of our calmness, the ripples in the pond begin to smooth and we have enough clarity to see right into our souls — to connect with that part of ourselves that is timeless and interconnected with all of creation. This wellspring restores, revitalizes and inspires us. Just as we need to recharge our various electronic devices from time to time, so too do we need to renew our very selves, plugging into a source of energy that will replenish and sustain us. In these moments, we connect with what is most true and real within ourselves. And it is in this act of going within that we draw the strength necessary to go back out into the world again to breathe life into everything around us and do what we were born to do.

Your Inner Pinocchio

- Pay attention to signals that your energy is running low; plan activities that nourish you back to life.

- Align yourself with methods that feel authentic. Attune yourself to what brings you the most of what you truly desire.

- Allow yourself to surrender what you think you know to open up to the mystery that is unfolding in your life.

- Pay attention to the ideas, thoughts and inspirations that land gently on you and beckon to be given a vehicle to enter the world.

- Create the time in your daily life to process and learn from your experiences, honor and develop your dreams, and take care of yourself in such a way that those dreams continue to come to you.

- Allow yourself to be truly in the moment, allowing it to unfold without judging it, labeling it, or getting lost in your thoughts about what it means or what you believe should be happening next, or instead.

- Contemplate what you have already experienced and ask yourself how you can build on it to create some intrigue and adventure.

- Learn to become comfortable with silence, to listen more than talk, and to allow yourself to become an instrument that helps others recognize their own greatness.

- You will not succeed in bringing out the best in others if you insist on doing everything yourself.

- You will not bring out the best in yourself if you continue to insist on doing things you are already good at.

- Move out of your comfort zone and be willing to experience the exhilaration and anxiety of not knowing, once again.

Chapter 12

The Adventure Never Really Ends

*There will come a time when you
believe everything is finished.
That will be the beginning.*

*~ Louis L'Amour,
American author (1908-1988)*

I've often wondered what the next chapter in Pinocchio's story would have been about. He became real. Then what? Upon realizing your greatest dream, unearthing your most precious treasure, having your most fantastic wish granted, what would you do next?

I don't think the adventure ever ends, the challenges ever cease, or the possibilities ever exhaust themselves. We are in a continuous cycle of self-discovery that begs us to dive deeper and to jump higher. And we are not alone. We are never alone. Through both animating genius and our puppets, we are all interconnected, woven together by both truth and illusion. We can serve to propagate one, the other or both. And though we must look within to find our answers, we must also never underestimate what we can accomplish when we join forces with one another.

This is where I believe leadership comes in. It must start with oneself and expand outward. Leaders are people who have the ability to shine a light on their surroundings and everyone around them. The light emanates from within them, a product of the unique combination of their talent, energy and passion. The very best leaders are those who help others ignite their own sparks so that they, too, may serve as a beacon of hope, inspiration and courage. Illuminated by this light, our paths become brighter and we are able to clearly see any obstacles that lie before us so that we may swiftly and effectively overcome them and grow stronger in the process. This light also allows us to recognize and bring out the strengths in ourselves, as well as in others, that will allow us to persevere and emerge victorious in the face of our greatest challenges and setbacks.

Life is a sort of splendid torch which I've got to hold up for the moment, and I want to make it burn as brightly as possible before handing it on to future generations.

~ George Bernard Shaw, Irish playwright and co-founder of the London School of Economics (1856-1950)

Exercising true leadership does not require that you have an advanced degree, a fancy title, people reporting to you, or even that you are part of an organization at all. Any community of people — a nation, a city or state, a corporation, a civic group, an association, a school, or a family — provides us an opportunity to join forces in such a way that we

When we let our own light shine, we unconsciously give other people permission to do the same. As we are liberated from our own fear, our presence automatically liberates others.

~ Marianne Williamson, spiritual activist, author, lecturer, and founder of The Peace Alliance

tap into and unleash our collective greatness. But first we must awaken to it. We must realize that there is so much more to us than we think there is — perhaps so much more to life itself than we ever knew. As we dare to dream bigger, the possibilities that swirl around us draw closer. And as we complement each other's unique talents, abilities and gifts we are able to do things we never imagined were possible.

Of course we will be met with challenge, adversity and even peril. We will have our ups and downs, but as we join forces we can bolster and sustain each other through them.

As we rise up to the challenges and opportunities that face us as a society, as organizations, communities and families, we must realize that WE are the leaders we have been waiting for.

The more we rely on others to come up with solutions, the further we get from the solutions each and every one of us holds within. We are all pieces of an intricate puzzle, and every single one of them is essential. We must take responsibility for what we have control over in our lives and make whatever impact is ours to make, even if that is only in our thoughts — in what we are paying attention to, in what we say and do, and in the example we set for others. We are collectively creating a reality that mirrors our thoughts. We must do what we can to keep that positive and constructive, so that our actions are that way as well.

We are living at a time when humankind can face whatever threatens it only if we, by which I mean each of us, manage to revive, with new energy and a new ethos, a sense of responsibility for the rest of the world.

~ Vaclav Havel, Czech playwright, essayist, the 10th and last President of Czechoslovakia

Leadership is about answering the call of Spirit to accomplish extraordinary things for, with, and through people. There is an abundance of tools, techniques, approaches and models out there on how to lead. But the essence of leadership is not in the domain of the intellect. It is in the heart.

**We follow people not because of what they do,
but because of who they are.**

Even "proven methods" for leadership fall flat unless they are employed by an individual who is strongly connected to the animating force within that gives form to a unique contribution of style, talents and passions. As we endeavor to practice leadership in every aspect of our lives, no matter what our vocation or role, the brilliance we were born with pours forth in such a way that it allows others to see and remember their own brilliance. We become real, and through our examples help others unearth the masterpieces in their own marble as well.

Many people die with their music still in them. Why is this so? Too often it is because they are always getting ready to live. Before they know it, time runs out.

~ Oliver Wendell Holmes, American physician, professor, lecturer and author (1809-1894)

There is something within you that is waiting to be rediscovered and unleashed. As you do, your life and everything in it will be transformed — first through yourself and then through the impact you will have on others. I challenge you to find a way to bring more of who you are to everything you do.

**Please don't wait another minute
to give yourself fully to your life's adventure.**

The world needs you now.

*For more information about my workshops, lectures,
products and services, please visit*
www.DianeBolden.com,
where you can subscribe to receive free articles and video posts.

Recommended Resources

Allard, Suzanne. Odyssey High Performance Solutions: http://www.odysseyhps.com/about/bios/suzanne-allard

Allen, David. *Getting Things Done: The Art of Stress-Free Productivity*. New York, NY: Penguin Group, 2001.

Allen, James. *As a Man Thinketh*. Ilfracome, England, 1901. For more information: www.asamanthinketh.net

Arntz, William, Betsy Chasse, and Mark Vincente. *What the Bleep Do We Know?* Lord of the Wind Films, LLC and Captured Light Industries, copyright ©2004. For more information: www.whatthebleep.com

Arrien, Angeles. *The Four-fold Way: Walking the Paths of the Warrior, Teacher, Healer and Visionary*. New York, NY: HarperCollins, 1993.

Beck, Martha. *Finding Your Own North Star: Claiming the Life You Were Meant to Live*. New York, NY: Three Rivers Press (Random House), January 2002. For more information: www.marthabeck.com

Beck, Martha. *Steering by Starlight: Find Your Right Life, No Matter What!* New York, NY: Three Rivers Press (Random House), March 2008. For more information: www.marthabeck.com

Bennis, Warren. *On Becoming a Leader: The Leadership Classic*. Cambridge, MA: Perseus Publishing, 1989.

Bennis, Warren & Robert J. Thomas. *Leading for a Lifetime: How Defining Moments Shape Leaders of Today and Tomorrow*. New York, NY: Harvard Business Press, 2007.

Bennis, Warren and Burt Nanus. *Leaders*. New York, NY: Harper & Row, 1985.

Blanchard, Ken. *Leading at a Higher Level: Blanchard on Leadership and Creating High Performing Organizations.* Upper Saddle River, NJ: Prentice Hall, 2006.

Block, Peter. *Stewardship: Choosing Service Over Self Interest.* San Francisco, CA: Berrett-Koehler Publishers, Inc., 1993.

Byron, Katie & Stephen Mitchell. *Loving What Is: Four Questions That Can Change Your Life.* New York, NY: Three Rivers Press, 2003.

Champion, Vickie. Feeding the Heart, Phoenix, Arizona: Business coach and consultant. http://www.vickiechampion.com/

Chopra, Deepak. *The Seven Spiritual Laws of Success: A Practical Guide to the Fulfillment of Your Dreams.* Novato, CA: New World Library, 1994.

Chopra, Deepak. *The Spontaneous Fulfillment of Desire: Harnessing the Infinite Power of Coincidence.* New York, NY: Harmony Books, 2003.

Collodi, Carlo. *The Adventures of Pinocchio.* Originally a serial between 1881 and 1883, later published as a book for children in 1883. There are many more recent, illustrated editions.

Cohen, Alan. *I Had It All the Time: When Self-Improvement Gives Way to Ecstasy.* Haiku, HI: Alan Cohen Publications, 1995. For more information: www.alancohen.com

Cohen, Alan. *Dare to Be Yourself: How to Quit Being an Extra in Other People's Movies and Become the Star of Your Own.* New York, NY: A Fawcett Book, published by The Random House Publishing Group, 1991.

Covey, Stephen. *The 7 Habits of Highly Effective People: Powerful Lessons in Personal Change.* New York, NY: Fireside, Simon & Schuster Inc., 1990.

Covey, Stephen. *Principle-Centered Leadership*. New York, NY: Fireside, Simon & Schuster, 1992.

Diamond, John. *Your Body Doesn't Lie*. New York, NY: Grand Central Publishing, Hachette Book Group, 1989. For more information: www.drjohndiamond.com

Dispenza, Dr. Joe. Evolve Your Brain — *The Science of Changing Your Mind*. Deerfield Beach, FL: Health Communications, Inc., 2007.

Dyer, Wayne. *You'll See It When You Believe It: The Way to Your Personal Transformation*. New York, NY: Harper Paperbacks, August 21, 2001. For more information: www.drwaynedyer.com

Ford, Debbie. *The Dark Side of the Light Chasers: Reclaiming Your Power, Creativity, Brilliance, and Dreams*. Riverhead Books, a division of Penguin Group (USA), June 1, 1999. For more information: www.debbieford.com

Greenleaf, Robert. Greenleaf Center for Servant Leadership. Westfield, IN, 1970. For more information: www.greenleaf.org

Hawkins, David R. *Power vs. Force*. New York, NY: Hay House, June 1995. For more information: www.veritaspub.com

Hill, Napoleon. *Think and Grow Rich*. New York, NY: Random House Publishing, 1937.

Kouzes, James K. and Barry Z. Posner, *The Leadership Challenge*. San Francisco, CA: Jossey-Bass, A Wiley Imprint, 2007. For more information: www.leadershipchallenge.com

Lippincott, Kristen. *A (Really) Brief History of Time*. New York, NY: Fast Company, May 31, 2000.

Livingston, Sterling. Pygmalion in Management. *Harvard Business Review*, September-October 1988.

Mackay, Harvey. *Swim with the Sharks Without Being Eaten Alive: Outsell, Outmanage, Outmotivate, and Outnegotiate Your Competition.* New York, NY: A Fawcett Columbine Book, published by Ballantine Books, 1988. For more information: www. harveymackay.com

Millman, Dan. *The Way of the Peaceful Warrior.* Novato, CA.: H. J. Kramer, New World Library, September 2000.

Roosevelt, Theodore. "The Man in the Arena," speech given at the Sorbonne, Paris, France, April 23, 1910.

Rosenthal, Robert and Lenore Jacobson. *Pygmalion in the Classroom: Teacher Expectations and Pupils' Intellectual Development.* Irvington Publishers, Inc., 1992, expanded edition; Holt, Rinehart and Winston, Inc.,1968.

Strick, Melanie. President and Founder of Success Connections, Inc. For more information: www.SuccessConnections. com

Thoreau, Henry David. *Walden,* or *Life in the Woods.* Boston, MA: Ticknor & Fields, 1854.

Tolle, Eckharte. *The Power of Now: A Guide to Spiritual Enlightenment.* Novato, CA.: New World Library, 1999. For more information: www.eckharttolle.com

Williamson, Marianne. *The Gift of Change: Spiritual Guidance for a Radically New Life.* New York, NY: HarperCollins Publishers, 2004.

Williamson, Marianne. *Healing the Soul of America: Reclaiming Our Voices as Spiritual Citizens.* New York, NY: Touchstone, 2000.

CPSIA information can be obtained at www.ICGtesting.com
Printed in the USA
LVOW051522130712

289921LV00001B/284/P